Economic Statecraft

Economic Statecraft

Human Rights, Sanctions,
and Conditionality

CÉCILE FABRE

Harvard University Press

Cambridge, Massachusetts
London, England
2018

First Printing

Library of Congress Cataloging-in-Publication Data
Names: Fabre, Cécile, author.
Title: Economic statecraft : human rights, sanctions,
and conditionality / Cécile Fabre.
Description: Cambridge, Massachusetts : Harvard
University Press, 2018. | Includes bibliographical
references and index.
Identifiers: LCCN 2018001855 | ISBN 9780674979635
(hardcover : alk. paper)
Subjects: LCSH: Economic sanctions—
Moral and ethical aspects. | Economic assistance—
Moral and ethical aspects. | Conditionality
(International relations) | Human rights—
Economic aspects.
Classification: LCC HD87 .F355 2018 |
DDC 327.1 / 11—dc23
LC record available at https://lccn.loc.gov/2018001855

Contents

Economic Statecraft

Introduction

IN THE PAST SIXTY YEARS OR SO, traditional powers such as the United States, European states, and China, and international multilateral institutions such as the United Nations, the African Union, the European Union, the International Monetary Fund, and the World Bank have routinely resorted both to economic sanctions and to conditional offers of material help in their dealings with one another and with less powerful states. Newspapers are filled with stories of sanctions against (inter alia) Russia, Iran, North Korea, Venezuela, Angola, Liberia, and Côte d'Ivoire. Aid and lending conditionality, for their part, are a staple of development assistance.

Those practices are sometimes referred to as "economic statecraft." They are hardly new. For example, in 432 BC Athens imposed trade sanctions on the city of Megara—an ally of Corinth, whose naval expansion greatly worried the Athenians. According to some scholars, Athens's decision contributed to the outbreak of the Peloponnesian War. A thousand years later, Justinian forbade the exports of goods that might confer strategic advantages on the Byzantine Empire's enemies, while his successors imposed a wholesale embargo on trade with Egypt and Syria. Italian city-states of the Middle Ages, such as Genoa, Venice, and the members of the Hanseatic League, as well as the papacy itself, routinely used embargos and boycotts as a way to bend their enemies to their will. In the modern era (to give but two examples), King Louis XIV offered subsidies to King Charles II in exchange for an offensive alliance between France and England against the United Provinces; a century or so later, the young American republic resorted to sanctions against the United Kingdom during the War of Independence.[1]

Economic statecraft works best if it is used in combination with diplomatic negotiations and is often toothless unless it is backed by the threat of military force. Yet, although it is only one of the many tools of foreign policy, it does warrant normative scrutiny, in just the same way as do the use of military force and the conduct of negotiations. For it consists in issuing threats (to sever trade relations) and in making offers (of material assistance) that, quite often, recipients have little choice but to accept. To the extent that threats and coercive offers are morally problematic, so is economic statecraft.[2]

To illustrate some of the issues at stake: on what grounds, if any, may nuclear powers justifiably resort to sanctions as a means to prevent other states from developing a nuclear arsenal? To what extent does the fact that economic sanctions occasion collateral harm to civilian populations constitute a moral reason *not* to impose them? If (as some say) all human beings have a human right to aid, or a right to their debt being forgiven, on what grounds are donor and lender countries morally justified in making those offers of assistance conditional on liberal reforms that might be antithetical to a recipient's culture? More generally, does economic statecraft in its various guises constitute a morally unacceptable interference in the internal affairs of sovereign states? Or, on the contrary, is it a justified tool in states' and international organizations' arsenal?

My aim, in this book, is to provide an account of economic statecraft as a tool for the enforcement of human rights. Human rights are the linchpin of the international normative order. Many states regard—or claim to regard—them as a central component of their foreign policy. Dozens have voted for and / or signed the international charters and documents in which they are set out, notably (and inexhaustively) the 1948 Universal Declaration of Human Rights, the 1966 International Covenant on Economic, Social and Cultural Rights, the 1966 International Covenant on Civil and Political Rights, the 1979 Convention on the Elimination of All Forms of Discrimination Against Women, the 1989 Convention on the Rights of the Child, and the 2006 Convention on the Rights of Persons with Disabilities.

And yet, human rights are honored at least as much in the breach as in the observance. It behooves us, therefore, to provide an account of what may justifiably be done, indeed must be done, in response. Put differently, it behooves us to provide an account of justified human rights enforcement.

Why economic statecraft, though? For two reasons. First, as a matter of fact and as my opening examples suggest, it is a key foreign policy tool. Moral and political philosophers—myself included—have devoted considerable energy to the ethics of war. In so doing, they have neglected alternatives to war, foremost among them the use of economic instruments. I hope to contribute to filling that gap.[3]

Second, as a matter of norm and as we shall see later on, rights to property on the one hand, and rights to material assistance on the other hand, are themselves human rights. They impose on third parties duties not to interfere with property transactions as well as duties to provide assistance. Yet, economic sanctions stand in tension with the former, while conditional offers of assistance stand in tension with the latter. It thus pays to investigate whether sovereign actors (or associations thereof) may justifiably seek to defend human rights in general by using means that are tantamount to depriving people of that to which they have presumptive rights—put differently, by doing that which those sovereign actors are under presumptive duties not to do. Seen in this light, the problem of economic statecraft is a particular instantiation of a more general problem, to wit, how to reconcile one's commitment to a particular value with the necessity of violating that value for its very sake.

In dealing with the problem, I shall argue that political actors such as states, coalitions of states, and international organizations are sometimes morally justified in resorting to economic sanctions, conditional aid, and conditional lending as a means to enforce human rights. In fact, they are sometimes under a moral duty so to act. To illustrate: I shall defend the view that some of the highly targeted sanctions that have been imposed against, for example, the leadership (widely construed) of North Korea, Russia, Syria, and Venezuela are justified. Turning to aid and lending conditionality, I shall defend the view that major sovereign donors such as the IMF, the World Bank, and their members sometimes may justifiably tie the delivery of assistance to the fulfillment by recipients of human rights–promoting conditions.

To some, all of this might seem obviously true. Of course, they might agree, we must protect human rights; and of course, if economic sanctions and aid conditionality help us do that, we may, indeed must, make use of them. Who could possibly object? Why write a whole book on this?

It is one thing intuitively to think that this kind of policy is morally sound; it is another altogether to provide a fully developed justification for it. In fact, as a cursory glance at the empirical literature suggests, interfering in trade relationships and subjecting the provision of economic assistance to respect for human rights are far more controversial than they first appear. Those measures can be very costly both on those at whom they are targeted and on those whom they unwittingly catch in their net. Yet it is far from clear that they are effective. As a result, they have been extensively criticized. Indeed, as we shall see, they are morally justified in fewer cases than seem at first intuitively plausible—precisely on human rights grounds, and even when they are meant to enforce those rights themselves.

I proceed as follows. In Chapter 1, I sketch out the account of human rights on which the remainder of the book relies, with particular emphasis on property rights and rights to material assistance in the form of both aid and loans. In Chapters 2 and 3, I turn to economic sanctions. In Chapter 2, I argue that sanctions are justified as a means to stop and deter human rights violations. I discuss two of the most standard objections to sanctions, namely that they are disproportionately costly to the innocent and that they are ineffective. In the light of those objections (which, I argue, are not as powerful as they may seem), I qualify my defense and conclude in favor of highly targeted measures.

In Chapter 2, I assume that the sanctions are imposed either by the United Nations or by a sanctioning party that exercises territorial and / or personal jurisdiction over at least some of the agents against whom the sanctions apply. These are standardly called primary sanctions. In Chapter 3, by contrast, I focus on so-called secondary sanctions, whereby a sanctioning party seeks to restrict the economic activities of agents who are not subject to its jurisdiction. I argue that the considerations that support primary sanctions also support secondary sanctions.

Chapters 2 and 3, thus, provide a normative account of economic sanctions—or economic threats. In Chapters 4 and 5, I examine the ethics of economic offers. Even though threats and offers are often used in tandem, it is necessary to address them separately.[4] In Chapter 4, I argue that aid conditionality as a means to enforce human rights is morally justified—though only to the extent that it maximizes chances that the rightful recipients of aid will indeed get the aid, and that the aid will be effective in the long term. In Chapter 5, I examine the ethics of attaching conditions to loans and debt relief. When a lender is under a duty to loan or to forgive debts, lending and debt conditionality admit of the same normative treatment as aid conditionality. In fact, and perhaps surprisingly, even if a lender is under a duty to provide aid for free but instead resorts to lending—thus in dereliction of its primary duty—it may still impose on the borrower conditions aimed at enforcing human rights.

As we shall see throughout, decisions to impose economic sanctions or to condition aid and / or lending on respect for human rights are routinely based on moral condemnation of the unjust policies that they are meant to stop. Those who conduct those policies (or their supporters) often retort that their accusers are guilty of exactly the same sin, indeed are often themselves partly responsible for the very same human rights violations that they condemn. In Chapters 2 to 5, I argue in effect that the objection lacks bite against the accuser's decision to resort to those measures. But as we shall see in Chapter 6, the objection sometimes—but only sometimes—gains purchase against expressions of moral outrage.

As the foregoing remarks make clear, I focus on economic statecraft as a means to protect human rights. Accordingly, I do not attend to the use of economic incentives as a means to secure advantageous trade deals and / or investment opportunities—in other words, to economic diplomacy writ large. For example, I do not examine the ethical issues raised by the imposition of tariffs and / or import quotas, or by the resort to export subsidies. Nor do I examine conditionality as a means to advance broader geopolitical goals such as getting another political actor to align its foreign policy goals to ours, or thwarting that actor's own geopolitical ambitions. Moreover, I restrict my inquiry to peacetime economic statecraft. Thus, I do not consider (for example) the ethics of embargoes, currency manipulation, or preferential lending, as a means to fight a war. Nor do I consider the ethics of boycotts by individual agents (what some have called ethical consumerism). Nor do I examine the ethics of what one may call indirect economic statecraft, as when a state mounts a cyber-attack on another state's economic and financial institutions to bend that state's regime to its will. Rather, my focus is on the use of direct economic instruments by sovereign political actors, international organizations, and multinational actors against other sovereign political actors.[5]

These may seem unduly restrictive constraints on the scope of my inquiry. However, they make the project more manageable. More importantly, focusing on peacetime statecraft is justified precisely insofar as it is the preferred foreign policy instrument of major powers; and focusing on direct economic statecraft is justified because and insofar as it raises specific ethical problems, such as the legitimacy of interfering in two parties' freedom to trade with one another or of withholding much needed material assistance, which indirect economic statecraft does not raise.

Let me end this Introduction with some remarks on methodology. This is a book of analytical political philosophy. As such, I engage in conceptual analysis of its key terms, aim to argue rigorously from premises to conclusions, and focus on the moral norms that ought to regulate economic statecraft. I do not address in any depth the questions of institutional design raised by the implementation of those norms. To the extent that I do discuss institutions and legal regimes, I do so mainly with a view to discerning whether they are morally justified at the bar of just economic statecraft.

Furthermore, I make extensive use of both hypothetical and empirical examples. Hypothetical examples inevitably simplify the matters at hand, particularly when they describe cases involving only one or two individuals and yet are used to extrapolate to large-scale phenomena. Nevertheless, they have an important role to play in analytical political philosophy, for they force us to be clearer as to what our intuitions are and how best to defend them. Empirical examples, for their part, present their own challenges. Each case is enormously complex: attention must be paid to the political, social, macroeconomic, microeconomic and cultural features of the country at issue; and thought must be given to its domestic and foreign policy. Moreover, using contemporary examples risks making the book outdated rather quickly; using historical examples risks giving the impression that the book is not in tune with contemporary politics. I have tried to strike compromises between those conflicting demands—uneasily but necessarily so. With that in mind, when I speak of extant or current practices, I mean "practices in use over the last thirty years or so, and/or current at the time of finishing this book—December 2017." It is possible that, by the time you read this, the facts as described here will have changed. Were that the case, sentences such as "in the light of those facts, sanctions against Y are justified" should be read as "given that the facts were so and so, sanctions against Y were justified then," or "*if* the facts are so and so, sanctions against Y are justified."[6]

In other words, I aim to engage in empirically informed political philosophy—rather than in a philosophical analysis of particular, highly context-specific cases. The line between those two kinds of philosophical inquiry is not as hard and fast as I make it seem. In his wonderful book *Ethics and Public Policy*, Jonathan Wolff couches the difference in roughly those terms. A philosopher who hopes directly to guide policy makers and citizens in the short term must take the latter's moral commitments at face value—even if she thinks that those values are misguided. But there is another kind of philosopher—one who seeks to show that those values are misguided, or that those values are indeed "the right ones" but that (notwithstanding their claims to the contrary) policy makers and citizens fail to live up to them. That philosopher may have to reconcile herself to the fact that she will not make much of a difference, here and now, to policymaking. She can only hope, in the longer term, to change those values or the ways in which people judge whether they live up to those values.[7]

This book is an exercise in the latter kind of philosophy. As a result, some of the complexities of various actual policy decisions will be inevitably lost. In return, my hope is to bring some clarity to the normative principles that (I argue) should guide our reflection as scholars, politicians and citizens, whenever we hear our leaders advocate or denounce the use of economic tools as a means to enforce human rights.

Without further ado, then, let us begin.

CHAPTER ONE

Human Rights

L ET ME RESTATE HERE THE BOOK'S THESIS: Political actors such as states, coalitions of states, and international organizations are sometimes morally justified in resorting to economic sanctions, conditional aid, and conditional lending as a means to enforce human rights—though in fewer cases than is often thought. Indeed, they are sometimes under a moral duty to do so—though, once again, in fewer cases than is often thought. In this chapter, I set the stage for my defense of that thesis. I begin by sketching an account of human rights. I then delineate the conditions under which those rights may justifiably be enforced. The chapter concludes with a very brief reminder of the book's overall structure.

Human Rights

A First Cut

Human rights are often described as those moral, pre-institutional rights that human beings have merely by dint of being human.[1] For the sake of intellectual honesty, I should say at the outset that I am deeply skeptical of this view, which strikes me as objectionably speciest. I do not think that I have a right not to be killed merely by virtue of being human, any more than my dog has a right not to be killed merely by virtue of being a dog. We both have a right not to be killed by dint of the fact that we both have an interest in a continuing life. Admittedly, mine might be more important than his; moreover, I may well have a greater range of rights than he does. If so, this is not because I am a human being whereas he is merely a dog; rather, this is because I have certain properties, such as the capacity for rational and moral agency, which he lacks. Imagine a non-human creature, with four legs, six arms, and an eye at the back of what seems to be a head, and which has the capacity for rational and moral agency. I see no reason to believe that she would not have a right not to be enslaved, a right to freedom of expression, and so on.

Some of the features that most humans have, and which they may well share with nonhuman creatures, ground the rights we normally think of as human rights. These rights are rights to what we need in order to lead a life worthy of the kind of beings we are—in short, a flourishing life. We would do better to call those rights fundamental rights, rather than human rights. I suspect that some readers might disagree. Since the language of human rights is both consensual and familiar, I will adopt it throughout. But let it be noted that the normative conclusions I reach here apply, mutatis mutandis, to those very same rights as held by nonhuman creatures, whoever and whatever those creatures may be.

Those rights, I contend, protect interests that are constitutive of a flourishing life for us, the kind of beings we are. To lead such a life is to enjoy some degree of well-being as well as some degree of autonomy—that is to say, to have the capacity to frame, revise, and pursue a conception of the good with which one can identify. Human rights are rights to the freedoms and resources that we need in order to lead a flourishing life so construed. More precisely: they protect our interests in enjoying the freedoms to dispose of our body, develop our mind, articulate our thoughts, and form relationships with one another. They thus include (inter alia) the rights not to be killed, tortured, raped, and assaulted; rights to freedom of speech, freedom of movement, and freedom of association; the right to education. In addition, human rights protect our interest in having some degree of control over the material resources that are necessary to our well-being and without which we would not enjoy those freedoms. Those rights are property rights (notably the right to use property and the right to transfer it), as well as rights to a decent level of income, housing, and health care. Furthermore, human rights protect us from arbitrary denial of those freedoms and resources—and thus include the right to a fair trial, as well as the right to equality before the law (with concomitant prohibitions on gender-based, race-based, religion-based, disability-based, sexuality-based, and nationality-based discrimination). Finally, human rights protect our interest in shaping the social and political environment in which we live, and thus include the political right to vote and, more generally, to participate in the political life of our community, and in so doing jointly to determine our community's future.[2]

So far, so good: we have human rights to the freedoms and the resources without which we cannot lead a flourishing life; those rights are universal in the sense that we all have them, irrespective of national-cum-political borders, that is to say, irrespective of our membership in this or that political community. Before I flesh out rights over resources in greater detail, I need to make two additional clarificatory points. First, to say that someone, P, has a right to x is to say that P's interest in x warrants special protection absent reasons to the contrary. Put differently, rights are presumptive—not in the epistemic sense that the burden of proofs lies on the shoulders of whomever wishes not to protect x, but in the substantive sense that P's interest in x warrants special protection unless there are countervailing reasons not to give it such protection.

Those countervailing reasons include (inter alia) the fact that the right has been forfeited (as when the holder of a right to x acts in such a way that his interest in x no longer warrants special protection). They also include the fact that the right is defeated by weightier considerations (as when the holder of a right to x has not acted in such a way as to lose protection for x but where there are countervailing reasons in favor of not protecting x). Finally, reasons for not protecting x also include the fact that the right is alienated (by dint of the fact P consents to not having x protected or, alternatively, consents to some other party making a decision as to whether or not x will be protected).

Note that there are important differences between cases in which a right is forfeited and cases in which it is defeated. To say that P forfeits his right to x is to say that P has acted in such a way that he no longer has that right and that he is not wronged, therefore, if his interest in x is not protected. By contrast, in some cases, to say that P's right to x is defeated is to say that P still has that right but that the right is justifiably infringed. In so far as P still has a right to x, not protecting his interest in x leaves a moral remainder that will have to be made good on. In other cases, P's right is defeated such that P no longer has that right—though not by dint of having done something wrong. Thus, I have a moral right to drive on whichever side of the road I want (as flowing from my more general right to freedom of movement) until the government coordinates users of the road by setting down rules. It would be odd to say in this case that my moral right to drive on whichever side of the road I want has been infringed such that I still have it. It will be necessary at times to distinguish between cases in which rights are forfeited, alienated, and defeated. Unless otherwise specified, I use the phrase "presumptive right" to denote all sets of cases. Since all rights are presumptive, I will affix this adjective to the word "rights" only when expository clarity demands it.[3]

The distinction between rights that are defeated (as it were) by countervailing considerations and rights that are not can be couched in the following way. Not all infringements render our life less than flourishing. Thus, the right to private property includes a right to sell one's property to whomever one wishes and whenever one wishes, absent reasons to the contrary. Some of those reasons might issue in costly but not harmful outcomes. For example, suppose that the state tells me that, if I decide to sell my house, I must allow time for the buyer to carry out various checks. I do not need to bypass that timeframe to enjoy a flourishing life, and the state is not harming me by so acting. Nevertheless, the measure is a restriction on my right to property and, as such, is a costly measure—albeit not a harmful one.

Other restrictions are harmful. Consider the following example, which I adapt from the real-life case of the shootout between the French police and the perpetrators of the November 2015 terrorist attacks in Paris. Suppose that a gang of terrorists has broken into my apartment in my absence while on the run from the police. In the ensuing siege, the police repeatedly attempt to blow up the door and fire over a thousand bullets through the windows. Once the siege is over, the whole building is declared unsafe and inhabitable. However strong the defeating considerations in support of the police's action, it remains the case that my property right to live in my apartment has been infringed, to the point where I am left homeless: there is a moral remainder, which the state ought to rectify. Throughout the book, absent further specification, when I speak of the costs that agents are made to incur, whether justifiably or not, I mean the costs attendant on being deprived of that to which we have presumptive human rights.

The second clarificatory point is this. I take respect for human rights to be a requirement of justice. Yet, in the eyes of more radical egalitarian thinkers, the conception of justice that I take as my starting point falls far short of what justice demands. Justice, they will press, requires that individuals have equal opportunities to achieve what they plausibly regard as a flourishing life, whereas in my account, so long as a certain threshold of flourishing is achieved, inequalities above that threshold are morally permitted.

I am sympathetic to the claim that a state of affairs in which some have less than others merely by dint of bad brute luck is profoundly wrong, so much so as to call for action. However, there are strategic reasons for starting from a less demanding account of our duties to one another. In particular, human rights are endorsed by many different theories of justice and thus allow for philosophical ecumenism. Moreover, the duties they impose are duties that the community of nations takes as its own. Articulating an ethics of economic statecraft in the light of those commitments is an important task—particularly if, as I argue at various points, it turns out that some of our extant practices of economic statecraft are at variance with those commitments. Accordingly, whenever I speak of justice, I shall mean justice as the realization of human rights to the freedoms and resources we need to lead a flourishing life. When I speak of an unjust regime, I mean a regime that violates human rights so construed.[4]

Rights and Resources

In this book, I argue that economic sanctions and conditional offers of assistance are morally justified as a means to enforce human rights, under various conditions that I delineate throughout. This implies that foreign policy actors are justified in interfering in property transactions (when they impose economic sanctions) and in withholding material assistance (when they resort to aid or loan conditionality) to that end. Yet, as we just saw, both property transactions and material assistance are protected by human rights. To assess whether and when those human rights warrant infringing, for the sake of enforcing those rights themselves or other human rights, we need to have a more precise sense of what they are.

RIGHTS TO MATERIAL ASSISTANCE

Rights to material assistance—or socioeconomic rights, as they are sometimes called—are set out in all the aforementioned international declarations, charters, and covenants. For my purposes in this book, the following two points will suffice. First, socioeconomic rights are not simply rights to receive those resources passively. So construed, they would imply that a just world is one in which individuals can justifiably be maintained in a state of dependency on the more affluent. This would not be compatible with what a flourishing life entails. To lead such a life, you recall, is to have the capacity to frame, revise, and pursue a conception of the good with which one can identify. Long-term dependency is antithetical to this ideal. Socioeconomic rights, thus, include rights to a social minimum such that their holders are protected from the harmful effects of unemployment, disability, and ill health; but they also include rights to the resources needed to live as independently as possible (such as education, retraining, etc.). The point needs stressing, for although individuals who suffer human rights violations are in some important sense victims, they must also be seen as agents of their own empowerment. My use throughout of the term "victims" should only be seen as an expository shortcut for "individuals who suffer human rights violations."

Second, theories of justice tend to focus on the right to be *given* resources—unemployment benefits, health care, housing benefits, food in the global context, and so on. This is misguided: socioeconomic justice also includes a right to borrow the resources we need. Suppose that I do not have money right now, yet desperately need to drink or eat. You, on the other hand, do not have spare food or water, but you do have spare cash. If you lend me the money now, I can pay you back later today. As economists put it, I face a liquidity constraint (since I cannot pay for what I need as I need it) but I am solvent (since I have enough assets to pay what

I owe in the long term). Under those circumstances, you are not under a duty to give me the money. But you are under a duty to lend it to me. For if what motivates a duty to give when I do not have money at all is the fact that I will die unless I eat, then it stands to reason that this very same fact grounds a duty to lend. Let us call those loans mandatory loans— mandatory, that is, at the bar of justice.[5]

Suppose now that I cannot pay you back later—or, at any rate, not without seriously jeopardizing my prospects for a flourishing life. You are under a duty of justice to give me the money yet refuse, offering instead to lend it to me. Given that you will not honor your first-best obligation to give, you are under a second-best obligation to lend. By lending me money, you would get repaid—or, at any rate, there would be an expectation that you would get repaid. Offering me a loan is thus less costly to you than giving me the money. It would be inconsistent on the one hand to place you under a duty to give, thereby incurring cost c, and yet to exempt you from incurring a lesser cost $c - n$ should you default on your first-best duty to give.[6]

PROPERTY RIGHTS

The claim that you are under a duty to give or lend me what I need implies that you must divest yourself of some of the resources currently in your possession. Do you not own those resources, though?

The right to property is recognized as a human right by, inter alia, the 1948 Universal Declaration of Human Rights (art. 17), the European Convention on Human Rights (art. 1, Protocol 1), and the 1987 African Charter on Human and Peoples' Rights (art. 14). This is far from uncontroversial: the right is omitted from both the 1966 International Covenant on Civil and Political Rights, and the 1966 Covenant on Economic, Social and Cultural Rights. Admittedly, property rights stand in tension with socioeconomic rights. However, the tension dissolves if one makes the former conditional on fulfilling the duties attendant on the latter. To illustrate, consider the risks of serious harms caused by short-term financial speculation in foreign currencies and securities transactions. Suppose for the sake of argument that justice requires that a tax on such exchanges be systematically levied, as a means both to curb those transactions and to create a pool of resources from which to remedy those harms. Under those circumstances, and on the assumption that agents rightfully own the funds that they seek to sell, they can exercise their right to transact subject to paying the tax.[7]

Those remarks suggest that it is misleading to say (as most of us have said for years) that the needy have rights against the affluent that the latter give them the resources they need, since this implies that the affluent own those resources and are under a duty to transfer their ownership rights to the needy. Instead, we should construe the duty of the affluent as a duty to fulfill their function as trustees, in this instance by disbursing the resources to their rightful owner. The point applies both to the duty to provide assistance for free (in which case we may say that recipients have the full set of ownership rights over the latter, without time constraints) and the duty to lend resources (in which case we may say that recipients have a right to use the loaned resources over the duration of the loan).

The claim that agents have property rights over the resources in their possession only if they fulfill their obligations of justice does not tell us why they do have those rights in the first instance. Providing such an account is beyond the scope of this book. I take it for granted that we all have a very strong interest in being able to exercise some degree of exclusive control over the resources we need in order to lead a flourishing life. Interestingly, however, there is no reason to suppose that property rights must be privately and individually held. Not only is it compatible with justice that we should publicly and jointly own some resources: under some circumstances, justice may in fact demand that we should so own them.[8]

What, though, does owning something involve? Incidents of ownership (to borrow Tony Honoré's classic phrase) include (inter alia) (a) Hohfeldian claims in respect to things and / or money, which correlate into duties that third parties not interfere with one's use thereof; (b) Hohfeldian powers to change one's bundle of claims, and so on, over money or things, notably by giving, receiving, selling, and buying; (c) Hohfeldian claims that third parties not interfere with the transfer of entitlements by, for example, physically seizing *g* or confiscating the money before or after the buyer and the seller agree to transact; (d) a claim against those third parties that they should recognize the transaction as valid.[9]

As human rights, property rights do not depend for their existence and normative importance on the presence of institutions, any more than my human right to freedom of movement depends on the fact that it is recognized by my state. That being said, a state-based property regime serves two important functions. For a start, it enables citizens, via the legislature and government, to specify the human right to own property, which is normally stated in a fairly abstract way. Not all such specifications are morally acceptable. Thus, denying women qua women access to private ownership is a human rights violation, irrespective of national and political contexts. But some contextual differences surely are morally permitted. Neither English law nor French law bans women from homeownership, yet they differ in various other ways. For example, English law distinguishes between freehold and leasehold, whereas French law does not. French property law regarding tenancy contracts is much more restrictive on landlords (or, depending on how you look at it, protective of tenants) than English law. (The point is not unique to property rights, of course: we encountered it with respect to the rules of the road earlier on.)

Moreover, moral property rights are important enough to warrant protecting through and by institutions with coercive powers of enforcement. (The same goes, incidentally, with most other pre-institutional rights such as the right not to be killed.) Legally enforcing moral property rights stabilizes them: enabling rights holders to rely on one another's compliance makes it possible for them to enjoy their rights of transfer and disposal, as well of use, with respect to their property.

There are two ways in which political officials with powers of enforcement as a matter of fact do, and as a matter of principle ought to, protect the rights to sell and buy. First, to reiterate, they can and ought to regard the transaction as valid. Suppose that you and I agree that I will sell you a painting: I am the rightful owner of that painting, and you are the rightful owner of the money you will give me for it. Those institutions are, or at any rate ought to be, disempowered (or as Hohfeld would have it, disabled) from conferring, post-sale, title to the painting on me, and title to the money on you. For were they so to act, they would fail to respect us as autonomous moral agents with the ability to enter into a transactional relationship with each other. As they are under a duty so to respect us, they lack the morally justified power to invalidate our decision to transfer the relevant rights and duties with respect to the painting and the money to one another.

Second, it is not enough that those institutions should regard you, and not me, as the rightful owner of the painting, and me, and not you, as the rightful owner of the money. They must also enforce our property rights against third parties over the relevant goods through the law. Conversely, however, they are under an obligation not to subject me to penalties for selling my painting to whomever I wish.

RIGHTS AND TRADE

To recapitulate: individuals wherever they reside have rights to the freedoms and resources they need to lead a flourishing life, including some property rights; subject to fulfilling their obligations of assistance, they enjoy a personal prerogative to give priority to their own projects.

Taken together, those two points yield the view that individuals have a presumptive right to trade with one another and to enjoy the fruits thereof, across borders. Suppose that the British government were to say that British citizen Ben's interest in disposing of his resources is strong enough to be protected by the relevant rights so long as he does not trade with Russian citizen Rodia, on the mere grounds that Rodia is Russian. This would restrict Ben's autonomy on the arbitrary basis (from the point of view of justice) of his political membership in the UK. Crucially, moreover, it would also restrict Rodia's autonomy, on the similarly arbitrary basis of his political membership in Russia.[10]

Human Rights and Duties

WHICH DUTIES?

So much, then, for rights. Rights correlate with duties. More precisely, they correlate with duties not to impose or contribute to imposing undue costs, a fortiori undue harmful costs, to their holders—as when you kill me without warrant. They also correlate with duties not to enable or facilitate the imposition of such costs by third parties. Thus, you are under a duty not to supply my attacker with the gun he needs in order to kill me; you are also under a duty not to supply him with some good if, were you to withhold that good, he would desist or at least find it harder to kill me. For ease of exposition, I shall sometimes speak of a duty not to impose a cost tout court. When I do so, absent clarification to the contrary, I shall have in mind both a duty not to impose a cost and a duty not to enable or facilitate its imposition.[11]

Rights also correlate with duties to rescue their holders from undue harm. Most straightforwardly, as we saw above, they include duties to provide assistance to those who need it, as when you give me the food without which I would die. But the duties that are correlative of socioeconomic rights are only a subset of the duties of assistance. Other such duties include duties to let third parties impose on us the costs attendant on rescuing those in need. Suppose that you desperately need food. I have a surplus of it, but I am not in a position to give it to you (say it is out of my reach). Nevertheless, I am under a duty to let third parties divest me of that surplus for your sake. Finally, and to anticipate the next section, duties of assistance also include a duty to deprive wrongdoers of freedoms and / or resources to which they have a presumptive right, as a means to help someone or in the course of helping someone in need (subject to the requirements of no undue sacrifice, proportionality, necessity, and effectiveness). Those duties are sometimes referred to as duties to protect. For ease of exposition, I shall sometimes speak of a duty to provide assistance (or duty of assistance) tout court. Unless otherwise stated, I shall have in mind all three kinds of assistive duties.

Duties not to contribute and duties to assist might seem overly demanding, in either form. However, they are limited in two different ways. First, recall that justice only stipulates that individuals have rights to the resources needed for a flourishing life: it permits duty bearers to confer greater weight on their own projects than on other people's similar projects once they have contributed to the collective task of meeting the demands of justice. Second, individuals' duty to contribute to meeting the demands of justice is subject to a "no-undue sacrifice" proviso, in virtue of which agents are not under an obligation to lead a less than flourishing life as the price to pay for helping those in need. In other words, duties of assistance impose relatively moderate costs on the affluent.[12]

This simple point raises an interesting and difficult question—namely, whether the no-undue sacrifice proviso also applies to agents who must impose serious costs onto another innocent person in order to avoid losing their own prospects for a flourishing life. Suppose that I am being attacked and am at serious risk of a debilitating and lifelong impairment. I can protect myself only by throwing you, who are wholly innocent of my predicament, in front of my attacker, in which case you would be afflicted by that same impairment. In so doing, I would be using you as a means only to my ends. Or suppose that I am at risk of sustaining a broken arm unless I take steps that will cause your own arm to be broken as a collateral side effect. Common sense morality tells us that I may not so act in the first case. I am not morally justified in deliberately imposing a serious cost on you, above and beyond the no-undue sacrifice proviso, as a means to avoid incurring that cost myself. However, common sense morality also tells us, as per the doctrine of double effect, that I am sometimes morally justified in imposing a greater collateral cost on you than I am justified in imposing a deliberate cost, for the sake of my escaping scot-free. (I say "sometimes," because I do not think that I am justified in collaterally killing you, the innocent bystander, when attempting to save my life.)

Now suppose, by contrast, that unless I give you almost all of the resources at my disposal, you will die of a debilitating illness. Common sense morality tells us that I may justifiably withhold those resources from you: in so doing, I would merely allow a serious cost to befall you rather than cause it—and that I may sometimes do. More generally, common sense morality tells us, as per the doctrine of acts and omissions, that other things equal, imposing a cost on another person is morally worse, when it is wrong, than allowing a cost to befall that person.

I accept the verdicts of common sense morality in those cases. I also accept another one of its verdicts, to the effect that individuals who are significantly responsible—a fortiori culpable—for the fact that some other individual does not lead a flourishing life, are under reparative duties to provide those resources. This is so whether the wrongdoer wrongfully caused harm to that person or wrongfully allowed harm to happen to them. Reparative duties, thus, differ from assistive duties. Both consist in transferring resources to those who need them. But reparative duties may be appropriately more onerous than assistive duties, precisely because they fall on those who are responsible for those needs—whereas assistive duties fall on innocent bystanders.

Importantly, the claim that wrongdoers are under reparative duties—or, to put it differently, that victims of wrongdoings have rights to remedy—does not constitute a departure from accepted international norms. The point is particularly salient in the context of this book: the world as we know it is marred by profound injustice—an injustice moreover that is deeply entrenched in the law, since extant legal property rights originate in wrongful acquisition, usually at the point of guns.

More controversially, beneficiaries of injustice also owe some reparations to the victims of that injustice. After all, those victims need assistance as a matter of right; we need to identify duty bearers and unjust benefits provide a way to do so—indeed a fairer way to do so, other things being equal, than to simply impose the fulfillment of the duty to nonbeneficiaries. Those reparations may include apologies for past wrongdoings as well as some financial assistance. To the extent that my defense of duties to impose sanctions or to condition aid or loans on respect for human rights is addressed to political actors as they currently operate here and now, it is a defense of reparative duties as much as of assistive duties.[13]

WHOSE DUTIES?

Suppose all of this is true. It remains to be seen by whom those duties must be discharged. At one extreme, some hold the view that they can be discharged only by officials of states, multistate organizations, or groups aspiring to exercise political and legal control over a territory. Consider, for example, the case of a soldier who, in the course of fighting a war or while participating in a UN peacekeeping mission, rapes enemy civilians. On this view, the soldier can be accused of violating the victims' human right not to be raped. By contrast, a civilian serial rapist would not be accused of violating human rights, even if he were doing so in the course of his work as a nongovernmental organization (NGO) or a private multinational corporation employee. He would be charged with violating a right tout court, but not a human right.

At the other extreme, whoever violates the aforementioned rights, whether or not in an official capacity or in the course of discharging official duties, can be described as violating human rights. On this view, which Marinella Capriati aptly labels the "universal scope thesis," human rights are universal not just in the sense that all human beings have them, but in the sense that all human beings are held under the corresponding duties.[14]

In between those two views, lies a range of conceptions. Some hold, for example, that individuals who, as citizens, fail to support just institutions can in principle be charged with human rights violations—for example, when they vote in favor of an apartheid regime, or to dismantle welfare provisions for the homeless. They cannot be so charged, however, if in the course of their daily life they discriminate against ethnic minorities (for example, as hotel owners, by refusing to rent a room to a African American couple), or if they fail to save the life of another person at very little cost to themselves (for example, by walking past a child who is obviously at risk of drowning in a pond). On such a view, they would act wrongly—indeed, they could be charged with violating a moral right. But they would not be violating a human right.

The universal scope thesis strikes me as correct. What distinguishes human rights from other rights is the importance of the interests that they protect—not the status of the duty violator. Admittedly, more often than not, those rights violations are the outcome of the acts and omissions of many agents—in some cases dozens of thousands of those agents—from the leader who authorizes a genocide to the munitions factory workers, thanks to whose labor the genocide can actually take place, or from the government that cuts off foreign aid altogether to the individual consumers in the West whose lifestyle is sustained by forced labor abroad. It is also true that ordinary citizens, consumers, and workers often do not know, and cannot reasonably be expected to know, that their acts and omissions are parts of a causal chain leading to the wrongful undermining of other agents' fundamental interests. Nevertheless, those citizens, workers, and consumers (yes, you and I) can aptly be described as contributing, objectively speaking, to human rights violations. Moreover, to the extent that they intentionally contribute to practices that, they can reasonably be expected to know, result in or constitute human rights violations, they can be said to be individually responsible for those violations even if they do not intend them. Thus, I can reasonably be expected to know that most of the goods I buy and consume are in my possession thanks to the commission of grievous human rights violations abroad. Not only do I contribute to those violations: I share responsibility for their occurrence, albeit to a lesser extent than those who wield a gun. The questions (to which I shall return throughout the book) are (a) what I am under a duty to do as a result, and (b) what may be done to me as a result.[15]

Institutions

The claim that individuals are the fundamental units of concern and respect, and thus the bearers of rights and their correlative duties, does not imply that institutions are irrelevant from the point of view of justice. The following three points are worth bearing in mind. First, as I intimated above, human rights need to be specified and enforced. The specification point applies not just to property rights but to almost all human rights. Thus, the right to vote and run for office, or the rights to freedom of association and freedom of speech, are subject to various restrictions and stipulations in various countries. As we shall see later on, what counts as a reasonable specification of a given human right is often open for debate. This does not undermine the point at issue, which is that institutions can, under certain conditions, act as a specification mechanism—as well as an enforcement mechanism.

Second, institutions coordinate individual efforts at respecting rights. This is consistent with the universal scope thesis. According to the thesis, individuals wherever they are in the world are under duties to protect the rights of others. Typically, they discharge their duty via the tax-raising and distributive powers of their state. Resource transfers in turn are made to whichever institution is best placed to direct them as required by justice. When the task of disbursing the aid to those who need it falls on the latter's fellow citizens, this is not on the particularistic grounds that they have a special obligation to look after them, but, rather, on the instrumental grounds that they are best placed to do so by dint of their proximity and shared subjection to the same coercive institutions.[16]

I say that they typically discharge their duties via their state—but not always. For in many parts of the world, state officials are unable or un-

willing to protect the human rights of their own citizens, indeed often actively violate those rights. The next-best-placed institutional agent is
under a duty to step into the breach by protecting those citizens from
abuse at the hands of their state and by offering them the assistance they
need. Often, the next-best-placed agent is another state, or international
or regional institutions (and their member states) such as the United
Nations, the European Union, and the African Union, or indeed international financial institutions (IFIs) such as the IMF, the World Bank, or the
African Development Bank. Often, too, development assistance is provided largely—in fact, sometimes almost exclusively—by nongovernmental organizations. This raises a number of ethical issues. In particular,
NGOs are not democratically accountable to those on whose behalf or for
whose sake they act. Partly for this reason, and as Jennifer Rubenstein
powerful shows, they are often a second-best solution to the problem of
delivering justice—at least compared to a well-functioning, transparent,
and accountable democratic government.[17]

Third, as we also saw earlier in this chapter, individuals have the
human right to form political associations—via the exercise of their political rights—and to shape their collective political, social, and economic
environment, once and so long as those duties have been fulfilled. In other
words, they enjoy rights of self-determination. Once again, however, there
is nothing in extant norms to suggest that the territorially bounded nation-
state is the only morally acceptable form of political organization. Sub-
state institutions and multilateral suprastate organizations such as the EU
are both compatible with a commitment to human rights.

Irrespective of the nature of those institutions, the key point is this. Individuals acting together as members of a group in general, and a sovereign political community in particular, do so via that group's institutions
and its individual officials. Those officials' rights, duties, powers, and lib-
erties supervene on those individuals' rights, duties, powers, and liber-
ties. Their role is to help ensure, to the best of their abilities and within
the constraints of their own institutional positions, that all individuals
wherever they are in the world, securely enjoy those rights and fulfill their
duties.

If I were accurately to reflect in my writing the methodological and
moral individualism of the book on the one hand and the relationship

between individuals and institutions on the other hand, I would have to
make statements of the following kind throughout:

> Individual citizens of a sovereign political community C1, via ap-
> propriately situated political officials acting through the relevant
> institutional channels, sometimes may justifiably impose economic
> sanctions and/or make conditional offers of material assistance on
> individual citizens of another sovereign community C2. Indeed, they
> are sometimes obliged to do so.

Expository precision is a virtue, but so is concision. At times, of course,
it will be necessary to distinguish individual citizens from specific officials, and mid-ranking officials from leaders. But whenever I can, I will
use the labels "Sender," "Donor," and "Lender" to denote both the regime and the individual citizens of the political community on whose
behalf that regime's officials impose sanctions and offer conditional assistance. I will use the labels "Target," "Beneficiary," and "Borrower" to
denote regimes and individual citizens of the political communities
who are subject to those sanctions and receive those conditional offers.
Those collective nouns (to which I will attach singular verbs) are merely
expository tools: my use thereof should not be read as a way, wittingly or
not, to introduce through the back door the thought that states are corporate agents whose acts can be treated, morally speaking, as independent
from the acts of (some of) their individual members.

One final terminological point. Throughout, I shall refer to individuals who are subject to the jurisdiction of a state as that state's citizens. In an important way, it is a misnomer. Residents and tourists who
pass through a country are also subject to the jurisdiction of that country's authorities, against which they have important rights. At many
junctures in the book, however, the term "citizen" will seem more apt
than "resident" or "member," let alone "an agent who is subject to the
jurisdiction of the state." Let it be noted that, depending on the context
(and in particular, on whether nationality is relevant), I shall have in
mind "residents," "individuals passing through," or "nationals," or all of
those at the same time.

Enforcing Human Rights

A First Pass

This book is about some of the economic means by which sovereign actors (or associations thereof) seek to defend human rights—means which are tantamount to depriving people of that to which they have presumptive rights. It presupposes that interfering with someone's freedom or depriving her of some resource is justified if she violates some agent's human rights, or unjustifiably fails to protect that agent from rights violations at the hands of third parties, or would discharge her duty to protect if faced with the threat of interference or loss of resources. In all three cases, the agent has forfeited her rights to the relevant freedoms and resources.

Defense of rights is an important justification—or a just cause, in the parlance of just war theorists—for depriving someone of that to which they have a presumptive right. Note, though, that it does not provide agents with an all-things-considered justification for so acting. Defender may have a just cause for killing Attacker if the latter is unwarrantedly threatening her life. However, she may not do so, all things considered, if by killing Attacker she would also kill a thousand innocent bystanders. Or Defender may have a just cause for inflicting some physical harm on Attacker as a means to block him from punching her on the nose. However, she may not kill him to that end. Defender's move, in other words, must not constitute a disproportionate response to the good she thereby secures (blocking Attacker's attack), vis-à-vis Attacker himself and vis-à-vis innocent bystanders. In addition, if Defender can thwart Attacker's attack by other means—for example, by arguing with him and thus convincing him to desist—she must do so. Finally, her move must stand a reasonable chance of succeeding in blocking the attack.[18]

One final point about rights enforcement. The overwhelmingly majority of officials (whether they act on behalf and at the behest of sovereign states or of international organizations) routinely commit or allow the commission of human rights violations. This uncontroversial diagnosis might be thought to generate a difficulty for my arguments throughout the book. Either only agents who are not themselves serious wrongdoers may justifiably enforce those rights in general and by way of economic statecraft in particular—in which case hardly anyone may justifiably do so in the world as it is. Or serious wrongdoers may justifiably enforce those rights—which seems very counterintuitive.

I can see the force of the very last point. However, imagine that both Andrew and Ann are unwarrantedly imprisoned by Villainous Kidnapper. Andrew attempts to rape Ann. Although Villainous Kidnapper is guilty of the grievous wrongdoing of kidnapping toward Andrew, she may forcibly prevent him from raping Ann without thereby wronging him. In fact, she is under a duty to Ann to do so—on the twofold grounds that one is under a duty to protect others from serious harm and that one is under a reparative duty to protect those who are exposed to serious harm as a result of one's action (in this case, the act of locking both rapist and victim in the same room). Or consider a police officer acting on behalf of a seriously unjust regime. Were his commanding officers to order him to arrest a murder suspect, he would be entitled to do so notwithstanding the fact that they might also, the next day, order him to torture a political opponent to the regime.

The issue at stake here—which I simply cannot tackle in this book—is that of state legitimacy and authority. More precisely, it is the issue of the grounds on which, if any, an illegitimate state has the moral authority to enforce rights and duties. I stipulate here for the sake of argument that it sometimes does—put differently, that the mere fact that a regime is a rights violator does not thereby make it impermissible for its officials to prevent third parties from committing rights violations themselves.

Enforcing Rights under Conditions of Uncertainty

Many philosophers who write on the ethics of defense seek to establish what agents may justifiably do to or for one another in the light of the facts as they are, whatever agents know or believe about the facts. However, political actors whose foreign policy decisions are under scrutiny here often act under conditions of epistemic uncertainty, and the best that they can do is to ground those decisions in beliefs that they have formed in the light of the evidence available to them. It is also what they *ought* to do. Refusing to act on the basis of evidence and proceeding to make costly, a fortiori harmful decisions on the basis of unsubstantiated beliefs, is morally wrong to the extent that it evinces disrespect for other persons—even if it turns out that those decisions are objectively justified in the aforementioned sense.

Suppose, though, that there is so little evidence that Defender simply cannot form a grounded belief as to whether or not, for example, Attacker is about to violate her right not to be killed. Or suppose that she cannot form a grounded belief as to what she needs to do in order to stand a chance of thwarting him. Or suppose that she can form grounded beliefs about all of those things, but there is a risk that, by attempting to kill Attacker, she will cause grievous and wrongful harm to another and innocent person. She might not even know that there is such a risk; or she might know that there is, but cannot assign to it a probability that it will eventuate. Defender, in other words, acts under conditions of uncertainty—indeed, in some cases, under conditions of ignorance. The question, then, is what she may or ought to do, given that she runs the risk of wronging Attacker or an innocent third party if she acts, and of losing her life if she does not.

Uncertainty of that kind pervades our lives. It has received comparatively little attention in moral and political philosophy—with the exception of environmental ethics. In that particular field, action-guiding principles for decision-making under conditions of uncertainty are known as precautionary principles. Those principles tend to have a tripartite structure: if some course of action (a) is, or is likely to be, damaging to, for example, the environment, and if (b) we do not have full knowledge of the causal connection between that course of action and such damage or of the probability that the damage will occur, then (c) we may not engage in that course of action regardless. Claim (c) covers different possible courses of action: we must altogether desist from proceeding, or we may proceed so long as we take steps to mitigate the likelihood that the damage will occur, or we must postpone proceeding until such time as we have better information.[19]

In the context of this book, the courses of action under consideration consist in the following. In the case of economic sanctions, they consist in interfering with agents' economic transactions, and/or in imposing on them the concomitant costs of such interference (via loss of income, depleted resources such as food shortages, etc.). In the case of assistance conditionality, they consist in threatening to withdraw or withhold resources, and actually doing so. In both cases, the aim is to enforce human rights.

When deciding whether or not to resort to economic statecraft under conditions of uncertainty, we must thus pay attention to the wrongful damage that those measures might cause—more specifically whether we would wrongfully deprive agents of the freedoms and the resources to which they have presumptive rights. What we must do depends on the degree of uncertainty under which we operate, the probability that the damage will eventuate, and the magnitude of both the damage that we risk causing and the damage that we risk not preventing if we do not act. Importantly, given that, other things being roughly equal, wrongfully imposing a cost on someone is morally worse than wrongfully allowing that cost to befall them, we ought not to resort to a particular course of action for the sake of protecting someone's rights if in so doing we risk infringing the rights of another person.

The foregoing remarks suggest that what we are morally entitled and obliged to do is highly contextual, contingent as it is on the specific facts of the case at hand. Absent further determination of those facts, we cannot reach a decisive verdict. What we can do in the present context, though, is articulate and develop those considerations in the context of economic statecraft, in an attempt to bring some philosophical order to the issue.

Conclusion

With those bits of conceptual and normative machinery in place, the book offers a qualified defense of economic statecraft as a tool for the enforcement of human rights. It begins with economic sanctions (or economic threats), proceeds to scrutinizing aid and lending conditionality (or economic offers), and ends with a discussion of hypocrisy and double standards in foreign policy in general, and this particular context in particular.

CHAPTER TWO

Economic Sanctions

ECONOMIC STATECRAFT OPERATES on agents' rights with respect to material resources. Insofar as it comprises economic sanctions, it constitutes an interference with agents' property rights in general and their rights to trade in particular. In extant practices, sanctions are standardly defended as a means to stop ongoing human rights violations; to deter the commission of future human rights violations; and to get the targets of those sanctions to align their rightful domestic and foreign policies to the sanctioning party's interests.

In this chapter, and in keeping with my overall approach in the book, I examine the first two rationales. I begin by offering a typology of sanctions and describing how they work. I then defend sanctions insofar as they apply to agents who commit or contribute to human rights violations, and as they are meant to prevent those agents from so acting or to make it more costly for them to so act. Next, I turn to sanctions as a mechanism for deterring putative wrongdoers from committing future violations. In a third move, I argue that sanctions may also sometimes be justifiably imposed on those who are not wrongdoers, on the grounds that the latter are under duties to shoulder some of the costs of protecting Target's victims. Having provided a defense of limited sanctions, I offer a partial rebuttal of the often-raised objection that sanctions are ineffective and therefore morally wrong.

Three caveats before I start. First, I restrict my account to the following kinds of sanctions: sanctions that are applied by the United Nations and sanctions that are applied by multistate organizations such as the European Union or the African Union, as well as by a sovereign state, against economic activities in which at least one of the parties is subject to the territorial or personal jurisdiction of these states. In Chapter 3, I shall address so-called secondary sanctions, which sovereign states, acting on their own and not as members of a multistate organization, impose against individuals and companies based outside their jurisdiction. In line with much of the relevant empirical literature, I refer to the sanctioning party as Sender and to the target of its policy as Target.

Second, I am concerned with cases in which Sender aims to enforce human rights thanks to sanctions. Cases in which it seeks to further other geopolitical ends but coincidentally succeeds in enforcing human rights are beyond the scope of my inquiry.

Third, I am interested in sanctions on transactions pertaining to privately owned goods and assets. When Sender decides not to sell to Target resources that it owns (such as financial services as provided by nationalized banks or natural resources located under Sender's territory), it is simply deciding not to transact with Target in the first instance. I shall consider some of the ethical issues raised by withholding opportunities for economic relationships when addressing the justice, or injustice, of sovereign lending in Chapter 5. For now, the private ownership assumption remains in place.

Preliminaries

A Typology of Sanctions

At the time of writing, the United Nations are operating fourteen different sanctions regimes, the EU twenty, and the United States twenty-seven—against sovereign states and officials thereof. Here are some examples of current regimes.[1] Following the annexation in all but name of Crimea by

Russia in 2014, the United States and the European Union applied a vast
array of sanctions against the latter. In particular, U.S.-based companies
may not export defense-related goods or services to Russia and Crimea,
and European nationals may not buy or invest in key sectors in Russia
or buy from and sell financial products to banks owned by the Russian
state. In November 2017, the United States and the European Union
imposed sanctions, in the form of bans on arms trade and asset freezes,
on Venezuela's leadership—in response to President Maduro's crackdown on the opposition.[2]

Better known still are the decades-long sanctions that the United States
has applied and renewed against Iran. To name but a few of those measures, in 1997 (via President William Clinton's Executive Order 13059)
U.S. nationals were banned from trading with and investing in Iran. In
addition, U.S.-based persons, irrespective of nationality, were also pro-
hibited from so acting, as are foreign-based subsidiary companies of
U.S. firms. Some of those sanctions were lifted following Iran's 2015
agreement with the world's main powers to slow down its program of
nuclear enrichment and destroy its stock of enriched uranium. However,
an array of measures remains in place.

Iran is not the only Middle Eastern country to be subject to sanctions.
Thus, the United States, the European Union, and the United Nations
have tried, unsuccessfully so far, to contain Syrian president Bashar al-
Assad's regime by resorting to a wide range of sanctions against him per-
sonally, his family, and his domestic allies. Those sanctions range from
asset freezes to bans on oil imports and restrictions on trade in various
technologies. Concurrently, Saudi Arabia, Bahrain, Egypt, and the
United Arab Emirates imposed various trade restrictions on Qatar in the
spring and summer of 2017, in response to the latter's alleged support for
transnational Islamist terrorism.[3]

Looking farther east, the United States, the United Nations, and the
European Union have imposed several rounds of economic sanctions on
North Korea in response to the latter's development and adoption of a nu-
clear program and policy of grievous rights violations against its people.[4]

Finally, the African Union (AU) and the Economic Community of West
African States (ECWAS) have imposed sanctions against a number of
African states. To give but two examples, in 1997 the ECWAS subjected

Sierra Leone to an arms embargo; in 2015, the AU imposed sanctions against Burundi. In the majority of cases involving sanctions against an African regime, African regional organizations have imposed their own sanctions in parallel with, indeed often preceding, similar moves by the UN, the EU, and other sovereign actors. Interestingly, the AU and the ECWAS have tended to focus on unconstitutional regime changes (and concomitant violations of political rights) within their member states as the basis for resorting to sanctions.[5]

Economic sanctions, thus, interfere in economic relationships between consenting economic parties for the sake of bringing about foreign policy goals. They standardly divide into trade restrictions and financial restrictions. Trade restrictions consist of export and import restrictions, tariffs, and wholesale embargos. Financial restrictions include freezing assets, banning investment in Target, banning Target's agents from investing in Sender, and locking Target's agents out of Sender's financial institutions. Trade and financial sanctions can be more or less comprehensive, or (put conversely) more or less targeted, with respect both to their objects and to affected individuals. Suppose that Sender decides to block all financial loans by Sender's banking institutions to all of Target's agents. The measure is targeted with respect to its object but comprehensive with respect to affected individuals. Furthermore, sanctions can be more or less stringent, in that they can restrict a particular activity to varying degrees. Suppose that Target's leaders invest in the stock market via Sender-based brokerage firms and that Sender decides to ban such transactions. The measure is highly targeted with respect to its object and affected individuals, but it is not particularly stringent if those officials can use a brokerage firm elsewhere. By contrast, when Sender freezes all assets held by Target's leaders with all Sender-based institutions, it blocks all uses of those assets, thereby stringently constraining their owners.

We must supplement this typology with three further distinctions. First, we need to distinguish between, on the one hand, goods that Target uses to conduct its policy (e.g., military hardware) and, on the other hand, goods that Target would like to procure from Sender and that are important enough to its leadership that withholding them might prompt the desired policy change. I propose to categorize the former as "narrow strategic goods" and the latter as "wide strategic goods."[6]

Second, we must distinguish between single-purpose and dual-purpose goods. Single-purpose goods enable Target to pursue its unjust policy and serve no other purpose—such as weapons. Dual-purpose goods are needed for both wrongful and rightful ends. Oil is the paradigmatic example of such a good: it fuels both the vehicles that Target's military uses to round up political opponents and the civilian ambulances that ferry patients to emergency rooms.

The distinction between narrow and wide strategic goods cuts across the distinction between single-purpose and dual-purpose goods. Narrow single-purpose goods enable Target to pursue its unjust policy and serve no other purpose. Wide single-purpose goods are goods that only Target's rights violators covet, so much so that depriving them of those goods would induce them to change policy. By contrast, narrow dual-purpose goods are needed for both wrongful and rightful ends—oil being a primary example. Wide dual-purpose goods, for their part, are needed or wanted both by Target's rights violators and innocent residents, so that withholding them can be costly to the former as well as the latter.

Third, assume that Target's leaders have the resources to buy and import the goods that they need to commit rights violations—say, weapons. However, they do not have enough financial reserves to do so and at the same time to procure what they need in order to further some other political or social goals (for example, food or medical equipment). Suppose now that economic agents within Sender are willing to sell those other goods to Target at a discounted price or to provide them with loans— which in turn enables Target's leadership both to buy the weapons it needs and to procure those other goods. Call the latter "indirectly contributing goods": they are indirectly contributing to Target's unjust policy in the sense that their availability makes that policy less costly than it could have been had Sender's economic agents refused to trade with, or to offer loans to, Target.

Hence the following typology:

- Trade versus financial restrictions
- Narrow strategic goods (e.g., weapons) versus wide strategic goods (e.g., luxury goods; resources needed by Target's leaders to buy political support)

- Single-purpose goods (e.g., weapons; military technology) versus dual-purpose goods (e.g., oil)
- Directly contributing goods (e.g., weapons) versus indirectly contributing goods (e.g., goods at discounted price, loans)
- Comprehensive sanctions (against all agents and / or all goods) versus targeted (against some agents and / or some categories of goods)
- Less stringent sanctions (with respect to one kind of transaction in a particular sphere) versus more stringent (with respect to all transactions in that sphere)

A normative account of sanctions must bear those distinctions in mind, for as we shall see presently, different justifications apply to different kinds of goods.

What Sanctions Do

A normative account of sanctions must also be attentive to the ways in which they operate. In Chapter 1, I claimed that all individuals, wherever they reside, have property rights over the resources they need in order to lead a flourishing life. Furthermore, subject to meeting the demands of justice, they also have property rights over the resources they have acquired above and beyond that threshold. Those property rights are best understood in Hohfeldian terms. Finally, I argued that interfering with a freedom or withholding a resource to which agents have a presumptive right stands in need of justification. Taken together, those points make a case in favor of free international trade.

Now, when Sender's leaders pass legislation or issue an executive order in favor of sanctions, they change economic agents' bundles of ownership rights over money and goods. Agents within Sender who might want to sell goods to their counterparts in Target are denied the Hohfeldian power to do so, as well as the Hohfeldian claim not to be interfered with when doing so. They might also be denied immunity from punishment should they nevertheless go ahead. Moreover, insofar as selling a good g is a means for them to derive income, they lose opportunities to earn more money thanks to which they would be able to implement their conception of the good. Similarly, agents within Sender who wish to buy g from their counterparts within Target are denied the power to dispose of their money to those ends, and the aforementioned claim right and immunity. To the extent that g contributes to their conception of the good life, they too lose opportunities to implement the latter. The same applies, conversely, to Target's agents.

That very last claim is particularly important. A successful justification for sanctions must provide an account of which parties in the transaction under consideration may justifiably be deprived of the freedom to transact (bearing in mind that they have presumptive rights to transact in general). The point is not specific to sanctions: generally, any argument to the effect that some agent may justifiably interfere with an economic transaction between n parties must state whether all n parties, or only some, may justifiably be subjected to such interference. This applies to, e.g., prostitutional transactions, surrogate motherhood contracts, restrictions on the sale and purchase of dangerous goods, the imposition of tariffs and nontariff barriers, and so on. To illustrate by reference to prostitution: to say that the state may justifiably refuse to recognize a prostitutional exchange as valid is to say that both client and prostitute may justifiably be denied the Hohfeldian power to contract with each other with respect to sexual services. To say that it may justifiably ban such an exchange is to say that either the client, or the prostitute, or both are liable to being punished for so acting: perhaps only clients may be punished; or perhaps only prostitutes. In the case at hand, when we justify sanctions, we justify subjecting Sender's and Target's economic agents to being disempowered from transacting with each other; if sanctions are backed by the criminal law, a justification for sanctions must also show which of the parties may be punished for transacting.

Agents whose well-being depends on international trade although they do not directly participate in it also incur sanctions-related costs. A firm in Sender which cannot sell its wares to its regular buyers within Target may have to lay off some of its employees. Those employees might find it difficult to find another job and might lose personal income as a result, with detrimental consequences for their families, the local businesses that depend on their custom, and so on. Likewise, a firm in Target that cannot buy the goods it needs from its regular suppliers in Sender might not be able to survive—with similar effects on its employees. More generally, sanctions that impair Target-agents' access to international trade have knock-on effects on Target's economic growth, which in turn lowers tax revenues and, by extension, undermines Target's ability to provide essential services to its residents, maintain its infrastructures, and so forth. Again, the same considerations apply to Sender's agents.[7]

Admittedly, the imposition of sanctions on Target might well benefit agents in third-party countries who succeed in increasing their market share in Sender as a result of Target's exclusion.[8] Nevertheless, sanctions do constitute an interference with the freedom of trade of some, and impose costs on many. To justify their use in defense of human rights, thus, is to justify interfering with agents' presumptive right freely to trade with one another for the sake of those rights; it is also to justify the imposition of the relevant costs, as described in the previous paragraph, on citizens of both Target and Sender. In the next two sections, I defend targeted sanctions as a means to stop and deter agents from wrongfully contributing to human rights violations against Target's citizens.

Economic Sanctions as a Means to Stop Human Rights Violations

A First Cut

Consider the following plausible scenarios. (1) Target forcibly annexes a territory that belongs to another sovereign state, without just cause. (2) Target embarks on a genocidal campaign against an ethnic minority within its borders. (3) Target provides military assistance to an ally that is itself waging an unjust war elsewhere. (4) Target develops and tests nuclear weapons and regularly issues declarations of aggressive intent toward its traditional enemies. Were it to deploy those weapons, it would violate the human rights of dozens of thousands of innocent people. (5) Target adopts severely repressive measures against one of its minorities, though falls short of killing those individuals.

In cases such as these, sanctions are often presented in public discourse as preferable to a war whose consequences would be catastrophic: imagine what would have happened had NATO invaded Russia in defense of Ukraine's territorial integrity in the summer of 2014; or consider what would happen if the United States decided to launch a preemptive strike against North Korea. Unsurprisingly, in the relatively recent normative literature on the topic, defenses of sanctions as an alternative to war often proceed by appeal to the normative framework of just war theory. At first sight, this makes sense. In the first four cases above, relevantly situated agents within Target (its leadership, armed forces, etc.) respectively threaten to kill, directly kill, or contribute to killing innocent people. We might accept that there is a just cause for war but nevertheless think that war would be, all things considered, unjustified. If so, it is natural to inquire whether economic sanctions might be a morally acceptable alternative to war.[9]

That being said, although just war theory is helpful in such cases, we should remain wary of embracing it too quickly as our default normative framework, for two reasons. First, in the fifth case, Target's leadership does not use, or threaten to use, lethal force as a means to violate the rights of innocent people and thus does not (I believe) provide Sender with a just cause for war.[10] The question then is whether it provides Sender with a just cause for economic sanctions—and if so, whether the latter are, all things considered, justified. Ascertaining that war is not a legitimate response does not establish that economic sanctions are legitimate, for it may be that doing nothing, or adopting other measures altogether, would be morally preferable to both.

Second, even if sanctions are a justified alternative to war, there is an important difference between those two instruments of foreign policy. When we go to war, we kill and wound. When we impose economic sanctions, although we might end up killing people, we do so by interfering with contractual economic and financial relationships. A precise philosophical justification for sanctions must be sensitive to that distinction.

Now, I averred earlier that a normative account of sanctions must show that Sender is justified in deliberately preventing Target's agents from having trade and financial dealings with Sender economic agents with respect to good g, and in preventing its own economic agents from dealing with Target agents. In this section, I am concerned with agents within Sender and Target who commit or contribute to committing human rights violations. With respect to Sender, my concern is with those of its economic agents who contribute to Target's unjust policy. With respect to Target, I focus on two categories of agents: Target's political and military agents, such as its leaders, armed forces, and high-level civil servants, who authorize and / or directly contribute to the commission of rights violations; and economic agents within Target who, by dint of their financial and / or trade activities act as intermediaries between Sender's economic agents and Target's political agents. To illustrate, for now I am interested in President Bashar al-Assad and his officials, the Western companies who might quite like to sell him their wares, and the Syrian businesses who, if given a chance, would quite like to act as intermediaries in those transactions. I shall address the difficulties raised by the case of ordinary citizens and ordinary economic agents later on.

TARGET'S POLITICAL OFFICIALS

Let us start with Target's officials. I take it for granted that individuals may justifiably exercise lethal force under the aforementioned conditions against agents who unjustifiably subject them, or third parties, to wrongful *lethal* costs. In those cases, defenders may justifiably subject attackers to economic sanctions. Suppose as per scenario (2) above that Target's regime mounts a genocidal campaign against a minority within Target. Suppose that Target's civilian leaders and combatants contribute to the genocide to such a degree that Sender may justifiably launch a military intervention and order its troops to kill them. War is not justified, all things considered, however, because (let us assume) it would constitute a vastly disproportionate response. Even so, a fortiori, Sender may justifiably subject *those* agents to a lesser cost to the same end—of which sanctions-related cost are a kind. In particular, Sender may justifiably refuse to sell to Target's leaders the resources that they need to carry out the genocide (such as military technology). It may also justifiably freeze those leaders' assets insofar as those assets are used to fund their unjust policy: by so acting, those agents have forfeited their presumptive property rights over their assets.

Consider now a case where there is no just cause for war in the first instance. For example, suppose that Target's cyber warfare specialists have successfully infiltrated Sender's computer networks, causing some—

though not devastating—disruption to the provision of services such as electricity and water without their having a just cause for doing so. Or suppose that Target's leadership carries out repressive policies toward its citizens: it severely constrains freedom of speech and association, imprisons hostile journalists (though falls short of killing them), bans political parties that are flagrantly hostile to it (though it falls short of being a mono-party system), and so on. Those acts are rights violations. However, they are not backed by the threat of lethal force, and it is not plausible therefore to regard them as providing Sender with a just cause for going to war against Target, whether in self-defense (in the first case) or in defense of the regime's victims (in the second case). Accordingly, if sanctions are to be justified as an alternative to war as well as in and of themselves, it cannot be on the grounds that there is a just cause but that a war would be disproportionate; rather, it must be on the combined grounds that there is no just cause for war in the first instance, that there *is* a just cause for sanctions, and that the latter would meet the aforementioned conditions on justified cost imposition.

To say that Sender has a just cause for imposing economic sanctions is to say (in part) that it may justifiably deprive agents who are avoidably violating the human rights of some other party of the benefits of trade relations with its own economic agents, as a means to stop them. The cases I have just outlined, where there is no just cause for war but where Target's political agents commit or contribute to human rights violations, are of that kind. To the extent that Target's political officials do so act and that the sanctions-related costs that they incur meet the conditions of justified cost imposition, Sender may justifiably impose sanctions.

Note that the point applies to single-purpose narrow strategic goods such as weapons and to dual-purpose narrow strategic goods such as oil—in other words, goods without which those wrongdoers would not be able to carry out their policy. It also applies to wide strategic goods (be they single-purpose or dual-purpose) and indirectly contributing goods. Wide strategic goods are goods that Sender's economic agents are willing to sell and that Target's officials wish to buy, though they do not need them to commit human rights violations. Indirectly contributing goods are goods that Target's leaders and citizens are sold at preferential prices, or loans offered at preferential rates, which in turn enables Target's leaders to fund their preferred policies—in this context, their unjust policies—at a lesser cost. If denying those leaders access to those goods would get them to stop, it is hard to see why Sender may not justifiably do so.

Note, finally, that in my account there is as much reason to impose sanctions on liberal democratic regimes that act grievously unjustly than on authoritarian dictatorships. The point might seem obvious, but given that in practice democratic regimes are more reluctant to impose sanctions on other democracies than they are to impose them on autocratic regimes, it does bear stressing.[11]

TARGET'S AND SENDER'S ECONOMIC AGENTS

Justifying the imposition of sanctions on Target and Sender's economic agents is somewhat more complex. Suppose that Sender's economic agents trade with their counterparts in Target in the narrow strategic goods that Target's regime needs to carry out its unjust policy. In so acting, those agents wrongfully contribute to those rights- violations. The point applies not merely to Target's economic agents, but also to Sender's: as we saw in Chapter 1, individuals are under cross-border duties not to wrongfully contribute to violating human rights. Insofar as Target's agents and Sender's agents wrongfully contribute through their economic activities to Target's unjust policy, they have forfeited their presumptive right not to incur the costs of not being able to continue to do so—and Sender may thus justifiably impose those costs on them.

But now consider indirectly contributing goods as well as wide strategic goods. Economic agents who trade in those goods do not directly contribute to the human rights violations that justify sanctions. Rather, they respectively lessen the costs for Target's leaders of committing those acts and fail to provide Target's officials with an incentive to stop committing human rights violations. Thus, the connection between selling narrow strategic goods to Target's regime and that regime's unjust policy is strong, whereas the connection between that policy and selling indirectly contributing goods or wide strategic goods is comparatively weak. However, this does not seem an appropriate basis for holding weapons manufacturers under duties not to contribute to those rights violations while exempting other economic agents altogether. For as we saw in Chapter 1, duties not to contribute include duties not to enable or facilitate the commission of such violations by third parties. Those duties, moreover, are held by all of us, individually and institutionally. Accordingly, financial institutions ought not to provide favorable loan terms to dictators thanks to which the latter will be in a position to commit rights violations; economic agents within Target who do not directly contribute to the wrongdoings committed by their leaders but nevertheless act as intermediaries between the latter and Sender's suppliers of those goods ought not so to act either. By so acting, those agents also contribute to human rights violations and have forfeited their rights not to be subject to the costs of sanctions. If the best available evidence leads Sender to believe that institutionalizing those pre-institutional individual duties would serve the desired end, Sender may justifiably do so.

Some readers might think those points farfetched, particularly with respect to luxury goods: would it really matter to a dictator and his acolytes not to be able to shop at Harrods? Perhaps not. But if, in addition, those people are unable to buy Bentley cars, flats in Paris, and mansions on the French Riviera; if their personal assets are frozen in perpetuity; if they are turned into pariahs in the world of so-called high net worth individuals, perhaps it might begin to matter or, at any rate, to weaken their power base to such an extent as to offer a glimmer of hope for their victims.[12]

This view admits of an important qualification. Suppose that, were Sender to turn an individual, unstructured boycott into governmental policy, Target's leaders would commit further rights violations. For example, those leaders might regard Sender's decision as a form of diplomatic provocation and in response choose to escalate the conflict— whereas they would not have done so had they been merely faced with an unstructured boycott. In such cases, even if economic agents are under a duty to boycott and thus would themselves not be wronged by the policy, Sender (we might plausibly argue) has strong countervailing reasons not to go ahead, indeed is under a duty not to go ahead.

To recapitulate, I have argued that agents within both Sender and Target are under duties not to contribute to the unjust policies conducted by Target's regime. Under certain conditions, those agents' failure to fulfil those duties provides Sender with a just cause for resorting to economic sanctions against them. Put differently, the moral imperative of enforcing human rights at the very least dictates in favor of targeted sanctions—targeted, that is, at those who contribute to Target's unjust policies by providing Target's political actors with the resources they need or by making it easier for them to procure such resources. In some respects, this is not particularly controversial. However, it is worth noting that implementing a policy of targeted sanctions raises specific epistemic difficulties. In particular, it requires of sanctioning parties that they have some knowledge of decision-making processes and networks of power and influence (both political and economic) within Sender's regime—of who, in other words, is a legitimate target. Put differently, it is one thing for Sender to be objectively justified in targeting this or that individual within Target; it is another for it to be justified so to act in the light of the evidence.

Proportionality and Necessity in Economic Sanctions

The problem of uncertainty is compounded by yet another moral imperative—namely that it is not enough that Sender should have a just cause for so proceeding (if it is to act justifiably): the sanctions are also subject to the requirements of proportionality, necessity, and effectiveness.

I shall return to effectiveness later on. Necessity and proportionality are troublesome, particularly given that decisions must be made under conditions of uncertainty. Consider necessity first. Suppose that we could stop the North Korean leadership from developing nuclear weapons by cutting off oil supplies to North Korea (which in some views would topple the regime) or by freezing all of their assets. Other things being equal, the requirement of necessity stipulates that we should do the latter. The difficulty of course is that at the point at which we must decide what to do, we may not know whether there might be a less harmful yet equally effective measure.[13]

Consider now proportionality, which (in the context of this section) requires that the imposition of a sanction on a wrongdoer not be a disproportionate response to his wrongdoing.[14] As I noted in Chapter 1, the human rights violations that sanctions are meant to thwart are committed by a great many agents acting, or failing to act, together. When Target's leaders embark on this kind of policy, they do so with the complicity—or direct participation—of the police, the army, the bureaucracy, indeed, in democracies, of those of its citizens without whose support it would not be in power. Yet within each of those groups, we must distinguish between more and less influential, more or less responsible wrongdoers: the chief of police and the highest-ranking members of the military contribute in more significant ways to, for example, human rights abuses against the regime's opponents or against members of an ethnic minority, than rank-and-file policemen and soldiers. Within the citizenry itself, the owner of a television network who provides media support to the regime has far greater influence than a single voter. The same considerations apply to economic agents within Sender, thanks to whose activities Target's wrong-doers are able to commit those abuses. Thus, the CEO of an arms producer is not in the same decisional position as a worker on an assembly line.

To avoid the charge of disproportionality, a decision to impose sanctions must in principle tailor the sanctions regime in such a way that it will apply differently to different wrongdoers. In some cases, this is relatively easy to do. Consider, for example, trade in narrow strategic goods. Suppose that the aforementioned CEO wishes to secure a contract with Target's ministry of defense. Thanks to those weapons, Target's regime would be able successfully to threaten a neighboring country into blood-lessly relinquishing control over territory alongside the border. Selling weapons to wrongful (though bloodless) invaders is morally wrong, and procuring weapons to those ends is also morally wrong. As we saw above, both the CEO and Target's officials may justifiably be subjected to the costs attendant on not being able to trade with one another, subject to proportionality. In this case, Sender's policy takes the provision of strategic military goods as its object, on which it imposes targeted sanctions— targeted, that is, only at those who supply and procure those goods to this particular wrongful end. The cost of not being able to trade in those goods and losing one's business as a result is not disproportionate given what those goods are being used for.

Consider now sanctions against wide strategic goods—namely, those goods that Target's leaders would rather or can only procure from abroad. Or consider sanctions against indirectly contributing goods. Again, and intuitively at least, the cost such as it is for Target's leadership and the upper echelons of its bureaucracy, police, and army of not being able to procure luxury goods or to unlock millions of dollars held in foreign bank accounts is not disproportionate to, for example, the wrongdoing of violating fundamental human rights.

But consider, now, agents who make a minor contribution to those wrongdoings, such as the arms producer's menial employees or ordinary citizens who have voted for Target's regime. Clearly, they would be disproportionately affected by a comprehensive sanctions policy if as a result they would lose their jobs and would no longer be able to meet their basic survival needs. They would also be disproportionately affected, in relation to their own individual contribution, by comprehensive sanctions on basic necessities. To illustrate, in September 2017, the UN imposed sanctions on imports from North Korea—as a means to deprive the country's leadership of the revenues it needs in order to pursue its expansionist military policy (which policy, the UN justifiably believes, both already consists in, and threatens further, human rights violations). According to some reports, those sanctions are causing severe hardship to a number of Chinese textile traders on the border between China and North Korea. By facilitating North Korea's textile exports, those traders contribute to increasing North Korea's revenues; in so doing, they contribute to North Korea's human rights violations, and it is not inappropriate to regard their contribution as wrongful. However, their individual contribution not only is indirect, it is also marginal to North Korea's policy. To threaten their very livelihood and thereby put them at risk of dying (of starvation, untimely illness, etc.) is disproportionate in relation to their contribution.[15]

This seems fairly straightforward: in this case, sanctioning parties can fairly easily form a judgment as to whom their policy would affect and to what extent. If so, their decision to impose sanctions on those individuals is justified—or not—in the light of the evidence. All too often, however, they simply do not have the kind of evidence that would enable them to form justified beliefs about the degree to which a sanctions policy is a proportionate response. They might be relatively confident that a CEO's presumptive right to trade and derive the benefits thereof may justifiably be curtailed; they may be similarly confident that Target's regime and top decision-makers make a significant contribution to the human rights violations at issue, and thus may be locked out of Sender's banking institutions. At the other end of the scale, Sender may also be appropriately confident that the CEO's menial employees and Target's ordinary citizens would incur disproportionate costs through comprehensive sanctions. But this would not give Sender a reason to be similarly confident about the CEO's mid-level employees, or Target's mid-level civil servants and civil society actors—for it simply does not know what kind of job those employees do exactly and thus how they contribute to Target's human rights violations.

The claim that rendering those judgments is difficult does not entail that there is no truth of the matter. But even if there is a truth of the matter, we still need an action-guiding principle that is sensitive to those epistemic difficulties. Drawing on my earlier account of rights enforcement under conditions of uncertainty in Chapter 1, Sender's leaders must take into consideration (a) the extent to which, to the best of their knowledge, a policy of economic sanctions would lead them wrongfully to deprive some agents of the freedoms or resources to which they have rights; (b) the extent to which, to the best of their knowledge, not resorting to such a policy would lead them wrongfully to fail to protect other agents' similar rights; and (c) the degree of uncertainty under which, to the best of their knowledge, they operate.

Now, other things roughly equal, harming wrongfully is morally worse than wrongfully allowing harm to happen. Accordingly, the greater the degree of uncertainty, the more should Sender err on the side of not imposing sanctions. Often, however, things are not equal. For example, it may be that by not imposing sanctions, Sender would allow considerably worse harm to happen to Target's victims, and/or to considerably more of those victims, than the admittedly disproportionate costs it would inflict on wrongful contributors by imposing sanctions. In that case, Sender should err on the side of sanctions. But it must at the same time try to minimize the risk that it would wrongfully infringe the rights of Target's agents. One way to do this would be to opt for a policy of targeted sanctions—targeted, that is, either with respect to wrongful contributors within Target, or with respect to certain kinds of goods, or both.

To illustrate, consider the sanctions imposed by the European Union and the United States on Russia following the latter's annexation of Crimea and parts of Eastern Ukraine in 2014. Assume for the sake of argument (but, I believe, plausibly) that the Russian authorities violated the human rights of those Ukrainians who did not wish to be annexed. The sanctions can be construed as an attempt to make it harder for President Putin and his administration to continue to violate those rights. To this end, they targeted state-owned firms controlled by President Putin's circle in the three sectors most closely relevant to Russia's expansionist policies and need for revenues (energy, arms, and finances). They also targeted dozens of individuals specifically by issuing travel bans and decreeing asset freezes. Those individuals included a number of generals, top-flight businessmen close to President Putin, security and intelligence chiefs (in the case of EU sanctions), and high-level Kremlin officials. Clearly, though, the European Union and the United States could have decided to widen the scope of their sanctions, in particular by extending their reach to many other sectors. Had they done so, they would undoubtedly have imposed much greater costs on many more wrongful contributors within Russia. Absent evidence of those agents' specific contribution to their regime's expansionist policy vis-à-vis Ukraine, it made sense, morally speaking, to err on the side of caution—particularly as there was no evidence at the time that Russia's leadership regarded the annexation of Crimea as a prelude to a wholesale invasion of Ukraine. Had there been such evidence, a more comprehensive sanctions policy would have been justified in the light of the evidence—albeit not objectively so if, in fact, it would have turned out to be disproportionate.[16]

Economic Sanctions as a Deterrent

To recapitulate, Sender is sometimes justified in imposing economic sanctions on agents who contribute to Target's unjust policy, as a means to stop them from so acting here and now and, thereby, as a means to put a stop to those ongoing wrongdoings. Under conditions of uncertainty and given that it ought to proceed on the basis of the best available evidence, the kind of sanctions it may justifiably impose on which agents depends on as accurate an assessment as it can provide of the relative risks of wrongfully depriving those agents of that to which they have a right, versus wrongfully failing to protect Target's victims. The weaker the evidence, the more cautious it should be—and the stronger the case, thus, in favor of highly targeted sanctions.

In this section, I examine the imposition of sanctions as a means to deter the commission of future wrongdoings. There are similarities of course between putting a stop to an ongoing wrong and deterring a future wrong. In both cases, the agent seeks to thwart wrongs. In both cases, the requirements of necessity, proportionality, and effectiveness constrain the imposition of sanctions, which (combined with the fact that Sender may be operating under conditions of uncertainty) dictates in favor of targeted measures. However, there are some important differences between those two courses of action. Let us stipulate that at time t_1, Target embarks on a policy p of human rights violations. In this section, we are concerned with cases in which Sender imposes economic sanctions on Target at t_2 as a means to render credible its threat of further sanctions at t_3 should further human rights violations be committed at t_3. (Strictly speaking, Sender might impose economic sanctions at t_2 as a means to make credible its threat of a different and more serious harm—for example, a missile strike—at t_3. I focus on sanctions, in keeping with my overall focus in this book.)

Now, it may be that by stopping Target at t_2 from violating human rights at t_2, Sender would deter its leaders from committing further rights violations at t_3. However, in some cases, sanctions that are effective at stopping at t_2 the human rights violations to which they are a response will not deter the commission of further violations at t_3. Only harsher sanctions would do—though those harsher sanctions would be disproportionate to the human rights violations committed at t_1. Analogously, suppose that, at t_2, Defender can stop Attacker from punching her on the nose by violently twisting one of his arms. However, she will not succeed at deterring him from trying again at t_3. Only a threat of having his arm broken, made credible by having both of his arms violently twisted, will do it. Granted, Defender will stop as well as deter him by violently twisting both of his arms at t_2. But the question is whether she may do so given that, ex hypothesi, she need not do so in order to stop him from punching her on the nose at t_2.

The difference between stopping the commission of an ongoing wrongdoing and deterring future wrongdoings is even more salient when general, as distinct from special, deterrence is at issue. A special deterrence–based justification for sanctions needs to show the following: at *t2*, Sender may justifiably impose economic sanctions on Target's wrongdoers, in response to the fact that the latter embarked on policy *p* at *t1*, and as a means to deter them from committing further rights violations at *t3*. In general deterrence, by contrast, the imposition of a cost on a wrongdoer is meant to deter other putative wrongdoers from committing a wrongdoing. Suppose that Target's leadership embarks on unjust policy *p* at *t1*. At *t2*, Sender imposes sanctions on the leadership as a means to deter another regime, Target*, from adopting *p* at *t3*. This is harder to justify than special deterrence. To see this, suppose that Defender will succeed at stopping and deterring Attacker by twisting one of his arms. To deter other putative attackers, however, she needs to twist both of his arms. Even if we can show that she may block and deter him by twisting one of his arms, we will not have thereby shown that she may twist both of his arms—thereby harming him to a greater degree—as a means to deter other putative attackers. For after all, ex hypothesi, he will not be responsible for those future rights violations, so it is not immediately clear why he should pay the additional cost of thwarting them.

With those points in hand, we must attend to two issues: the justifiability of threatening at *t2* to impose economic sanctions at *t3* in case further human rights violations are committed; the justifiability of imposing economic sanctions at *t2* as a means to render this threat of further sanctions credible.

Before I begin, let me make two further clarifying points. First, in the context of this book, the question of general deterrence arises in two scenarios: either Sender wishes to deter the leadership's successors, or it wishes to deter the putative wrongdoers of another country, Target*. In the first scenario, cohorts of citizens in general and wrongdoers in particular within a given community overlap with one another. As a result, a policy of general deterrence vis-à-vis putative wrongdoers is likely to be merged with a policy of special deterrence vis-à-vis those individuals who acted wrongly at *t1* and are threatened at *t2* with further cost if they collaborate with putative different wrongdoers at *t3*. The conclusions I will reach regarding special deterrence apply to those same wrongdoers; the conclusions I will reach regarding general deterrence apply to those of their compatriots who have not yet but might commit rights violations at

$t3$. For ease of exposition, I focus on the second kind of scenario, where a general deterrence–based theory of economic sanctions needs to show the following: Sender's leaders are justified at $t2$ in imposing economic sanctions on Target's wrongdoers as a means to make their threat, at $t2$, of imposing sanctions at $t3$ on Target*'s wrongdoers credible.

Second, deterrent sanctions can be used to deter both leaders of dictatorial regimes and their henchmen and economic agents who contribute to those rights violations by, for example, selling arms, granting loans, and so on, to dictators. In practice, this is not always the case. Thus, to the extent that sanctions against Syria are a deterrent, they are an attempt to deter President Assad and his acolytes. They are not meant to deter Western arms manufacturers who might be tempted to sell him weapons in the future—even though they effectively prevent those manufacturers from trading with him. In principle, however, insofar as Western arms manufacturers would commit the wrongdoing of aiding and abetting President Assad by selling him weapons, we must remain open to justifying sanctions as a deterrent measure against those agents, as well as Assad himself. For ease of exposition, I will focus on sanctions that are construed as a means to deter Target's political leaders, but my claims apply, mutatis mutandis, to all other contributors to human rights violations.

Threatening Economic Sanctions

Suppose that Attacker attacks Defender at $t1$. Unless she disarms him at $t2$ by inflicting cost c on him, Attacker will attack her again at $t3$. So long as imposing c meets the constraints of necessity, proportionality, and effectiveness, Attacker may justifiably impose c on him. The fact that his attack will happen at some point in the future instead of now is irrelevant.

Suppose now that Attacker, who attacked Defender at $t1$, will attack her again at $t3$ unless she threatens him now, at $t2$, with inflicting c on him if he proceeds at $t3$. If she may justifiably thwart him by subjecting him to c at $t2$, thereby acting on his body, surely she may justifiably modify his incentives structure by threatening him with c at $t2$, thereby acting on his mind. Imposing a cost is not as bad as a threat thereof. If imposing a cost on him is justified defensively, so a fortiori is threatening him with the same or indeed lesser cost. In other words, the moral justifiability of threatening a cost is derived from the justifiability of protecting oneself.[17]

Let us apply those points to sanctions. As we saw above, Sender may justifiably impose sanctions on Target's leaders—for example, a stringent freeze of all the assets held by the latter in Sender's banking institutions. Under the same circumstances, it is justified in merely threatening at $t2$ to impose those very same sanctions against those agents, in response to their human rights violations at $t1$, as a means to deter them from committing or contributing to the commission of further rights violations at $t3$.

So far, so good. But now, suppose that Sender would not be justified in actually imposing those sanctions. May its leaders nevertheless threaten Target with it? On some views, one may not threaten to do something that one is not morally permitted to do. This is because (it is argued) the threat is not credible, and thus will not work, unless one forms the conditional intention to carry it out; but if it is morally wrong to do x, surely it is morally wrong to form the conditional intention to do x; and if it is morally wrong to form such an intention, it is morally wrong to threaten to do x.

This is the classic paradox of deterrence. Yet something seems to have gone awry here, as the following example suggests. Let us concede that Defender may not justifiably kill Attacker's innocent sleeping son as a means to protect herself from Attacker's wrongful lethal attack. Defender has good reasons to think that if she threatens to kill the child unless Attacker desists, Attacker will believe her and desist. It does seem that Defender may justifiably threaten to kill Attacker's son in this case—even though she would not be morally permitted to proceed if Attacker turned out not to take her threat seriously. The son is asleep and thus not harmed by a threat which, in any event, will not materialize. Attacker has no claim against incurring the cost of having to deal with this particular threat. It seems highly counterintuitive to say that, under those circumstances, Defender ought to allow herself to be killed.

If this is right, the fact that Sender may not justifiably impose sanctions against Target does not entail that it may not justifiably threaten to do so. In fact, there are good reasons for thinking that it is morally justified in doing so—namely that Target's leaders would be thereby deterred from committing further rights violations. Of course, threats of that kind raise

serious worries about the dangers of escalation. I will address those worries later on.[18]

Imposing Sanctions as a Credibility Mechanism

Deterrent economic sanctions are a means to make the threat of future
sanctions credible. So construed, they are a signaling measure. As we also
saw, there are moral limits to the kind and magnitude of the costs we are
permitted to inflict on other agents—including, in this context, signaling
costs. Those limits are set by the constraints of necessity, proportionality,
and effectiveness. Thus, Sender may justifiably impose economic sanctions at t_2 as a means to make its concomitant threat of future sanctions
at t_3 credible only if the cost so inflicted is necessary, proportionate, and
effective.

What kind of cost might that be? In some cases, the answer to that
question can be read off the permissibility—or not—of measures that are
meant to stop ongoing contributions to human rights violations. If imposing a cost is morally disallowed on the grounds that it is a disproportionate response to a given ongoing threat, imposing it as a means to deter
a similar threat is not permissible either. Thus, if Sender is not justified
in imposing sanctions on the basic necessities of life against wrongdoers
as a means to stop them from violating human rights, it is not justified in
imposing this particular kind of sanctions to signal at t_2 their willingness
to impose further sanctions at t_3.

In some cases, however, the claim that one may not impose a cost to
block a violation does not entail that imposing the same cost is impermissible as a credibility mechanism for dealing with future threats. For
example, Sender's sanctions might be a disproportionate means to
block human rights violations here and now, but once one takes into account the magnitude of the future violations they are deterring Sender
from committing, they might in fact constitute a proportionate response.

The Special Case of General Deterrence

Everything I have said so far applies to both special and general deterrence. But general deterrence raises a specific problem, for it seems to

permit imposing a cost on a wrongdoer as a means to deter other putative wrongdoers. To pure consequentialists, the mere fact that someone
is adversely affected as a means for the good of others is no reason not to
proceed. But for those who accept the broadly Kantian view that we must
always treat people as autonomous moral agents, general deterrence is
seriously problematic: treating people as a means for the good of others
seems antithetical to treating them with the respect they are owed as such
agents.

The objection threatens a number of extant practices. There is little
doubt that economic sanctions such as are imposed on aspiring nuclear
powers are meant to deter other regimes from embarking on military nuclear programs and, thereby, to increase prospects for peace and respect
for human rights. There is also some evidence to suggest that economic
sanctions have had some success in this respect.[19]

The best recent responses to the problem of general deterrence have
been articulated by Victor Tadros. In his view, we do not fail to treat
someone as a mean when we deprive him of that to which he has a presumptive right as a way to enforce his moral duties. Consider: A wrongdoer, T, is under enforceable remedial duties toward his victims, such that
it is permissible to deprive him of his freedom or to inflict some harm on
him as a means to protect them from his own repeated attacks (hence special deterrence). More strongly still, T also owes enforceable protective
duties to future victims of another wrongdoer, T*. If T refuses to fulfill
those duties, and if inflicting a cost on him makes it less likely that T*
will harm future victims, we may so act, thereby enforcing his duty to
protect—even though we thereby use him as a means: T is guilty of a
serious wrongdoing and thus has forfeited his right not to be used as a
means.[20] As applied to deterrent sanctions, the argument goes like this:
on account of the atrocities that they have authorized against Syrian civilians, President Assad and his acolytes are under remedial duties to protect
future victims of atrocities committed by other wrongdoers not connected
to the Syrian authorities. One way to enforce those remedial duties is by
imposing economic sanctions on Assad and his associates as a means to
deter other dictators from committing similar offenses in the future.

Now, I agree that we (sometimes) may treat agents in these ways as a
means to protect others. This in effect is what enforcing duties of good

Samaritanism amounts to, and I shall argue as much in the context of sanctions below. But herein lies the rub for deterrence. As I argued in Chapter 1, we all are under duties of assistance to one another—which include a duty to protect them from serious harm—subject to the no-undue-sacrifice proviso. If so, it is not clear how wrongdoers' assistive duties to putative victims differ from duties of assistance which all human beings owe to one other as a matter of justice. However, to justify deterrence is to justify imposing on wrongdoers a cost which, but for the fact that they committed a serious wrong, they would have a right not to incur. If all the deterrence view permits, as the price to pay for compatibility with the Kantian prohibition, is the imposition of costs which the innocent must also incur for the sake of others, it loses its distinctiveness as a theory of justified cost imposition on wrongdoers.

Let me put the point in the context of economic sanctions. President Assad and his acolytes are innocent of the rights violations that other would-be dictators in other faraway countries might routinely commit in the future against their own compatriots. It may well be that imposing sanctions on Assad and his associates would deter those dictators from embarking on this particular policy. But it is unclear why the mere fact that Assad and his acolytes have authorized the commission of atrocities in Syria places them under greater protective duties to the dictator's victims than, for example, the leaders of France and the United Kingdom who are, let us assume, as innocent of Assad of those putative wrongdoings. Put differently, it is not clear why the dictator's victims would have a grievance against President Assad specifically, which they would not have against the French and British leaders, on account of his unrelated wrongdoings.

The justification for general deterrence I have just rejected relies on the claim that wrongdoers owe duties of protection to future wrongdoers' victims. But Tadros advances another defense of general deterrence, which does not rely on that claim and which fares better, as follows: We all are under an impersonal obligation to combat human rights violations. However, a wrongdoer qua wrongdoer is under a stronger obligation of that kind than an innocent person. Precisely because he committed such wrongdoings, it is appropriate to impose greater costs on him than on the innocent for the sake of human rights. Insofar as deliberately imposing such a cost on him would deter future wrongdoers and thus would help thwart human rights violations, we may so act—instead of imposing a cost on an innocent person.

The argument is plausible only if we accept impersonal obligations in general. I strongly suspect (though cannot defend that view here) that we must do so. So let us apply the argument to economic sanctions. On this view, the reason why President Assad may be subject to the costs of economic sanctions rather than the French president or the British prime minister is that, by dint of his wrongful past contribution to grievous human rights violations, he is under a greater duty than they are to allow himself to be adversely affected for the sake of combating future human rights violations. If so affecting him would deter other putative wrongdoers, then we may, indeed must, do so (subject to requirements of necessity, proportionality, and effectiveness).[21]

The Problem of Escalation

In this section, I consider the worry that deterrence policies in general, and thus deterrent sanctions in particular, inherently risk escalating the conflict they are meant to solve and should therefore be rejected.

Consider special deterrence first. At $t2$, Sender imposes sanctions on Target as a means to impress on the latter's leadership that, should it resume its unjust policy at $t3$, further sanctions will be imposed then. Let us assume that to the very best of Sender's knowledge, these sanctions are a necessary, proportionate, and effective response. But suppose that circumstances change: Target's leadership is facing renewed popular dissatisfaction with its economic policy and launches a vast crackdown operation, with concomitant acts of assassination, torture, and so on, on its opponents, in defiance of Sender's threat. May Sender make good on its threat and thus harm those leaders with a further round of sanctions, at the risk of escalating the conflict?

At the bar of deterrence, Sender cannot justify its decision to make good on its threat at $t3$ by appealing to the fact that sanctioning Target's leaders at $t3$ would (for example) prevent them from violating their opponents' human rights again at $t4$. For even if sanctioning those leaders at $t3$ in this way would be effective and were justified on those grounds, it would not be justified as a deterrent measure. Sender is deterrence-justified in making good on its threat, thereby imposing on Target's leaders the costs of sanctions, only as a means to make credible its concurrent threat, at t_3, of further sanctions if Target commits similar wrong-doings at t_4. Yet, given that Target's leadership were not deterred by the t_2 sanctions, it is hard to see what would deter them at t_3. Perhaps Sender can prolong extant sanctions, hoping that Target's leadership will come to regard the attendant cumulative costs as too high a price to pay for re-offending. Alternatively, Sender can impose even more stringent and / or more comprehensive sanctions. Either way, there may well come a point where the signaling costs that Sender imposes on Target's leaders through further economic sanctions are ineffective (in the face of Target's persistent dereliction of duty) and / or disproportionate.

The problem of course is that Sender's leaders have little by way of evidence to form justified beliefs about the probability that the conflict will escalate and, if so, at what point the even tougher sanctions they will impose will no longer meet the requirements of justified cost imposition. In line with my earlier discussion of sanctions under those epistemic conditions, Sender should proceed with extreme caution. By applying sanctions of increasing scope and stringency, Sender's leaders run the risk that the conflict will escalate to the point where they would have to apply ever more stringent and comprehensive sanctions. But the more comprehensive and stringent sanctions are, the higher the risk that they will adversely affect both wrongdoers and the innocent in breach of the requirement of proportionality. The higher the risk of escalation, thus, the weaker the case for proceeding. The point, if cogent, does not apply merely at t_3, for Sender is faced at t_2 with exactly the same decision as to whether or not to impose sanctions as a means to back up its threat of future sanctions, without knowing whether Target's leadership will reoffend at t_3.

The claim that the higher the risk, the weaker the case for proceeding relies for its implementation on a roughly accurate assessment of probabilities combined with a roughly accurate assessment of the costs and benefits accruing from sanctions. A fortiori, given how uncertain Sender's leaders necessarily are about the relevant odds, and given how costly comprehensive sanctions can be, they should restrict sanctions to as targeted a set of measures as possible, namely, against Target's upper echelons and with respect to their financial holdings and the luxury goods they would like to procure. Lest this discussion should seem overly abstract, it is worth noting that, at the time of writing, it describes the kind of predicament in which the United Nations, China, the United States, South Korea, and Japan find themselves in relation to the North Korean leadership's adamant persistence with nuclear tests, notwithstanding repeated rounds of sanctions.[22]

So much for special deterrence. Suppose now that Sender imposes sanctions on Target's leaders at $t2$ as a means to impress on Target*'s leaders that they too will be subject to similar sanctions if they commit human rights violations at $t3$. However, at $t3$, Target*'s leaders proceed so to act. May Sender's leaders impose sanctions, running the risk of escalating the conflict?

The problem of escalation is slightly different in most cases of general deterrence. In special deterrence, Sender's leaders are faced with a repeat wrongdoer. As a result, they can plausibly infer that unless they escalate both their threat and the mechanism by which they make the threat credible, Target's leaders will offend again at $t4$. In general deterrence, however, the wrongdoer at $t3$ is Target*'s leadership, whereas the offender at $t1$ was Target's leadership. If Target* leadership did in fact commit human rights violations in the past but was not harmed as a result, Sender may treat it as repeat wrongdoer. If, however, Target*'s leadership would be a first-time wrongdoer at $t3$, then other things equal, it seems that Sender's leaders have fewer reasons to escalate the economic sanctions than they do under special deterrence—since they have fewer reasons to believe that this leadership (Target*'s) will offend. In such cases, given that, under special deterrence, the sanctions they may justifiably impose are already highly targeted both with respect to scope and wrongdoers, Sender have even fewer permissible sanctions tools at its disposal under general deterrence.

Sanctions and Noncontributors

To recapitulate, we have seen that economic agents who, by dint of their economic and financial transactions with Target's leaders, contribute to the latter's unjust policies, may justifiably be subject to economic sanctions. Furthermore, economic sanctions are also justified as a means to deter present wrongdoers from reoffending and future wrongdoers from so acting—though, in the case of general deterrence, one might have to accept impersonal obligations. However, under conditions of uncertainty, sanctioning parties must opt for highly targeted sanctions with respect to their objects and to the individuals against whom they apply.

It seems that the position I have defended so far blocks one of the main objections against sanctions, to wit, that they indiscriminately affect individuals who are not themselves acting wrongly. Although there certainly are cases in which comprehensive sanctions have a disproportionately costly impact on the innocent, targeted sanctions seem immune from that criticism.[23]

However, this optimism seems misplaced. Targeted sanctions, particularly on dual-purpose goods such as oil, do have detrimental effects on those who do not contribute to the human rights violations to which they are a response (for example, rising unemployment and concomitant loss of income, crumbling infrastructure as a result of Target's diminished resources, goods scarcity, and so on). In addition, some of the costs of sanctions are also incurred by agents within Sender who are not themselves directly involved in wrongful trade or financial relationships with Target's wrongdoers (for example, as when economic sanctions result in diminishing tax returns and thereby diminishing public investments in transport infrastructure, health, and education).

In this section, my aim is twofold. On the one hand, I argue that Sender is sometimes justified in deliberately imposing the costs of economic sanctions on agents who do not wrongfully contribute to Target's unjust policy. On the other hand, subject to compliance with the proportionality, necessity, and effectiveness requirements, it is also sometimes justified in collaterally subjecting to the costs of sanctions agents who neither contribute to Target's rights violations by dint of their economic activity nor are under a duty to protect Target's victims. In other words, the claim that economic sanctions are costly to individuals who do not themselves wrongfully contribute to Target's human rights violations is not, in itself, a decisive objection.

Justifying the Deliberate Imposition of Sanctions-Related Costs

Some agents do not contribute to Target's rights violations and yet (I now argue) are under duties to protect Target's victims. In Chapter 1, we saw that duties of assistance admit of three forms: duties to provide needed resources, duties to protect others from (unjustified) harm, and duties to bear the costs of assistance as provided by a third party. Suppose that Defender needs Rescuer's help against Attacker's lethal attack. Rescuer shoots at Attacker while running toward him, thereby knocking Bystander over. Bystander is under a duty to allow himself to be knocked over instead of stopping Rescuer in her tracks, thereby preventing her from saving Defender. This is so at the bar of two rather different principles of justice: at the bar of reparative justice if he has previously derived a wrongful benefit from Attacker's nefarious activities vis-à-vis Defender, and at the bar of assistive justice if not. In what follows, I develop and apply both points to the case of economic sanctions.

SANCTIONS AND ASSISTANCE

An important argument in favor of applying sanctions against noncontributors appeals to the ethics of assistance, construed not as the provision of aid but, rather, as exposure to costs. Suppose that Target's leadership, with the support of a powerful ethnic group, is planning a genocidal campaign against a rival and powerless minority. At the bar of justice, individuals who lead a flourishing life are under duties to provide assistance to those who lack such prospects, irrespective of borders. Target's victims clearly do not have a flourishing life. Consequently, Sender's citizens are under a duty of assistance to be willing to expose themselves to the costs of sanctions—so long as those costs do not exceed that which may reasonably be expected of them. The same applies to those of Target's citizens who are neither contributing to nor wrongfully benefiting from the plight of those victims.

Interestingly, the claim that Sender's innocent civilians are under a duty of assistance to incur sanctions-related costs also applies to self-defense cases. This might seem counterintuitive. Suppose that Target annexes part of Sender's territory and thereby furnishes Sender with a just cause for war, but that the war, unlike a properly designed sanctions regime, would constitute a disproportionate response to the human rights violations. May Sender proceed with sanctions? To illustrate, in March 2017, the Ukrainian authorities imposed a raft of sanctions against both Russian-owned financial institutions and Russian-backed separatist enclaves, in response to Russia's ongoing attempts to sever Eastern Ukraine from the rest of the country.[24] Had Ukraine responded by going to war against Russia, it is plausible that it would have been annihilated as a sovereign political community—on the equally plausible assumption that NATO would not have come to its help.

Now, here is an argument *against* sanctions in such cases: It is up to Sender's citizens to decide whether or not to surrender the territory—in other words, to alienate their jointly held rights to sovereignty over it. Suppose that citizens who live on that territory do not wish to live under Target's jurisdiction and would endorse sanctions, particularly if those citizens are not given the option to leave. Even so, Sender's decision not to stop Target's ongoing rights violations via sanctions is morally justified if it is taken according to legitimate procedures that take into account the preference of citizens who live on that territory, and if citizens who live outside that territory are not wrongful beneficiaries of Target's policy (and, thus, do not owe it to their compatriots as a matter of reparative justice to help protect their rights).[25]

This argument appeals to the general principle that nonunanimous collective decisions over jointly held rights will sometimes and unavoidably leave minorities unprotected. That general principle itself has considerable intuitive force, from which the argument under scrutiny derives much of its prima facie plausibility. On closer inspection, however, we should reject the argument, for even if Sender's citizens decide in their majority no longer to regard the annexed territory as their own, they do remain under duties of assistance to their erstwhile compatriots. The fact that they have relinquished their rights over that territory is irrelevant; what matters is that their erstwhile compatriots' rights are under threat, in just the same way as the rights of another citizenry altogether would be under threat were Target to invade that territory as well.

That said, whether sanctions are justified by appeal to some rights of Sender's citizens (in self-defense cases) or by appeal to some rights of Target's citizens (in other-defense cases), they are justified only if their costs are distributed as fairly as is feasible under the circumstances. A fair distribution dictates in favor of spreading the costs of depressed economic activity on the basis of ability to bear those costs, away from the poor and toward the better off. Economic sanctions can be costly to agents who are innocent in the sense that they neither contribute to nor benefit from the wrongdoings at issue. At the same time, those agents are appropriate targets of sanctions simply because, by some stroke of bad luck, their being harmed would protect Target's victims. Fairness dictates that the effects of sanctions on innocent agents who are already disadvantaged should be mitigated by, for example, raising taxes on the well-off. To illustrate, there are good reasons to believe that the 2003 war against Iraq had a very damaging effect on those who were already poor in the United States, and a considerably less bad effect on those who were already affluent. In fact, it helped enrich those who had shares in companies tasked with supplying the coalition forces. There are similarly good reasons to believe that the effects of the comprehensive embargo on economic activity with, for example, Iran are disproportionately felt by the poor rather than the rich. The fair thing to do, then, would have been for the Bush administration in 2003 onward to tax at a much higher rate than it did the profits realized by corporations involved in the war against and reconstruction of Iraq, and to divert those proceeds to roads, hospitals, income support, and so on. In the case of Iran, the fair thing to do would be to improve spending for those deprived populations who are bearing the brunt of the sanctions against Iran.[26]

Crucially, my claim is not that sanctions are justified *only* if their costly effects on the innocent are distributed fairly. In practice, it is unlikely that the condition would ever be met, either because individuals, not least the well-off among them, are generally deeply reluctant to pay more taxes, or because designing and implementing the right kind of welfare policies takes time, or for some other reason. Hence the qualification that the costs of sanctions should be distributed "as fairly as is feasible under the circumstances." Feasibility constraints include so-called soft constraints such as motivational, epistemic, and resources constraints, as well as hard constraints such as the laws of physics. What is feasible in any given case is highly context-dependent: Norway might be able to spread sanctions costs more fairly than the United States. Be that as it may, the key point is that considerations of fairness combined with feasibility constraints have a role to play in our overall evaluation of a sanctions policy.[27]

SANCTIONS AND REPARATIONS

As I noted in Chapter 1, wrongful beneficiaries are under reparative duties toward the victims of the wrongdoings from which they benefit. One way in which they can discharge those duties is by incurring the costs of a policy whose aim is to protect victims. The point straightforwardly applies to economic sanctions. Agents in Sender and Target who have wrongfully benefited from Target's policy and / or from the economic relationships that directly or indirectly enable Target to carry out this policy are under reparative duties to protect Target's victims. To the extent that sanctions on the economic activities that those agents engage in would help protect those victims, they are morally justified, even though those economic activities neither directly nor indirectly enable Target's leadership to carry out this policy. For example, consider the security apparatus within Target, whose activities make the leadership's oppressive policies possible. Dozens of thousands of people who are not themselves employed by the security apparatus nevertheless benefit from its activities. To the extent that those people are not themselves victims of Target's policies, they can be aptly described as unjust beneficiaries of those activities and can be appropriately held under prima facie reparative duties to Target's victims. Suppose that if Sender were to impose sanctions on the exportation of consumption goods that those people particularly enjoy, there would be enough popular unrest to lead Target's regime to rescind its policy. Sender, it seems to me, would have a strong moral justification for so acting.

This broad-brushed claim warrants qualifying along five dimensions. First, unjust beneficiaries are under reparative duties other things being equal: it might sometimes be fairer to ask a vastly wealthy individual to provide a small amount of assistance to a victim of a wrongdoing than to make the same request of a modestly well-off individual who derived a very small unjust benefit from the wrongdoing.

Second, if Sender has a choice between imposing sanctions on unjust beneficiaries and imposing them on unjust contributors, other things being equal it ought to opt for the latter—on the grounds that, again other things being equal, contributing to a wrongdoing is morally worse than wrongfully benefiting from it.

Third, considerations of reparative justice in principle help support sanctions against both Sender's and Target's innocent (though wrongfully benefiting) agents, since both are under reparative duties to Target's victims. Depending on the facts of the case, however, sanctions might be more likely to work if they are applied against Target's innocent agents than against Sender's, simply because the hardship endured by the former and the resulting popular dissatisfaction are much more likely to induce Target to change its policy.

Note, fourth, that if those who are under duties of assistance at time $t1$ to protect Target's victims by exposing themselves to the costs of sanctions fail to discharge their duties, they acquire a new reparative duty at $t2$ to make good on their previous dereliction by protecting those victims again—which reparative duty they might be in a position, once again, to fulfill via a sanctions policy. The ground for the new reparative duty is twofold: it is the fact that duty-bearers failed to do at $t1$ what they were morally required to do, and the fact that, by not providing assistance, they are now better off than they would have been otherwise and have thus derived an unjust benefit from their moral dereliction. Furthermore, it stands to reason that they are under duties to incur greater costs at $t2$ than they were under a duty to incur at $t1$, precisely because they were derelict at $t1$.

Finally, when defending sanctions as an means to stop and deter agents from wrongfully contributing to human rights violations, I argued in favor of highly targeted sanctions, both with respect to their objects and with respect to the individuals to whom they apply, in the light of the requirements of proportionality, necessity, and effectiveness, and bearing in mind the fact of uncertainty. Other things equal, the point holds for reparative cases as well.

Justifying the Collateral Costs of Sanctions

A FIRST CUT

As I intimated at the outset of this section, economic sanctions are often costly on agents who are not under a duty to incur their attendant costs. And as I posited in Chapter 1, one may justifiably impose such costs on another party so long as those costs are not disproportionate to, inter alia, the goods one brings about. Consequently, sanctions that, by dint of their comprehensiveness or stringency, are particularly costly to the wholly innocent are unjust to the extent that those costs, though not imposed deliberately, are disproportionate. Unsurprisingly, sanctions against dual-purpose goods such as oil are more likely to violate the proportionality requirement than sanctions against single-purpose goods such as missiles.

It is true that, as a matter of fact, embargos are usually "tempered" with humanitarian exceptions covering food and other basic necessities. However, these exceptions generally do very little to alleviate the enormous hardship endured by already impoverished civilians who are neither responsible for their leadership's policies nor are under duties to incur those costs. The sanctions that the UN put in place against Iraq in the days following the latter's invasion of Kuwait, and which lasted until May 2003, are a case in point. Countless reports, some commissioned by UN agencies such as UNICEF or the UN itself, have pointed to a catastrophic decline in the provision of basic services such as health and education, and to the near collapse of the economy. This led the UN to adopt its oil-for-food program, whereby the Iraqi regime was allowed to sell oil in exchange for which it could buy basic necessities. Although the program enabled the delivery of roughly $28 billion worth of humanitarian aid, there is strong evidence that its implementation was marred by serious corruption and that the poorest of Iraqis did not get the help to which they were entitled.[28]

Some might perhaps object that Sender is not accountable for the costs accruing to Target's civilians as a result of the leadership's decision to carry on with its unjust policy. On that view, more generally, intervening agents bear sole responsibility for the costs they impose, even if those costs can be traced to some anterior event for which other agents are causally responsible. But this seems false. To give a familiar example, if I throw my still-lit cigarette butt into a bucket knowing, or even merely supposing with a high degree of plausibility, that you will subsequently pour petrol on it, thereby triggering a bush fire, there is a sense in which I share responsibility for the fire. Admittedly, that alone does not establish that I am acting wrongly. For example, suppose that I know, though you don't, that triggering a fire here will help control and destroy a much bigger fire, by burning its natural fuel first. I know of your pyromaniac obsession and deliberately throw my cigarette into the bucket. I am responsible for the ensuing smaller fire, but act justifiably. By parity of reasoning, it may well be that Sender acts justifiably by imposing sanctions that, it knows, will (collaterally) harm Target's innocent civilians as a result of the leadership's wrongful decision not to give in. But it is still responsible in some sense for those costs and must take them into account when deciding whether sanctions are justified overall.[29]

Two final points. First, sanctions can be costly to agents within Sender too. Some of those agents directly trade with Target. Others, however, do not: the costs that they incur as a result of sanctions are indirect and, in some cases, severe enough that they cannot reasonably be held under a duty to incur them. At a macro level, they might incur costs as a result of depressed economic activity within Sender, itself the result of the sanctions. At a micro level, they might suffer hardship as a result of, for example, their spouse going bankrupt for not being able to trade with Target. Are sanctions nevertheless justified in such cases? Yes, on the same grounds and under the same conditions as govern the imposition of collateral sanctions-related costs on Target's innocent agents. This is so whether Sender resorts to sanctions as a means to protect itself from Target's rights violations, or whether it does so to protect Target's own citizens from their leadership's policy.

Second, when sanctions impose costs on both Target's and Sender's innocent civilians, Sender may sometimes adopt a sanctions regime that is less costly to its own civilians and more costly to Target's than other options. It may do so on the grounds that Target's civilians, unlike its own, are beneficiaries of the sanctions, or on the grounds that, although both sets of agents benefit from it, Target's civilians do so to a greater extent than its own. For example, consider the economic sanctions that have been repeatedly inflicted against North Korea. As already noted, there is evidence to suggest that those sanctions (via the regime's intervening agency) have inflicted collateral damage on ordinary North Koreans, Chinese traders, and those agents' dependents. Many of those individuals do not contribute to the North Korean regime's nuclear policy and are ex ante beneficiaries of the sanctions: ordinary North Koreans clearly have an interest in their regime's being stopped; furthermore, should there be an outbreak of hostilities on the peninsula, ordinary Chinese individuals who live in close proximity to the border would be among the primary victims of the resulting influx of North Korean refugees into China. And yet, it is also plausible to surmise that ordinary North Koreans would benefit from the sanctions (if the latter were successful at stopping North Korea's regime) to a greater degree than ordinary Chinese. As a matter of fact, the Chinese authorities did vote for those sanctions at the relevant UN Security Council meeting, knowing that they would harm both North Koreans and its own civilians. I do not know whether, when they did so, they applied a greater discount on sanctions costs incurred by ordinary North Koreans civilians than on those accruing to ordinary Chinese civilians. As a matter of principle, however, it would not have been impermissible for them to do so.

Crucially, this is not tantamount to allowing Sender's regime to give priority to its compatriots' interests qua compatriots—a claim that would not be acceptable at the bar of human rights. Rather, the point is this. Sometimes the costs that result from a given course of action have to be distributed between agents who benefit from that course of action and agents who stand to lose from it or who will not gain from it as much. In such cases, those who benefit the most (irrespective of their nationality) may justifiably be expected to bear the greater share of the cost. This, of course, is subject to a number of conditions, to do in particular with the magnitude of the costs incurred by both sets of agents.[30]

THE IMPORTANCE OF CONSENT

Is the consent of Target's innocent civilians required for Sender justifiably to impose sanctions on their regime/community on humanitarian grounds? Those civilians—particularly opponents to the regime—might welcome Sender's decision to freeze all assets held by Target citizens, including their own, even though they are not responsible for Target's wrongdoings. This might be for two reasons: because they oppose their regime, and because Sender's policy would protect them from Target's attempt to seize those assets as a means to silence them and/or to fund its repressive policies.[31] Still, whether or not their consent is required, morally speaking, is another matter. Here, we must distinguish between the following two cases: (1) the victims of the sanctions policy are also the victims of Target's regime, and it is their plight that provides Sender with a just cause for sanctions; (2) the victims of the sanctions policy are not the same as Target's victims.

The claim that victims' consent is required elicits considerable skepticism in the relevant literature—on the grounds that in cases involving multiple victims, we simply do not and cannot know how many such victims would have to consent for the requirement to be satisfied.[32] Moreover, to say that a majority of victims would have to consent seems both too restrictive on interveners and too permissive vis-à-vis minority victims, particularly if the latter would stand to benefit to a much greater extent from the intervention than the opposing majority. Conversely, to say that only some victims need consent (but that such consent nevertheless is required) seems too permissive of interveners and too restrictive vis-à-vis majority victims, particularly if the latter would stand to benefit to a much greater extent from the intervention than the opposing minority.

The questions, then, are whether explicit consent is required, what counts as evidence for the claim that consent (whether explicit or not) has been validly given, and how we should handle scenarios where some victims reject sanctions while others welcome them. On this latter point, and assuming that consent of some kind is necessary, much would depend on the number of victims who validly consent and on the magnitude of the costs that sanctions would impose on those who do not validly consent.[33]

My main concern here is with establishing what kind of consent matters (assuming that consent of some form matters at all), and how we can ascertain that it has been given. Suppose that the victims of the sanctions policy are also the victims of Target's regime. I do not think that the explicit consent of those victims (however such consent may be obtained) is necessary to render the policy just. Insisting on explicit consent would deny those who are simply not in a position to offer such consent the (ex ante) benefits of the policy. By implication, those who are the most vulnerable to human rights violations and, thereby, the least able to offer (or withhold) consent, would be left wholly unprotected. Put more bluntly still, on the view that explicit consent is necessary, the worst the human rights abuses, the less permissible the sanctions policy. This, it goes without saying, seems perverse.

However, victims' presumptive consent is required. This is so in virtue of the following general two-pronged principle: first, one may help another person only if she does or would consent to it, and second, in the absence of clear and unambiguous information to that effect, one is morally justified in helping her only if one has strong reasons for believing that she would consent to it. The more serious the human rights violations that provide Sender with a just cause for sanctions, the greater reason there is to believe that victims would consent to sanctions if they could be asked, and thus the lower the evidentiary threshold for presumptive consent.[34]

Suppose now that the victims of the sanctions policy are not the same as Target's victims. Consent—whether explicit or presumptive—is not a necessary condition for the justified imposition of collateral sanctions-related costs on the innocent either—any more than, in war, a just belligerent must have the consent of innocent civilians in order justifiably to kill them, collaterally, in the course of bombings. So long as the costs thus occasioned are proportionate to the ends achieved, the just belligerent may so act. The same considerations apply to sanctions. In both cases, however, the innocent are morally justified in defending themselves from such threats: although their right not to incur those costs is justifiably infringed, they still retain it precisely because the costs are high enough that they are not under a duty to suffer them. In the case of war, civilians are justified in killing the just combatants at whose hands they would otherwise die. In the case of sanctions, this may mean that they are justified in subverting the sanctions regime, such as by engaging in illicit trade as a means to procure the goods they need and of which they are deprived.[35]

Finally, is the consent of Sender's innocent citizens required for Sender justifiably to impose sanctions on economic activities with Target, thereby subjecting them to collateral costs? To illustrate, suppose that Target's policy violates the human rights of Sender's citizens. The latter, thus, are victims of the wrongdoing that gives rise to a just cause for sanctions; insofar as the latter policy adversely affects them as well, albeit collaterally, their presumptive consent is needed. The same considerations apply when the victims of Target's unjust policy are Target's citizens themselves or, indeed, third parties.

Some might be tempted to hold that the evidentiary threshold for consent is higher in the other-defensive case than in the self-defensive case.

Perhaps they might hold that it is more reasonable to suppose that agents would want to help their compatriots than it is reasonable to suppose that they would want to help distant strangers. As a matter of fact, I do not doubt that such would be the preferences of a majority of people. But those preferences would be morally misguided. Consider the following variant of William Godwin's classic rescue case. You and I—both British citizens—are in front of a burning building in which another British citizen is trapped alongside a Congolese citizen. You are in a wheelchair and cannot go in. I can go in, but can rescue only one person. As I would run a high risk of dying, I am not under a duty to rescue either one of them. I am willing to do it but realize that if I do it and die, you too will incur fairly high costs: you depend on me to push your wheelchair and take you away from the site, and there is a high risk therefore that you will be killed as the building collapses. In this particular case, where neither you nor I are under a duty to incur those costs for the sake of rescuing one person from death, I may attempt the rescue only if you consent to being put at risk in this way. But I am not under a more stringent duty to obtain your consent for the sake of saving the British citizen than I am to obtain it for the sake of saving the Congolese citizen. True, I may desist from rescuing either. But at the bar of human rights (which, you recall, are universal in scope), it remains the case that if I decide to rescue one of the persons trapped inside, with your consent, nationality ought to have no bearing on my decision to save one rather than the other; nor does it have any bearing on my duties with respect to either putative beneficiary and to you. Mutatis mutandis, there is no reason to treat the sanctions case differently.[36]

Uncertainty, Once More

To recapitulate, I have argued that economic sanctions are sometimes morally justified as a means to enforce human rights, notwithstanding their costs to both Sender's and Target's populations, even though not all of their citizens are causally and morally implicated in the human rights violations to which they are a response.

Before I address the issue of effectiveness, let me make one final point about uncertainty, with respect to the requirement of proportionality.

When discussing sanctions against agents who contribute to Target's un-just policies, I argued that the more uncertain Sender is that sanctions are a necessary, effective, and proportionate response to those wrong-doings, the stronger the case for applying highly targeted sanctions. The same considerations apply, mutatis mutandis, to sanctions insofar as they target agents who are under reparative or assistive duties. More-over, Sender must also be attentive to the fact that the damage it would inflict on agents who contribute to Target's policy, on those who are under reparative and assistive duties, and on the innocent, might not be proportionate to the aims it seeks to achieve. Here too, the less certain Sender is that its sanctions policy is a proportionate response in all of those senses, the more cautious it ought to be.

Which sanctions Sender may justifiably use in any given case depends on further and specific features of that case. Consider again the UN sanc-tions on textile, minerals, and seafood imports from North Korea, which have been thought to be deeply harmful to hundreds of thousands of or-dinary North Koreans, many of whom are not contributing to their re-gime's unjust policy, who, indeed, are victims thereof. However, there are some reasons to think (at the time of writing) that failure to stop the North Korean leadership might lead to a continental war in the Far East—a war, moreover, in which hundreds of thousands of people would die.

Are those sanctions justified, notwithstanding the damage they cause, in the light of those reasons? I am inclined to think not, but not on grounds of proportionality—rather, on grounds of evidence to the effect that sanc-tions against North Korea have hitherto proved ineffective. (I shall return to this point in the next section.) For on grounds of proportionality, and again in the light of the relevant available evidence (the regime's adamant refusal to desist with tests, its bellicose posturing, the U.S. administra-tion's fanning the flame, etc.) the harms that would ensue if there were a regional conflict would be so severe as to provide a reason for compre-hensive sanctions.[37] Of course, it may be that, by the time you are reading this, the North Korean leadership will have been toppled bloodlessly. If so, it will have turned out that those relatively comprehensive sanctions were objectively unjustified on proportionality grounds. But this does not undermine the claim that, in the light of the evidence, the converse was true in the autumn of 2017. By the same token, comprehensive sanctions might be unjustified on proportionality grounds, in cases in which the evidence points to a relatively limited threat to human rights—even though it might turn out to be objectively justified if the threat is in fact of greater magnitude.

Ineffective, Therefore Unjust?

We have just seen that some who are not wrongdoers may justifiably be subjected to sanctions at the bar of reparative and assistive justice. At the same time, however, we have also seen that under conditions of uncertainty, sanctioning parties ought to resort to as targeted a sanctions regime as is possible in the light of the human rights violations it would otherwise fail to forestall.

In this section, I examine another important objection to sanctions, namely that they are not an effective way of enforcing human rights. Insofar as imposing a defensive or deterrent cost on others is justified only if it stands a reasonable chance of success of parrying the threat to which it is a response, if the factual claim is correct, then sanctions are not justified. Or so the objection goes.

The objection turns on the factual veracity of its empirical premise— namely that sanctions are ineffective. This is a hotly contested debate and I will not enter the fray here.[38] Rather, I will assume for the sake of argument that sanctions are not effective at protecting Target's victims and that Sender has very good evidence to that effect. In many cases, this seems plausible. Political leaders who are blacklisted by Western governments use aliases, shell businesses, offshore companies, and criminal networks to circumvent sanctions; they also off-load the costs of sanctions on their most vulnerable compatriots while terrorizing them into not rebelling, and continue to act wrongly. There are also good reasons for doubting that sanctions effectively deter economic agents from contributing to those human rights violations. This is particularly true of Target's economic agents, many of whom are subject to severely repressive campaigns and who, more often than not, live in considerable poverty. The thought that comprehensive sanctions might deter those people from contributing to those grievously wrongful deeds by, for example, not taking jobs in certain businesses beggars belief.

The question, then, is whether we can infer from the claim that sanctions are ineffective that they are also unjust. To answer this, we must revisit the distinction between using sanctions as a deterrent and using them as a way to block agents from wrongfully contributing to ongoing human rights violations. Consider deterrent sanctions first. Their very rationale is that they should deter Target's and Sender's agents from contributing to, or committing, human rights violations in the future. If they fail to deter and yet occasion collateral costs—and a fortiori harms—to the innocent, then they are unjust qua deterrent measures. To the extent that relatively comprehensive sanctions against North Korea have so far failed to deter its leadership from committing human rights violations, they are unjustified qua deterrent measures.

The case of sanctions that seek to stop ongoing human rights violations is more complex. Recall that in Chapter 1 I argued that agents may justifiably deprive another agent of that to which he has a presumptive right, on the grounds that they are thereby defending their or someone else's rights. I also averred that they act justifiably so long as they stand a reasonable chance of parrying the threat—in other words, of being effective. Suppose that Attacker is about to kill Defender without warrant. She can parry the attack by killing him. Subject to all other conditions being met, given that her attack is effective, she may proceed. But now imagine that Attacker has arranged to buy the gun he needs to attack Defender from Gun Seller. Defender can stop Gun Seller from selling the gun to Attacker only by physically and harmfully restraining him from going to their meeting point. In so doing, she succeeds in protecting herself from Gun Seller. However, if Attacker can procure a gun from another source, Defender would not succeed in protecting herself from Attacker's threat by restraining Gun Seller. The question then is whether she may justifiably restrain Gun Seller.

The example suggests that we need to distinguish between the imposition of a narrowly effective cost and the imposition of a widely effective cost. One imposes a narrowly effective cost on another agent when one successfully prevents that agent from contributing to a threat; one imposes a widely effective cost on him when, by preventing him from contributing to the threat, one also and thereby parries that threat.

Let us apply this point to sanctions. Consider the case of narrow strategic goods such as the weapons that Target needs in order to kill its opponents; or consider indirectly contributing goods such as the money Target generates through favorable trade deals and thanks to which it can buy those weapons. Suppose that if Sender applies sanctions against arms trade with Target, Target will procure military equipment elsewhere. Sender's policy is ineffective in the wide sense. But it is effective in the narrow sense, such that Sender is justified in so acting. As Elizabeth Ellis powerfully shows, to say otherwise is to say that Sender must allow its arms manufacturers to continue to sell to Target if sanctions would not work. But this cannot be true. The fact that President Assad and his regime are able to violate the human rights of ordinary Syrians notwithstanding our arms embargoes clearly does not in itself permit us to help him by allowing our arms manufacturers to sell him those goods. The same point applies to similar sanctions as applied by the European Union and the United States against the then president Mugabe of Zimbabwe, which have long been criticized for being ineffective. It would also apply to the sanctions those parties applied in the autumn of 2017 against arms trades with Venezuela, should President Maduro manage to buy weapons from another source. Even if those sanctions are ineffective at blocking the threat posed by those leaders, they may well be effective at preventing these arms manufacturers and similarly situated economic agents from helping them violate rights. It is only if they are ineffective in that narrow sense that the objection goes through.[39]

Here is a case in which the fact that a given sanction against narrow strategic good is ineffective in the wide sense at stopping Target's leaders seemingly provides a reason against it. Suppose that sanctions against narrow strategic goods not only do not work, but in fact make things worse in the following way: as a result of our refusal to sell our own equipment to its forces, Target procures more devastating weapons elsewhere. Whether or not we may justifiably lift sanctions to spare further harm to Target's victims and in so doing enable its leadership to pursue its policy raises the deeper question of the conditions under which one may justifiably collaborate with wrongdoers. I will not take a stand on this here. But assuming for the sake of argument that we may *not* impose sanctions in such a case, note that the worry is not that sanctions do not work: the worry is that they cause far more harm than good. What grounds the objection is not so much the requirement of effectiveness as the requirement of proportionality.[40]

So far, I have argued that ineffectiveness does not provide a blanket objection to defensive sanctions with respect to narrow strategic goods. What about wide strategic goods and indirectly contributing goods? Agents who trade in those goods are justifiably targeted on the grounds that they are under a moral obligation to make it costly for Target's leaders to pursue their policy by withholding from them the goods (unrelated to their wrongdoings) that they want. Suppose Target's leaders are willing to bear those costs and carry on violating rights despite the fact that the personal assets they hold in Sender's banks are frozen. The sanctions are ineffective in the sense that they do not eliminate any threat at all. Yet, they occasion costs to third parties, notably collateral costs that the latter have not done anything to warrant. Are they nevertheless justified? We might think not, for surely costs and particularly harmful costs that are pointless in that sense can never be justified—can they?

Perhaps they can, though. Economic sanctions are not used merely to block or deter the commission of human rights violations. They are also used as a way to express condemnation of those deeds. Sanctions as imposed on apartheid-era South Africa or the grain embargo imposed on the USSR by the Carter administration following the former's invasion of Afghanistan in 1979 are good examples of this particular policy. Likewise, decisions to freeze the assets of direct perpetrators of human rights violations often have largely symbolic value.

Whether sanctions are justified in such cases depends on the extent to which it is permissible to impose their attendant costs, not merely on wrongdoers themselves, but also on innocent parties, for the sake of getting one's message across. I am doubtful that expressive sanctions are justified in as many cases as they seem to be employed. Consider again the case of North Korea. Assume as per the evidence so far that some of the more comprehensive sanctions severely affect the livelihood of ordinary and innocent North Koreans. If we have reason to believe that those individuals do not consent to the sanctions, asking them to bear the burden of our expressive aims does seem morally disproportionate and thus unjustified.

Suppose that in a given case, imposing expressive sanctions would be proportionate. They would still have to be effective (if they are to be justified). And, interestingly, it may well be that to be effectively expressive, those sanctions must be quite onerous on Sender's agents, perhaps more onerous even than on Target's agents—precisely as a sign that Sender is taking human rights seriously. The aforementioned grain embargo was quite detrimental to U.S. agro-interests—a fact that served to emphasize the administration's strong stand in the wake of the invasion of Afghanistan. If so, justifying expressive sanctions amounts to justifying deliberately imposing the relevant and possibly asymmetrical costs, to those ends, on Sender's agents.[41]

It seems that there are good reasons for so acting. Faced with such grievous wrongdoings, we must at least do something, if only to show that we are not indifferent to victims—subject here again to considerations of proportionality, necessity, and (context-sensitive) effectiveness. In cases such as these, the ineffectiveness objection has force only if Sender's sanctions policy is ineffective at conveying condemnation of Target's wrongdoings. Interestingly, even if Target's regime succeeds at hiding from its population the condemnatory intent behind the sanctions, thereby rendering the sanctions ineffective in a Target-focused sense, the sanctions might nevertheless be effective at conveying Sender's outrage to the rest of the world. So long as the proportionality and necessity conditions are met, this might suffice to justify the policy. The only theoretical example of wholly ineffective condemnatory sanctions I can think of are sanctions adopted in complete secrecy. I cannot think of a single actual example of such measures.

Conclusion

In this chapter I have argued that a justification for economic sanctions must take into account the fact that they constitute an interference in global trade in general and in economic agents' presumptive right freely to transact with one another in particular. Economic sanctions are justified—I argued—as a means to block or deter human rights violations or to express our condemnation thereof, subject to the requirements of necessity, proportionality, and effectiveness properly construed. In the light of those requirements and the difficulties inherent in decision-making under conditions of uncertainty, we should favor very limited, highly targeted sanctions against agents whom we have strong evidence to believe are making a significant contribution to human rights violations. We should be correspondingly very reluctant to resort to more comprehensive sanctions that are likely to inflict considerable harm on individuals who, we also have strong evidence to believe, do not contribute to those wrongdoings.

In some respects, the conclusions reached here align with extant practices—for example as regard to decisions to freeze the assets of key members of highly repressive regimes or to impose arms embargos. Good examples include targeted financial sanctions on, for example, President Putin, President Assad, or President Mugabe—and their respective circles of advisers, top-level policy makers, and friends and relatives; sanctions on arms and military technology trades against those regimes as well as (inter alia) North Korea.

In other respects, my conclusions do not align with extant practices. For example, I have expressed considerable skepticism of decisions comprehensively to ban any kind of investment, including on dual-purpose goods, in the light of the damages those decisions wreak on local economies and thereby civilian populations. The paradigmatic example of unjustified sanctions is the policy adopted by the UN and its most powerful members against Iraq following the First Gulf War; others include far-reaching sanctions imposed on North Korea, which, if the evidence at hand is correct, impose very severe hardship on its most destitute citizens for rather meager results.

CHAPTER THREE

Secondary Sanctions

SO FAR, I HAVE RESTRICTED my account to the following kinds of sanctions, those that are applied by the United Nations and those that are applied by multistate organizations such as the European Union or the African Union, as well as by a sovereign state, against economic activities in which at least one of the parties is subject to the territorial or personal jurisdiction of the sanctioning parties. In this chapter, I focus on so-called secondary sanctions, whereby Sender seeks to restrict the economic activities of agents, none of whom are subject to its territorial and / or personal jurisdiction, on the grounds that they trade with or invest in Target. To illustrate, recall the sanctions that the United States has imposed on economic relationships with Iran, North Korea, and Cuba. Relevant to this chapter, and at the time of writing, non-U.S. companies that invest in Iran's energy sector are liable to (inter alia) being frozen out of the U.S. banking system. Furthermore, agents based outside the United States may not reexport to Iran goods that were initially exported from the United States, if those goods would have fallen foul of export restrictions had they been exported directly from the United States—and this even if the reexporters did comply with legislation in their own country. Criminal penalties against such agents have sometimes been sought. Regarding North Korea, on March 16, 2016, President

Obama issued an executive order as a retaliatory measure against one of Pyongyang's ballistic missile tests. The order sought to extend the reach of extant U.S. and UN sanctions to persons who are not subject to the territorial and personal jurisdiction of the United States. Since then, a number of commentators have called on the U.S. administration to impose secondary sanctions against Chinese firms and banks as a means to induce the Chinese leadership to adopt much tougher (primary) sanctions against North Korea. Indeed, further secondary sanctions were endorsed by the U.S. Treasury in the summer of 2017.

In the case of the U.S. sanctions against Cuba, not only are U.S. nationals and U.S.-registered firms subject to comprehensive trade and financial restrictions; in addition, under the terms of the 1996 Cuban Liberty and Democracy Act (or Helms-Burton Act) any U.S. agent can sue in American courts anyone, irrespective of nationality and residence, who has traded in or benefited from property confiscated by Fidel Castro's regime from U.S. citizens after the 1959 Cuban revolution. Under the terms of the 1992 Cuban Democracy Act (or Torricelli Act), no vessel that has docked in Cuba can load or unload goods in a U.S. port for 180 days unless furnished with a special license to do so by the secretary of the Treasury.[1]

My aim in this chapter is to provide a defense of secondary sanctions as a response to human rights violations. As we shall see below, at the bar of human rights, one of which is individuals' jointly held right to self-determination, individuals, via their state, ought to have some degree of jurisdictional authority over their territory and over one another as fellow citizens. It is therefore appropriate to inquire whether a state may justifiably impinge on another state's jurisdictional authority by means of secondary sanctions. Indeed, threats to impose such sanctions are widely regarded as particularly controversial. For example, the European Union has expressed serious concern at the expanding extraterritorial reach of U.S. sanctions policy against Russia.[2]

My inquiry proceeds as follows. I make a preliminary case for secondary sanctions by drawing on my defense of primary sanctions. In the following two sections, I tackle two concerns about secondary sanctions: the concern that they are not sufficiently sensitive to the distinctive features of global trade, and the concern that they ride roughshod over multilateralism as a morally desirable conduit for enforcing human rights worldwide. I qualify my defense of secondary sanctions in the light of both concerns.

Justifying Secondary Sanctions

The Issue

As we saw in Chapter 2, primary sanctions are justified as a means to enforce human rights. As we also saw, a successful justification for sanctions must show that all the parties in the transaction under consideration may justifiably be deprived of the benefits of that transaction. Here is a simple example to illustrate the issue at hand. The European Union has imposed a raft of sanctions against the Syrian state, its regime, and its president. Those sanctions target the supply to those actors of (inter alia) arms, telecommunications monitoring and interception equipment, and equipment related to the exploitation of gas and crude oil.[3] Suppose that Ben, a British citizen located in Britain, exports telecommunication equipment to Syrian businessman Sami, who sells it to Syria's armed forces. By imposing sanctions against those transactions, Britain (as part of the EU) refuses to recognize Ben's and Sami's contract of sale as valid in its courts of law; by enforcing those sanctions, it coerces at least one of them, if not both, not to transact with each other—or at least makes one of them, if not both, vulnerable to criminal and civil penalties. This is a case of primary sanctions.

Now suppose that Sami also buys telecommunications equipment from Russian citizen Rodia, who is trading from within Russia. Suppose that Russian citizens have political rights to shape their collective future. This implies that they have and exercise (via their state) some degree of territorial and personal jurisdictional authority, and thus (by further implication) have a right not to be subject to the personal and territorial jurisdiction of another state. The Russian leadership has consistently vetoed attempts by the UN Security Council to vote UN-wide sanctions on Syria. Rodia, in fact, acts in compliance with Russian law.[4] Hence the question at the heart of secondary sanctions: may the EU extend to

Rodia's economic relationship with Sami the sanctions regime that it imposes on Ben's transactions with Sami? It could so do in several ways. For example, it could lock Rodia out of EU-based financial institutions by refusing to recognize the transaction as valid and on that basis by including as part of his assets (and thus as collateral for loans) the money he will have generated from that sale. It could also subject him to criminal and civil penalties. Were it to do so, it would directly interfere in the economic and financial affairs of an agent who has a right not to be subject to its territorial and personal jurisdiction. The question is whether it may so act.

With respect to Sami, secondary sanctions are no different from primary sanctions. To see this, let us assume that the EU is justified vis-à-vis Sami in preventing its own private economic agents from trading with him, on the grounds that Sami's business activities directly help Syria's regime commit grievous human rights violations. The EU is equally justified vis-à-vis Sami in preventing Rodia and other foreign economic agents who are not subject to its political or territorial jurisdiction from trading with him. The fact that Sami engages in separate transactions with a Russian businessman rather than a British businessman is irrelevant to the permissibility of sanctioning him.

The key issue, then, is whether the EU's imposition of secondary sanctions on Rodia's transactions with Sami would be justified vis-à-vis Rodia and, if so, would be subject to a higher justificatory burden than its imposition of primary economic sanctions on Ben's transactions with Sami. After all, Rodia is not subject to its political and/or territorial jurisdiction and he is compliant with Russian law. On what grounds, if any, may the EU justifiably arrogate jurisdictional authority over his economic relationship with Sami?

The Presumption in Favor of States' Jurisdictional Sovereignty

Respect for jurisdictional sovereignty is a cornerstone of international law. So long as a foreign court renders a judgment within its jurisdiction, other courts will not invalidate it by substituting their own domestic law, on the grounds that such judgment is an act of sovereignty, fully effective within the borders of that court's jurisdictional domain. In legal parlance, out of respect for state sovereignty and in due deference to reciprocity, courts ought to act with comity with foreign courts, even if they hold that, as a matter of fact, those foreign courts got it wrong. The principle holds for both criminal law and private law—notably, in the latter case, the law of contracts. Furthermore, although the principle mainly holds for courts, it should also hold for states whose laws courts enforce. State S1 acts with comity toward another state, S2, when it recognizes S2's jurisdictional sovereignty over its territory and, more specifically, when it instructs its courts to acknowledge that S2's courts have jurisdictional authority over that territory.[5]

At first sight, the principle of jurisdictional recognition does not seem to comport with human rights, since it rests on and instantiates respect for legislative sovereignty. However, as I suggested when discussing property rights in Chapter 1, one can be committed to human rights and at the same time support the principle of recognition of foreign jurisdictions, laws, and judgments in criminal as well as private matters. Indeed, the former implies the latter. The right to self-determination, which is jointly held by individuals qua members of a political community, is a human right. An important way in which individuals shape their community's future is, precisely, by determining what belongs to whom (so long as they do not thereby violate one another's or foreigners' human rights). For example, consider differences between the United States and the United Kingdom with respect to ownership of natural resources. In the United States, the federal government invites private companies to bid at auction for the right to exploit resources located under public land and keeps the proceeds of those auctions. In the United Kingdom, the Crown owns oil, gas, silver, coal, and gold, and the government grants licenses to exploit and develop those reserves. Other minerals may be privately owned and exploited without a governmental license. Endorsing human rights does not preclude accepting those differences and the principle of legislative sovereignty on which they rest.[6]

Lifting the Presumption

Against that background, the claim that secondary sanctions are morally justified implies that Sender may refuse to recognize that a law other than its own dispositively applies to those transactions. The question, then, is when it is morally entitled to apply its domestic legislation beyond its borders.

As a matter of law, states are empowered to do so according to five principles. According to the first four principles, a state may so act if it has a connection of a relevant kind with the object or individual to whom it wants its legislation to apply. Those connections are the following:

Nationality principle with respect to persons, whereby a state's laws govern the conduct of a national of that state, wherever that person lives.

Protection principle, whereby a state's laws aim to protect that state's vital interests irrespective of the nationality or residence of the agents to whom the laws apply.

Passive personality principle, whereby a state's laws aim to protect nationals of that state, wherever those nationals are under threat and irrespective of the nationality of the threateners.

Principle of goods territoriality, whereby Sender bans the reexportation of goods initially produced on its territory that would have been subject to sanctions had they never left that territory before being sold to Target's agents. This is so even when the final transaction takes place outside its territory and is conducted by individuals who are not subject to its jurisdiction.

In addition, a state under some circumstances enjoys:

Universal jurisdiction, whereby a state's laws aim to protect anyone in the world from the commission of so-called international crimes such as war crimes, crimes against humanity, and piracy.

Under the principle of universal jurisdiction, the state need not have a territorial or political connection to the target or beneficiary of its laws: rather, it is connected to the act to which its laws pertain by that act's very nature as being of concern to all states and, more deeply, to humankind as a whole.[7]

As I now show, each of those legal principles rests on secure moral grounds; but even when so grounded, not all can justify secondary sanctions.[8] Consider the nationality principle. All individuals, wherever they are in the world, have human rights to the resources and freedoms they need in order to lead a flourishing life; they are under the corresponding duties to everyone else in the world. On the plausible assumption that they cannot properly discharge those duties absent a state, it makes sense to allocate to a given state the task of ensuring that they so act, via the conferral of nationality. This does not preclude other jurisdictions from enforcing those duties when appropriate, but it does mean that the state of nationality may step into the breach with the consent of the jurisdiction where the crime was committed, and absent its consent if it is unwilling to prosecute. Thus, British citizens suspected of pedophiliac abuse abroad against non-British children may justifiably be punished by British courts—on the grounds that some jurisdiction has to take on the task of protecting children against sexual abuse wherever and by whomever it occurs in the world, and that Britain might as well do it as far as British citizens are concerned. Quite clearly, the nationality principle allows Sender to impose sanctions against its nationals and, by extension, on companies based on its territory. Equally clearly, however, it does not support sanctions against third parties such as Rodia in my illustrative case.[9]

Contrastingly, the principle of goods territoriality does support sanctions against any party, irrespective of nationality or residence at the time the transaction is made. Target's regime needs resources to conduct its policy (fuel, weapons, money, etc.). It also needs resources for other purposes, lack of which might induce it to discontinue its policy. Again, as we saw in Chapter 1, we all have duties not to contribute to human rights violations by supplying to perpetrators the resources they need. By implication, Target's victims have a right against the world at large that the flow of relevant resources to Target be stopped. In this case too, it makes sense to devolve to each state the task of controlling the ways in which the resources that are produced in its territory and which Target needs are used. Sender may thus apply sanctions with respect to those resources at the point at which those resources are on its territory. Once those resources have left Sender's territory, it is up to the states on whose territory they end up to exercise such control. Should they be unwilling or unable to do so, however, Sender may step into the breach. With respect to those goods, the principle of goods territoriality furnishes Sender with a justification for sanctioning third parties.[10]

By implication, however, the principle does not support sanctions against third parties' transactions over goods that do not originate in Sender's territory. To justify secondary sanctions with respect to those goods, we must turn to the protection principle and the principle of universal jurisdiction. The protection principle can be deployed in support of Sender's reach beyond its territorial and personal jurisdiction when Sender acts in defense of the human rights of its own citizens. To the extent that Target's economic agents contribute to violating those rights and that the sanctioning party has evidence-based reasons for believing that they are contributing, they may justifiably be subjected to sanctions at the hands of the latter. By parity of reasoning, so may third-party agents who contribute to those rights violations by trading with Target's agents. Sender, thus, is not more justified in preventing its own citizens from contributing to those rights violations by trading with Target than in preventing third parties from doing exactly the same. Return to Rodia, who sells EU-sanctioned telecommunications equipment to Sami. If Rodia's business were located in EU territory, we would not say that he should be sanctioned to a lesser degree than Ben, a British national trading from Britain with Sami. We would, or at any rate should, regard nationality as irrelevant. For consistency's sake, territorial location is also irrelevant. When combined, as they are in Rodia's case, nationality and territorial location are equally irrelevant.

The principle of universal jurisdiction, for its part, can be deployed in support of Sender's sanctions in those cases in which Target violates the fundamental human rights of parties other than Sender's own citizens—for example, an ethnic minority within Target, or the citizens of another sovereign state. By transacting with Sami, Rodia enables wrongdoings that are regarded as international crimes. At the bar of the principle, Rodia has forfeited his right to enjoy the benefits of this kind of trade and may justifiably be subject to relevant sanctions. This is not as controversial as it might seem. Thus, a legal system in which some human beings are treated and exchanged as chattels is not morally justified. Nor should we regard as morally justified a legal system sanctioning the wholesale coercive appropriation by a section of the population (say, men) of property initially owned by another section of the population (say, women). Grievously unjust foreign dispositions with respect to property rights can legitimately be discarded at the bar of the principle of universal jurisdiction—indeed, have been so discarded, as when (for example) British courts refused to enforce a Nazi statute depriving fleeing German Jews of their citizenship.[11]

Of course, the more restrictive one's conception of international crimes, the narrower the range of morally appropriate sanctions under the principle of universal jurisdiction—and the less likely it is that Sender will be justified in applying sanctions against third parties contra the latter's domestic law. The worry (if it is a worry) is particularly acute when economic sanctions are applied in response to human rights violations that are not severe enough to justify war. Most scholars of international criminal law rely on precisely such a narrow definition: in law, only the most grievous violations of international law, such as war, torture, forced disappearances, genocide, crimes against humanity, slavery, and piracy count as international offences and thus fall under the remit of universal jurisdiction. The sanctions applied by the EU against Syria are a very good example, as are the sanctions imposed by the United States against the Republic of Sudan following (inter alia) its genocidal campaign in Darfur. Although those sanctions are of primary nature in the main, the United States has taken steps to extend its reach to third parties.[12]

. However, as a matter of morality, a commitment to human rights implies a commitment to extending the normative reach of universal jurisdiction beyond those crimes. If human rights truly are universal, such that individuals hold those rights and bear the corresponding duties irrespective of borders, so is the right to enforce them. Indeed, to restrict the right to enforce human rights to the victims' state would be problematic for at least two reasons. First, it would leave unprotected those whose state officials are the worst culprits. Second, human rights violations are, or at any rate ought to be, of deep concern to all of us, wherever they occur, against whomever they are committed, and by whomever they are perpetrated. To widen the scope of the principle of universal jurisdiction accordingly is to do them proper justice.

The Problem of Global Trade

So far, my argument for secondary sanctions has relied on a very simple, indeed simplistic, case: one agent, Rodia, sells goods to another agent, Sami. We also assume that the policy is proportionate and that it stands a reasonable chance of success (where it is appropriate to apply the latter requirement). The case is simplistic because even if Rodia's company manufactures those goods, it buys some of the materials and components from other suppliers, not all of whom may be located in Russia—most of whom in fact will be located abroad and outside the jurisdiction of the EU. Those materials and components themselves are likely to have been assembled abroad as well. May those agents be justifiably subject to sanctions as well?

In my account of human rights, those agents are under a pre-institutional duty to help block Target's unjust policy. If they fail to discharge that duty, they act wrongly and may justifiably be harmed through sanctions (subject to appropriately deployed considerations of necessity, effectiveness, and proportionality). The question then is twofold: whether agents in far-flung corners of the world who somehow contribute to Target's unjust policies may justifiably have their prospects for a flourishing life undermined via sanctions, and, if not, whether sanctions against them are nevertheless justified on other grounds.

The problem clearly is not unique to secondary sanctions. As we saw in Chapter 2, it also arises for primary sanctions, where Sender might have to decide whether to impose sanctions on all businesses that trade with its own agents and in so doing enable the latter's trade relationship with Target. Nor is the problem unique to sanctions tout court: it also arises in the context of war, where we might have to decide whether, for example, we may justifiably harm individuals who contribute to our enemy's war effort by working in munitions factories, paying taxes, and so on. Still, secondary sanctions seem far more vulnerable to this kind of objection than either war or primary sanctions, precisely because the nature of global trade is such that a consistent policy of secondary sanctions would apply to far more agents located in many more parts of the world.

One might think that agents whose economic activities, loosely constructed, somehow contribute to the manufacturing of the goods over which Rodia transacts with Sami (and for which Rodia himself is subject to sanctions) may not justifiably be subject to sanctions, for two reasons. First, consider the causal connection between, on the one hand, the activities of a worker on an assembly line in China in charge of putting together processors for telecoms equipment, only some of which will be sold to Rodia, and, on the other hand, Sami's getting the equipment. This connection is too tenuous to support the claim that those workers are actually contributing in any meaningful way to the exactions committed by the Syrian regime. Second, those individual workers are unlikely to know—indeed cannot be expected to know—that they are contributing, via a long chain of global trade, to the nefarious activities of Target's leaders (in the case of narrow strategic goods) or that they are failing to deprive those leaders with an incentive to rescind their policy (in the case of wide strategic goods). Surely (some will press) it would be unfair deliberately to target them with sanctions for so acting.[13]

Consider the point about ignorance first. It presupposes that an agent's frame of mind at the point at which he acts is relevant for establishing whether or not we may deliberately harm him as a means to prevent him from so acting. On that view, if I do not know, and could not reasonably be expected to know, that I am contributing to a wrongdoing, then I may not be defensively harmed. As we saw in Chapter 1, however, subject to considerations of proportionality, effectiveness, and necessity, deliberately imposing some cost on agents is morally justified if the latter contribute to violating rights. On this view, the fact that those workers are ignorant of the ways in which their economic activity contribute to other regimes' unjust policies does not exempt them from being subject to the costs of economic sanctions in general and secondary sanctions in particular.

Consider next the claim that those workers' contributions are simply too minor to warrant subjecting them to those costs. We encountered that claim in Chapter 2. There, I conceded that the menial employees of businesses that trade with the citizens of unjust regimes do not make significant enough a contribution to those violations to warrant deliberately harming them via sanctions. The point is even more apt in the present context. For example, someone whose job consists of screwing the plates of metal that will, by a long circuitous route, end up encasing Rodia's telecoms equipment has not thereby lost his right to the material resources he needs to lead a flourishing life—resources that he would lose if sanctions were imposed on him. Even if that worker is in fact under a preinstitutional duty of justice to President Assad's victims not to carry out this kind of work, it is plausible that the costs he would suffer through sanctions would be disproportionate to his wrongful contribution to President Assad's unjust policy.

I accept that claim. Note, however, that this concession is compatible with three points. First, it is compatible with endorsing the deliberate imposition of sanctions-related costs on economic agents for whom those costs would not be disproportionate. Second, it is compatible with the view that imposing collateral costs on those ordinary workers is justifiable, again subject to considerations of proportionality. Third, it is compatible with the view that the imposition of secondary sanctions under conditions of uncertainty is subject to precautionary considerations. Those three claims were defended in Chapter 2 in the context of primary sanctions. Mutatis mutandis, they also hold for secondary sanctions.

Secondary Sanctions and Multilateralism

To recapitulate: arguments in favor of primary sanctions, whereby Sender restricts transactions between its own residents / nationals and Target's economic agents as a means to block and forestall grievous human rights violations by Target's regime, also support in principle Sender's imposition of those sanctions on secondary agents who are not subject to its personal or territorial jurisdiction.

At this juncture, many will undoubtedly object that even if economic sanctions are morally justified as a means to enforce human rights worldwide, secondary sanctions are not. This is because (they will argue) secondary sanctions are in tension with two fundamentally important justified tenets of the international legal order, namely the principle of sovereign equality between states and the principle of noninterference by states in the domestic affairs of other states.[14] By contrast, the imposition of economic sanctions by a multilateral institution is morally defensible.

Such an institution, comprising and representing as it does the community of states, is not restricted, jurisdictionally, to territorial borders, and its decisions are thus appropriately binding on all of its members. Moreover, it is precisely because global trade involves a wide range of economic agents across national borders into the commission of grievous wrongdoings that global multilateral institutions are uniquely placed to coordinate and impose the necessary sanctions.

Whether or not secondary sanctions are illegal under international law, my concern is with their morality. As it happens, I do not think that it is a necessary condition for defensive sanctions to be morally justified that they should be authorized by multilateral institutions with global jurisdictional reach. As I concede, however, there are cases in which multilateral authorization is morally necessary. Let me take both points in turn.

On the first count, jettisoning the requirement of multilateral authorization seems particularly apposite when sanctions are applied in self-defense. Compare with the view that, under the terms of Chapter VII of the UN Charter, the UN is the primary arbiter of interstate disputes. All the same, Article 51 unambiguously states that nothing in the charter should be taken to undermine a state's right to defend itself unilaterally from unwarranted aggression. There is strong normative support for this view: both as individuals and as members of collectives, we do have the right to defend ourselves from (wrongful) lethal and military threats. To say *a contrario* that we must wait until authorized by (something like) the United Nations is to leave us at the mercy of its members' willingness and ability to protect us. This is wrong. After all, domestically (as it were) even if the state does have a monopoly over the means of legitimate violence in a given territory, citizens of that state may kill their (wrongful) attacker in self-defense without waiting for the police to arrive. By parity of reasoning, Sender is not under a moral obligation to seek authorization from a multilateral body such as the UN before applying self-defensive sanctions, even if those sanctions apply to parties that are not subject to its territorial or personal jurisdiction.

Nor, in fact, is it under a moral obligation to do so before applying other-defensive sanctions. Consider wars of humanitarian intervention. As a matter of principle, multilateral authorization is not a necessary condition of their being just. If it were, a unilateral, unauthorized intervention by a member state to stop a genocide (in Rwanda for example, or in Sudan) would be unjust for that reason alone. In the light of the wrongful and serious harms that such an intervention would thwart, this evinces a somewhat fetishistic normative attachment to multilateralism.

That said, it does not follow that multilateral authorization is never morally required. Sender may not be in a position to know whether or not its sanctions regime meets the requirements of necessity, proportionality, and (when appropriate) effectiveness. Its leaders might be tempted grossly to distort available evidence to suit their ends, or at least be strongly and plausibly suspected of doing so. Sender may also run up against fierce opposition from other political communities whose residents / nationals would be subject to its policy. The problem arises for primary sanctions. But it is particularly pressing with respect to secondary sanctions, for two reasons. First, those sanctions interfere in the very complex networks of transactions that characterize global trade, and it is therefore much harder to assess how well they fare at the bar of necessity, proportionality, and effectiveness. Second, Sender may well be right that sanctions in general and secondary sanctions in particular would be necessary, proportionate, and effective, but, for the sake of its own nationals, it may be tempted to design the provisions of its secondary sanctions regime in a way that systematically, unnecessarily, and wrongfully disadvantages those third parties.

Insofar as multilateral institutions are likely to be more transparent and impartial than sovereign states acting unilaterally, and to command greater compliance than the latter, they might be better suited for the task of protecting individuals from human rights violations at the hands of their own or a foreign regime. But by implication, the authority to impose secondary sanctions is entrusted to and may be wielded by whomever is best suited for that task. Suppose that those institutions are unable or unwilling so to act, that unilateral state action is likely to be both more effective in this particular case, *and* that it will not undermine multilateral institutions in the longer run. Under those conditions, it is not rendered unjustified for being unauthorized. The case of Sudan illustrates the point well: in the face of (inter alia) China's repeated refusal to vote in favor of sanctions at the UN Security Council, the United States has unilaterally extended its own sanctions against President Bashir's regime to agents outside its jurisdiction: this does not in itself render its decision morally unjustified.[15]

The argument against the claim that multilateral authorization is a necessary condition for the justified imposition of sanctions is all the more plausible the more grievous the human rights violations which Target's regime is carrying out. In this respect, it is contingent on the facts of the case at hand. However, there are situations in which multilateral action is morally necessary. To wit: Target poses a threat to collective security, and in so doing commits or enables human rights violations; there are conflicting understandings of the extent to which Target does indeed pose such a threat; and the less morally risky way of parrying that threat is through the multilateral imposition of sanctions (and thus not merely through the multilateral authorization of a sanctions regime that might be imposed by one party). The conflict between North Korea and much of the remainder of the international community of states in 2017 is a case in point and worth revisiting. On September 11, 2017, the UN Security Council unanimously voted in favor of further economic sanctions against North Korea, in response to the latter's policy of nuclear and missile tests.[16] Nuclear proliferation, the Security Council stated, is a threat to international peace and security (and, thereby, human rights). Some UN and other officials worried, moreover, that the North Korean leadership was willing to use nuclear weapons against its neighbors South Korea and Japan, as well as the United States—at the costs of possibly hundreds of thousands of lives. Other officials believed, by contrast, that faced with the prospect of destruction, the North Korean leadership would be content merely to have nuclear capability and willing to settle into a pattern of nuclear deterrence. Either way, it seemed fairly clear in September 2017 that the unilateral imposition of sanctions, notably by the United States, had failed to stop North Korea. Equally, however, it also seemed that had the United States acted unilaterally, in the face of disagreement (and lack of information) about the North Korean's resolve, it would have deprived itself of the support of North Korea's hitherto staunchest allies, China and Russia—and in so doing increased the risk that, partly due to misunderstanding and miscommunication, the conflict would escalate. This, it seems to me, provides as good an illustrative argument as any of the importance of multilateralism and the dangers of unilateral secondary sanctions.

Conclusion

In this chapter, I have focused on the neglected case of secondary sanctions, whereby the sanctioning party interferes in the economic activities of agents who are not subject to its territorial and personal jurisdiction. Granted, states and associations thereof should be granted some degree of jurisdictional sovereignty. However, a commitment to human rights implies a commitment to lifting the presumption in favor of sovereignty in the realm of economic transactions, in those cases in which the multilateral imposition of economic sanctions is not morally required. Other things being equal, good examples of justified secondary sanctions in extant practices include unilateral U.S. sanctions against Sudan. Secondary sanctions against Iran and Cuba, for their part, are objectionable not on the grounds that they are imposed by the United States against agents who are not subject to its jurisdiction but, rather, on the grounds that sanctions as applied against those targets are unjustifiable tout court.

CHAPTER FOUR

Conditional Aid

W E HAVE JUST SEEN THAT economic sanctions—in other words, economic threats—are sometimes morally justified as a means to enforce human rights. Put differently, agents' rights to trade with one another are conditional on the fulfillment both of their obligation not to contribute to violating other agents' human rights and of their assistive and reparative obligations to those agents. Economic sanctions—which constitute an interference with agents' decisions with respect to the resources in their possession—are a way of enforcing those obligations.

Property rights, of which the right to trade is a subset, are only one kind of rights with respect to material resources that all human beings have. Rights to economic assistance are another. Accordingly, in this chapter and in Chapter 5, I turn to the conditionality of economic offers. I argue that individuals' rights to economic assistance are conditional on the fulfillment of similar obligations to other agents. Consequently, under certain limited conditions, the well-off, via their states and international organizations, are morally entitled—indeed, sometimes obliged—to condition the fulfillment of their duties of assistance to the fulfillment by recipients of their own obligations of justice. As we saw in Chapter 1, rights to such assistance include both the right to be given and the right to be loaned the relevant resources. The former correlate with what I call duties to aid, while the latter correlate with what I call duties to lend. I address the case of aid conditionality in this chapter, and the case of lending conditionality (and, concomitantly, debt-forgiveness conditionality) in Chapter 5.

By "aid" I mean transfers of resources from sovereign donors and international associations thereof (such as the IMF, the World Bank, or the African Development Bank) to sovereign beneficiaries, toward promoting the latter's political, social, and economic development, with no expectation that the latter will repay the aid. By "resources" I mean not merely money but also technical assistance. My definition is narrower than the various definitions at play in the empirical literature, where aid can include loans—though, to qualify as aid, a package must include a certain share of free transfers or concessionary loans.

Aid conditionality has taken different forms since 1945. Broadly speaking, in the two decades or so following World War II, the United States and the USSR used aid as a weapon with which to fight the Cold War and to this end provided aid to countries willing to align themselves against their arch enemy. In the 1960s and 1970s, it became less tied to the superpowers' geopolitical aims and more closely connected to fighting poverty in developing countries. Furthermore, whereas in the 1980s the conditions imposed by donors centered on market liberalization, the 1990s witnessed a growing emphasis on political and legal reforms as a necessary step to getting aid. Thus, the United States, the United Nations, and the European Union and its member states fund a number of development programs to help those whose human rights are under the most serious threats. When so doing, they condition the delivery of aid on the recipients' future compliance with a number of requirements. In particular, they insist that recipient regimes on the one hand should not be engaged in human rights violations and on the other hand should use the aid so provided to promote their citizens' human rights.[1]

My aim in this chapter is to defend aid conditionality so construed. I begin by offering a typology of the ways in which it is deployed, and then identify the conditions under which it is morally justified. It might seem as if human rights aid conditionality is wholly unobjectionable: if one is committed to human rights—it might be thought—of course one can use aid as a tool to enforce them. However, aid conditionality is routinely subjected to two objections: the objection that it exhibits lack of respect for its beneficiaries, and the objection that it is ineffective. I reject those objections, though qualify my defense of conditionality accordingly.

Before I begin, four features of my account of human rights to assistance are worth restating here. First, I posit that the well-off are not under duties of assistance to individuals who already lead a flourishing life; nor are they under such duties if providing assistance would impair their own prospects for such a life.

Second, my account raises the question of how best to allocate those duties. The well-off are under duties to transfer resources to the global poor via their own state institutions, either by bilateral arrangements from state to state, or by multilateral arrangements via, for example the United Nations' Development Programme. The task of disbursing the aid to those who need it largely falls on the latter's fellow residents—not on the particularistic grounds that they have a special obligation to help their needy compatriots qua compatriots but, rather, on the instrumental grounds that they are best placed to do so by dint of their proximity and shared subjection to the same coercive institutions. If and when they are unable and unwilling so to help, the obligation then falls on outsiders.

Third, the right to assistance is not merely a right to be lifted out of material poverty, it is also a right to the resources one needs for the secure exercise of civil and political rights. Thus, my human right to a fair trial has little worth if my country is too poor to afford a properly functioning justice system, or if my government systematically slashes legal aid. Equally, my right to vote has little worth if my government can only set up one polling station every 500 kilometers.[2]

Fourth, the requirement that conditionality be tailored to Beneficiary's long-term independence from Donor is crucial. As we saw in Chapter 1, in requiring that individuals be able to lead a flourishing life, justice thereby requires that they be able to achieve such a life by themselves and not live in a state of continuing dependency. The point is familiar in the context of domestic social policy, where the government's aim typically is to help welfare recipients move off welfare benefits if they can. It also applies mutatis mutandis to the global context: a state of affairs in which Beneficiary's citizens continue to be dependent, unnecessarily so, on Donor's citizens, is antithetical to justice. This will strike many scholars of global aid and development, as well as aid organizations, as obviously true, intent as they have long been on denouncing the aid trap in which the poorest individuals and their communities have been locked. To political theorists, however, who are used to speak of rights to *receive* assistance, the point is worth stressing.[3]

One final caveat. My aim is not to provide an account of justice in aid in all of its dimensions. My concern is to establish whether, if at all, a political actor is morally justified in resorting to conditionality as a means to enforce human rights. Moreover, in defending or, as the case may be, rejecting aid conditionality, I seek to defend or reject not just the decision to impose a condition on the delivery of aid, but also the decision not to deliver the aid if its putative beneficiary does not meet the relevant conditions. These are two separate tasks. As we saw in Chapter 2, threatening to impose a cost is not the same as actually making good on that threat. Similarly, conditioning an offer of a benefit on compliance with certain conditions is not the same as actually withholding that benefit. Issuing the condition does not, in itself, necessarily result in the occurrence of a cost—though it may sometimes be morally wrong, for example insofar as it evinces lack of respect for the other party. Withholding or withdrawing the benefit, by contrast, may well have seriously adverse effects on that party. Unless otherwise stated, when I speak of aid conditionality, I mean both the issuing of a condition and the decision to withhold or withdraw aid as a result of noncompliance.

Conditionality

Rights protect interests. To say that some agent—call him Bob—has a right, is to say that an interest of his—say, ϕ—is important enough to hold third parties under various duties to him to protect his interest in ϕ. To say that Bob's right to ϕ is conditional, thus, is to say that his interest in ϕ warrants holding third parties under such duties only if certain conditions are met.

We have already encountered conditional rights: the claim that economic sanctions are justified implies that economic agents' right to trade with one another is conditional on their not having contributed to human rights violations or on their meeting their assistive and reparative obligations. In the context of assistance, however, some features of rights in general and conditional rights in particular need highlighting.

Fiduciary and Nonfiduciary Rights

Suppose that Bob has a young child, Cora. Cora is dependent on Bob for her life prospects and has a right against Bob that Bob feed her, clothe her, and so on. However, Bob is very badly off and cannot fulfill his duties to his daughter without help. At the bar of justice, Cora has a right to assistance against the well-off. The well-off can best exercise their duties by transferring the needed resources to Bob himself (for example, via child benefits). On that view, Bob is entrusted with the task of discharging the duties of the well-off to his daughter. However, Cora is not the only right-holder in this case: Bob also has a crucially important interest as a moral agent—to wit, an interest in having the resources he needs in order to discharge the general obligation to help with which we have entrusted him. This interest is important enough to be protected by a fiduciary right against the well-off that the latter not only not prevent him from doing that which they tell him he is under a duty to do, but also enable him to do so.

Similar considerations hold for the relationship between residents of the same political community—different from familial relationships though that relationship is. In so far as the well-off members of a political community have been entrusted with the task of discharging universal obligations of justice to their needy fellow members, they have an interest in not being prevented from discharging those obligations. That interest is strong enough, I submit, to be protected by the relevant fiduciary rights. We will have to bear that in mind throughout, because our task is to evaluate the claim that rights to resources as held by citizens of this or that political community may depend on those individuals meeting various conditions. To do so, we need to know whether those conditions attach to those agents' own right to the resources that they lack but need to lead a flourishing life, or whether they attach to their fiduciary rights vis-à-vis those agents whom they under an obligation to help.

Conditional Rights

There are several candidate bases for conditionality, only some of which are relevant here. In particular, I set aside what one may call feasibility conditions. On some views, and depending on one's conception of feasibility, Bob does not have a right to ϕ if securing ϕ requires the deployment of resources that are not available; or if securing ϕ requires that third parties be sufficiently motivated to help yet are not in fact so motivated; or if securing ϕ requires violating another person's rights.

Relevant as those considerations are to a full elaboration of a theory of justice, aid conditionality as an instrument of foreign policy is not meant to respond to them. Rather, it is meant either to respond to what recipients have done in the past or are currently doing, or to induce them to act in certain ways in the future, or both. In the context of this book, it is meant to induce the recipients to fulfill their obligations of justice. Thus, we might say that Bob's right with respect to ϕ can be deemed conditional on his respecting—or not violating—Cara's human rights. Let us call this human rights–based conditionality.

In a different vein, in some theories of distributive justice, Bob has a right to the resources he needs to lead a flourishing life only if he is not causally and morally responsible for the fact that he lacks those resources. Let us call this no-responsibility conditionality—the core principle of which is at the heart of the dispute between so-called luck egalitarians and their critics, and (as we shall see) is thought by some to have a part to play in the provision of assistance to the distant needy.[4]

The distinction between human rights–based conditionality and no-responsibility conditionality needs refining in the light of five further intersecting distinctions.[5] First, we must distinguish between negative and positive conditionality. Negative conditionality consists of withdrawing aid one has started to provide, whereas positive conditionality consists of withholding aid in the first instance. To the extent that the costs of no longer receiving aid on which one has come to rely are higher than not getting aid the first place, other things being equal the justificatory bar is higher for discontinuing aid than for refusing to give it in the first place.

Second, we must distinguish between internal and external conditions. Internal conditions pertain to the way the aid is or has been used, whereas external conditions pertain to ends unrelated to such use. For example, Donor imposes an internal condition on the provision of aid when it says to Beneficiary, "If you do not use the resources you are asking for in this way, we will not give it to you" or "Because you have used the aid we gave you to commit human rights violations in the past, we will not give you any more of it." Contrastingly, Donor imposes an external condition when it says to Beneficiary, "If you embark on an unjust policy—a course of action for which you admittedly do not need the specific aid you are asking for—we will not help you."[6]

Third, we must distinguish between ex ante and ex post conditionality. Donor imposes ex ante conditions when it says to Beneficiary that the latter will get assistance at time $t5$, or that assistance will continue to be provided at $t5$, only if it fulfills a certain number of conditions between $t1$ and $t5$. Donor imposes ex post conditions when it gives or renews assistance to Beneficiary at time $t1$ subject to a commitment on the latter's part to fulfilling a certain number of conditions between $t1$ and $t5$. Obviously, ex post conditionality raises the issue of moral hazard: from the moment Beneficiary receives the aid and so long as it is confident that it will not need more of it in the future, it has little incentive to fulfill those conditions. No less obviously, Donor can protect itself from moral hazard by selecting Beneficiary on the grounds that the latter already has a good track record of fulfilling the relevant kind of conditions, or by delivering the aid in tranches. To the extent that ex post conditionality is selective in this way, it tends to merge with ex ante conditionality.[7]

Fourth, we need to distinguish between policy conditionality and outcome conditionality. For example, Donor might say to Beneficiary, "We will give you financial help only if you use it to fund free school meals to induce parents in very deprived areas to send their children to school." Alternatively, Donor might say to Beneficiary, "We will give you financial help so long as you achieve a school enrollment rate of 95 percent of school-age children."[8]

Finally, aid and its attendant conditions can be more or less comprehensive, or more or less targeted. For example, conditions can relate to very specific projects such as improving school enrollment or to large-scale reforms such as a wholesale restructuring of Beneficiary's energy sector.

In summary, here is a typology of conditionality:

- Human rights–based conditionality versus no-responsibility conditionality
- Negative conditionality (withdrawing aid unless conditions are met) versus positive conditionality (withholding aid unless conditions are met)
- Internal conditions (the resources must be used as intended and required by human rights) versus external conditions (Beneficiary must, as the price for getting aid, respect human rights though need not use the aid to this end specifically)
- Ex post conditionality (giving aid at t_1 and asking that conditions be met thereafter) versus ex ante conditionality (giving aid at t_5, or in tranches between t_1 and t_5 so long as conditions are met from t_1 onward).
- Outcome conditionality (giving aid so long as Beneficiary achieves outcome o) versus policy conditionality (giving aid so long as Beneficiary conducts policy p)

With this typology of conditionality in hand, we are now in a position to examine whether and why conditionality in those various forms is a morally justified instrument for the enforcement of human rights.

Internal Conditionality

In standard cases of aid conditionality, Donor offers a package of economic and financial assistance to Beneficiary on the condition that the latter should conduct policies of Donor's choosing—in this context, respecting human rights. Beneficiary thus must opt between, on the one hand, getting the aid and taking steps which it might not have wanted to take otherwise, and, on the other hand, getting nothing while retaining its political independence from Donor.

Usually, and applied internally, conditionality ties the use of the aid itself to human rights–based outcomes and policies. It does so in the following ways: it is meant to ensure that the aid is not used to violate human rights (for example, to develop nuclear weapons as a tool for an expansionist foreign policy), or it is meant to induce Beneficiary's leaders to respect human rights (for example, to embark on poverty-alleviating measures or to develop a functioning justice system, thanks to the aid). Notwithstanding appearances to the contrary, these forms of conditionality differ from each other. The stipulation that you not use the money to kill your neighbor does not imply that you must use it to feed your child: it is entirely compatible with my granting you permission to use it to buy an expensive painting even though your child is starving. Of course, were you to buy the painting or, for that matter, to kill your neighbor instead of feeding your child, you would be violating your child's right to be fed. But you would not be using the money as a means to do so.

Suppose, then, that Donor stipulates that it will provide aid to Beneficiary conditional on Beneficiary's regime not using the aid to commit human rights violations. Or suppose that Donor provides aid at $t1$ and undertakes to continue to do so as long as Beneficiary's regime does not use it to violate human rights. If the regime cannot give Donor assurances that it will comply, Donor withholds the aid from that regime. If, once Donor has provided a first tranche of aid, Beneficiary's regime fails to comply, Donor withdraws the aid. Is Donor justified in so acting?

In Chapter 1, I averred that agents are justified in withholding resources if the recipient violates a third party's rights or unjustifiably fails to protect a third party from those rights violations. A fortiori, agents are justified in withholding the resources a would-be recipient would use to violate the rights of a third party. By parity of reasoning, Donor is morally justified in so acting vis-à-vis Beneficiary's regime, whose officials have forfeited their fiduciary right to aid. If so, and again a fortiori, Donor is morally justified in merely issuing the aforementioned condition. Finally, not only is Donor morally justified in so doing, it is under an obligation to do so. Otherwise, it would be facilitating and thereby contributing to Beneficiary's wrongful policies—in breach of its obligation not to do so. In addition, it would fail to help third parties outside Beneficiary who also have a right to the aid—in breach of its assistive obligations.

One might think that conditionality in that sense ought to be rejected, on the grounds that it unfairly penalizes Beneficiary's destitute members—who do need the aid—for their regime's unjust policy. On closer inspection, however, Donor would not act unfairly. For a start, some of those members might share some of the responsibility for those human rights violations—for example, if they would support the pursuit of homophobic policies thanks to the aid thus provided. Moreover, suppose for the sake of argument that Beneficiary's members are not responsible in any way for their regime's policy. Even so, if the aid were given to Beneficiary's leaders, ex hypothesi it would not be diverted to those individuals, since the leaders would use it to violate rights. Transferring it to those leaders would be both wrong tout court and wrongfully wasteful. In such cases, it behooves Donor to consider ways in which it can get the aid to the latter more effectively. This could take the form of delivering the aid to Beneficiary's regime subject to more stringent performance reviews. Alternatively, as per extant practices, Donor could bypass those institutional wrongdoers and get the aid more directly and efficiently to its rightful recipients—for example, via NGOs.

Suppose now that Donor conditions the delivery of aid on Beneficiary's regime using it to implement human rights–based reforms. Again, this is not controversial: that, after all, is what the aid is for. In fact, Donor would act wrongly if it did not impose such conditions. The question, though, is how it ought to frame them. As we saw above, Donor can either set outcomes to be reached or design policies to be followed. Consider outcome conditionality first. At the highest level of generality, Donor says to Beneficiary, "We will give you aid in the form of cash disbursements and technical expertise so long as you use it to meet the need of your destitute population. How you do this is up to you." In practice, of course, aid donors do not set as open-ended conditions as "so long as you meet the needs of your population." They are more likely to say something like, "We will give you the aid you need to achieve a school-enrollment figure of 70 percent of school-age children, so long as you use it for that purpose. How you do it is up to you." Either way, at first sight, internal outcome conditionality does not seem controversial, particularly if outcomes are defined broadly and if achieving those outcomes places Beneficiary's citizens in a good position to achieve independence from Donor.

That said, there remain some difficulties with outcome internal conditionality. To the extent that it is imposed ex post, it exposes Donor to moral hazard. Granted, Donor could guard itself against it by disbursing the aid in tranches subject each time and ex ante to the partial, staggered realization of the outcomes. Yet there are many reasons why Beneficiary's regime might fail to achieve those outcomes, many of which are beyond its control. It seems unfair to withdraw or withhold aid from its citizens on the grounds that they failed to achieve goals that, it turned out, were beyond their reach.

Faced with such difficulties, Donor could monitor Beneficiary's progress toward those outcomes, while bearing in mind the constraints it faces when seeking to realize them. Here, however, the difficulty is that a claim to the effect that Beneficiary did not make as much progress as could have been expected will necessarily rely on counterfactual judgments as to what it should and could have done otherwise.[9]

Hence the move, in practice, toward policy conditionality. Instead of conditioning the delivery of aid on Beneficiary using it to, for example, achieve a 70 percent school-enrollment rate, Donor conditions aid on Beneficiary using it to adopt a policy that is the best way to achieve this outcome, for example by using the cash to build more schools, thereby reducing the time it takes children to get to school.

This of course is a particularly specific policy condition, tailored to this particular example. Less specifically, aid donors often insist on the aid being used to bring about wide-ranging reforms, including market liberalization and the democratization of its institutions. However, there are reasons to be skeptical of such broadly defined policy conditions, insofar as measuring success and holding both Donor and Beneficiary accountable for the implementation of those measures is all the more difficult the less specific the conditions are. In fact, evidence suggests that aid is most effective when targeted at very specific policies, notably in the areas of health, education, sanitation, and reforms of the security sector.[10]

External Conditionality

Let us take stock. So far, I have defended the view that Donor may justifiably condition the fulfillment of its duty to provide aid to Beneficiary's citizens on the latter using the aid to fulfill their own obligations of assistance toward one another. Internal conditionality, I further noted, ought to target specific policies.

Suppose now that Donor conditions the delivery of aid on the adoption by Beneficiary of human rights–based policies for which the aid itself is not needed. In such cases, we cannot defend conditionality by appealing to the rationale for giving aid in the first instance. Rather, we must appeal to the moral imperative of protecting human rights in general.

Let us distinguish between two cases. In the first case, Donor's conditions relate not to the use to which the aid is put but to broader considerations of distributive justice. For example, at a micro level, the World Food Programme's team in rural Cambodia provides take-home food and vitamins rations to families who send their children to school instead of having them work in fields or keeping them at home to look after younger siblings.[11] At a macro level, donors such as the IMF and the World Bank have conditioned the delivery of aid to the realization of reforms that, they claimed, would help lift the destitute out of poverty. In this particular case, there are reasons to be hugely skeptical: those donors were routinely taken to task for fetishizing the free market and pushing through shock therapies of economic liberalization (out of commitment to the so-called Washington Consensus) without pausing to consider whether the "beneficiary" societies could actually handle the harmful economic and social consequences of those policies for their most vulnerable members. In many such cases, it is often said, had proper consideration been given to the specific cultural, social, political, and economic features of those societies, more effective and less harmful reforms would have been undertaken.[12]

Either those criticisms are well grounded or they are not. If they are not well grounded, external conditionality of that kind was justified in such cases. If they are well grounded when they apply to those context-specific measures, external conditionality may still be justified in principle so long as those donors are willing to take the aforementioned local factors into account.

In the second case, Donor's conditions relate not to the use to which the aid would be put or to the structural circumstances under which it would be used but to broader considerations of nondistributive justice—as pertain to civil and political rights. Conditions relating to respect for

political rights stipulate that Beneficiary must engage in governance reforms if it is to receive assistance—notably reforms aimed at improving
citizens' political participation, fighting official corruption, and intro-
ducing transparent governance. The Millennium Challenge Corporation,
a U.S. aid agency created in 2005 by the then president George W. Bush,
operates precisely on that basis. Similarly, both France and the United
Kingdom have tied the provision of aid to their former colonies in sub-
Saharan Africa to the adoption by the latter's regimes of policies conducive to civil and political rights. This kind of conditionality is justified
on the grounds that (as we saw in Chapter 1), the right to political self-
determination is a human right. Effective and meaningful self-determination
is incompatible with endemic political corruption and requires transparent governance.[13]

To illustrate civil rights conditionality, in 2014 the Netherlands and
Norway cut down aid to the Ugandan government in the wake of Ugandan
legislators' decision to pass harshly repressive antigay legislation. To say
that external conditionality is justified in this case is to say that the Netherlands and Norway were justified in withholding or withdrawing from
the Ugandan government the assistance it needed (and ex hypothesi would
have used) to help the Ugandan citizens, as a response to its unjust policy.
There is no suggestion (to the best of my knowledge) that those two donors meant to induce Uganda's legislators to rescind their policy. But
suppose that their decision can be so construed. Is it morally justified?[14]

Suppose that international donors know that the Ugandan regime will
not rescind its homophobic legislation in the foreseeable future. Even if
the regime would not misuse the aid, it is morally open to donors to refuse to engage with its officials. Note, however, that in this case conditional aid cannot be justified as an inducement: it must be construed, and
justified, as a form of symbolic condemnation. It must also be accompanied, if possible, with measures aimed at reducing poverty. In this particular instance, the donors diverted the aid away from the Ugandan
government toward NGOs and civil society organizations working
with the very poor. To the extent that some of those charities, notably
American evangelical organizations, themselves propagate homophobic
views and have been supportive of the legislation, entrusting them with
the task of disbursing the aid—thereby consolidating their position in

Ugandan civil society—seems even more misguided. More generally, re-directing aid to charities risks replacing one kind of dependency (on the state) with another (on those organizations). All we can say, then, is this: if, thanks to the redirection of aid, beneficiaries are not made worse off by conditionality, the latter is morally justified.[15]

In harder cases, the beneficiaries—more strongly put, the rights-holders—will not get the aid to which they are entitled, as a result of Donor's policy. This may happen when the nonstate organizations to which Donor directs the aid are in fact less efficient at distributing it than Beneficiary's officials. The question then is whether Donor may never-theless so act for the sake of inducing a policy change on the part of Beneficiary's regime.

At the very least, it may do so only if conditionality stands a reasonable chance of succeeding, for failing that, the suffering occasioned to already very destitute individuals would be in vain. But even if conditionality does stand such a chance, and indeed does prove successful in the end, that alone does not suffice to make the case in its favor, for it will not work immediately, if it does at all; meanwhile many will suffer who would not otherwise.

So the question remains of what Donor may do under those circum-stances. I do not think that one can reach verdictive conclusions on the justifiability of this particular kind of conditionality in abstraction from the specific details of the case at issue. That said, any moral assessment of external conditionality should take the following two considerations into account. First, and to put it bluntly, the question is whether enforcing civil rights (in this case, the rights of homosexuals and their advocates to be free from persecution) is important enough to warrant depriving the very destitute of resources to which they have a presumptive right. As I argued in Chapter 1, there are limits to the sacrifices we are under assis-tive duties to incur for the sake of others: imposing external conditions on the delivery of aid is morally unjustified if it would send indirect ben-eficiaries of hoped-for policy changes into wretched poverty.

The point applies whether or not those individuals support their re-gime's civil rights abuse. Some might think, on the contrary, that agents who contribute to such abuses—for example those who support harshly repressive measures against homosexuals—have forfeited their right to the assistance the withholding of which stands a good chance of yielding a justified policy change. However, as we saw in Chapter 1, the requirement of proportionality does not apply merely to decisions to interfere with wrongdoers; it also applies to decisions to withhold resources from them. In Chapter 2, moreover, we saw that agents who make a minor contribution to human rights violations would be disproportionately harmed if sanctions were to make it impossible for them to meet their basic needs. By parity of reasoning, they would be disproportionately harmed, relative to their contribution to civil rights abuse, if they were denied aid altogether.[16]

Second, moreover, some of the individuals who suffer as a result of Donor's decision to impose conditionality are direct ex ante beneficiaries of their regime's hoped-for policy change. Donor in effect is asking them to bear the cost of not having, in the short or medium term, the resources they need for the sake of having their rights to bodily integrity, sexual freedom, and so forth, recognized in the longer term. Whether they can justifiably be made to incur that cost depends on whether or not they consented to it. After all, it is up to them to decide whether they would rather live in wretched poverty for a while in the hope that the injustice of which they are victims will be redressed, than enjoy some material comfort though under the yoke of that injustice.

Of course, matters are not so simple. Donor has no way of knowing who, among the individual beneficiaries of its assistance programs, is wrongfully supportive of the unjust policy and who is not. Nor can it ascertain which direct beneficiaries of the hoped-for policy change, if any, would consent to the imposition of external conditions. Under those conditions, Donor once again has two options. On the one hand, it could impose external conditions and withhold aid until such time as Beneficiary's regime rescinds it policy. If it does so, it will act justifiably vis-à-vis those who are beneficiaries of assistance but wrongfully supportive of the unjust policy. It will also act justifiably vis-à-vis those who consent to incur considerable hardship for the sake of rescinding the unjust policy. However, its decision so to act will come at the serious moral cost of not giving aid to the innocent and to the nonconsenting victims of the unjust policy. On the other hand, Donor could decide not to impose external conditions and to continue to give aid. In this case, it will provide assistance to those who do have a right to it as well as to the victims who would prefer receiving such help at the cost of enduring injustice. In so doing, however, Donor will end up helping both individuals who are wrongfully supportive of the unjust policy and victims of injustice who would have been willing to suffer more hardship still for the sake of increasing chances of a policy change.

When addressing similar epistemic problems in relation to economic sanctions in Chapter 2, I argued that, other things being roughly equal, we should err on the side of caution. That is to say, other things being roughly equal, we should desist from imposing all but the most targeted of sanctions, at the risk of benefiting wrongdoers but as the price to pay for minimizing the risk of wrongfully harming the innocent. In a similar vein, other things roughly equal, we should continue to provide aid, at the risk of benefiting wrongdoers but as the price to pay for minimizing the risk that we would wrongfully allow harm to befall the innocent. Once again, however, other things might not be equal: the numbers of individuals who would be seriously harmed or who would greatly benefit, and to what extent, might well make a moral difference. In the light of those epistemic obstacles, one cannot reach firm, action-guiding judgments in abstraction from the details of the case. But one can at least keep in view some of the considerations that ought to be brought to bear in reaching such a judgment, on a case-by-case basis, such as (inter alia) the numbers of people helped or not, the numbers of victims of human rights violations, the likelihood that Beneficiary's regime will rescind its unjust policy, and the timeframe within which it will do so.

I should like to end this section by drawing attention to an important feature of my arguments so far and by dispelling a nagging worry. In practice, donors tend to make the delivery of aid conditional on beneficiary regimes respecting the human rights of their own citizens. In principle, however, my arguments apply mutatis mutandis to cases in which Beneficiary's regime is in breach of its obligations of justice to distant stranger—for example, when they support another unjust regime and are told that they will not have access to aid unless they change course. Thus, under the 1992 Cuban Democracy Act, the United States does not provide assistance to countries that support Cuba (save exports of medical supplies and food). It may well be that the United States errs, morally, in so doing. If so, it errs on the grounds that its own foreign policy decisions vis-à-vis the Cuban population are morally wrong. If, however, it were entitled so to act vis-à-vis Cubans, other things being equal it would also be entitled so to act vis-à-vis third parties that support the Cuban regime (subject, here too, to considerations of proportionality).

And now for the nagging worry. In Chapter 1, I argued that there is a sense in which every single needy individual in the world has a right to assistance against every single well-off individual in the world. As I also noted, duties to provide such assistance need to be coordinated—typically via the tax-raising and distributive mechanisms of a state. They also need to be allocated among states. It is not the case, thus, that destitute Ugandans have a right to be helped by Norway specifically. Rather, they have a right that some donor help them. In the absence of a global mechanism whereby the resources of the well-off across the world can be pooled and distributed to destitute individuals across the world, sovereign donors have to exercise discretion as to whom they should help. If so, why can they not simply pick and choose on the grounds that this putative beneficiary already complies with human rights? Why (to put the point differently) need Norway be concerned by the fact that, were it to direct the away from Uganda, many Ugandans might suffer terrible hardship—given that those individuals do not have a right to be helped by Norway itself?[17]

In response, we must distinguish a decision to withhold aid from a decision to withdraw it. Taking away from people resources on which they have come to rely is harder to justify, other things being equal, than not providing those resources in the first instance, insofar as it imposes on those people additional adjustment costs. When deciding to withdraw aid, Norway (and the Netherlands) would have had to weigh the aforementioned considerations more heavily than if they had never decided to provide it in the first instance.

That said, suppose that Donor has to decide whether to provide assistance de novo to a civil rights–violating regime as a means to induce the latter to respect those rights. It comes to the realization that those inducements simply will not work, but that the regime will direct the assistance to the destitute, and more effectively than civil societies organizations would. May Donor withhold the aid, on the grounds that it may instead justifiably provide it to rights-respecting regimes or to unjust regimes that would regard it as an inducement to implement rights-respecting reforms? Not always. What Donor may do depends, inter alia, on the number of individuals it would thereby help (by respecting their socio-economic rights to resources as well as, possibly, their civil right to be free from persecution), and on the severity of their needs, relative to the number of destitute individuals who would lose much-needed resources. Here again, those decisions can only be made on a case-by-case basis, in awareness of the fact that, under conditions of epistemic uncertainty, one may well get it wrong.

The Problem of Responsibility

To recapitulate, I have mounted a defense of limited aid conditionality— limited, that is, to narrowly specified conditions and to targeted policies. As we saw, withholding or withdrawing the aid in response to beneficiary regimes' refusal to comply with those conditions is not always morally justified. In this section, I scrutinize one of the most important arguments in favor of aid conditionality—which appeals to political actors' responsibility for the fact that they need aid in the first place.

A First Cut

In *The Law of Peoples,* Rawls asks us to imagine two societies, one of which is profligate in its use of collective resources while the other is not. A few generations later, Profligate, whose population suffers considerable economic hardship, asks Thrifty for help. Given that Profligate is responsible for its predicament, Rawls argues, Thrifty is not under a duty to help its members at the bar of justice. On this view, even if Donor is not morally justified in making the provision of aid at $t1$ conditional on future performance, it may refuse to continue to aid Beneficiary if the latter has put itself in a position where it will need such aid.[18]

No-responsibility conditionality so construed extends to global aid standard arguments in favor of luck egalitarianism. In that literature, it is purely backward looking: the mere fact that I made foolish investment decisions in the past and find myself homeless as a result is enough to warrant not helping me at the bar of justice, even if I will not make the same mistake again: it would be unfair of me (luck egalitarians argue) to ask you to help me under those circumstances. In the present context, the rationale for no-responsibility conditionality is not merely the unfairness of demanding of third parties that they subsidize our expensive mistakes. It is also that Beneficiary's past misconduct gives Donor reasons to believe that it will continue so to behave. In addition, no-responsibility conditionality offers a solution to the problem of moral hazard: if putative beneficiaries take note that donors are not willing to provide aid to wasteful regimes, they themselves are less likely to be profligate when the time comes for them to ask and receive aid.[19]

Those arguments have considerable intuitive pull: to pour resources into individuals and / or communities that will not use them properly is a morally condemnable waste given that resources are scarce and could be better used to help others elsewhere. However, the following three considerations should lead donors to be particularly cautious when holding Beneficiary responsible for the fact that it needs assistance. First, and as we already saw above, even when Beneficiary's need for aid can be traced solely to recent instances of domestic mismanagement, more often than not the most vulnerable of its citizens are not responsible for those past failures in the sense in which individuals can be held responsible for collective outcomes. This is clearly so in authoritarian regimes, where they do not have the right to vote. But even in nominally democratic regimes, it is by no means clear of all of those individuals that they can reasonably be expected to know that, by voting for this or that party, they were contributing to policies of gross mismanagement. The question, then, is whether tying aid to officials' responsibility is more or less likely to benefit the very poor. Sometimes it might: faced with the realization that they are held responsible for the predicament of their destitute citizens and that aid will be cut off unless they embark on the requested reforms, those leaders and their supporters may well change tack. If they would not, Donor may justifiably withhold the aid from them on grounds of responsibility (subject to considerations of proportionality when those supporters are also destitute), but it must look for alternatives.

Second, Beneficiary's officials are not themselves responsible in the relevant sense for their country's current predicament; rather, their predecessors are. If so, it is hard to see why those officials, here and now, could be predicted to fail on the basis of what their predecessors did or did not do. My point, note, is not that a regime cannot be bound by the decisions of its predecessors. On the contrary, under certain conditions, it can. My point is merely that the past performance of a set of officials is not necessarily a good predictor of the future performance of a different set of officials.[20]

Third, as a matter of fact, donor countries themselves are often partly and wrongfully responsible for the fact that beneficiary regimes are unable or unwilling to discharge their obligations of justice to their compatriots. As former colonial powers, their past policies have contributed to the current predicament of those regimes—and in ways that are benefiting their current generations of citizens. They still support oppressors in myriad ways: by selling them weapons, by buying oil from them, by giving them access to financial help, by providing them with technical and military expertise as called for by their unjust policies, by colluding in the endemic corruption thanks to which they maintain their networks of clients—the list goes on. Worse still, donor countries often make it particularly difficult for well-off members of beneficiary countries to discharge their obligations to their compatriots, not just by helping oppressors, but (inter alia) by closing down their own markets to imports from those countries, by enforcing multinational pharmaceutical companies' patenting rights in such a way as to render the cost of medicines prohibitive, and by exercising disproportionate and undue influence in the governance of international institutions. In so acting, donor countries are not just violating the rights of Beneficiary's destitute citizens to the resources they need for a flourishing life: they are also violating the fiduciary rights of Beneficiary's well-off members not to be thwarted in their fulfillment of their obligations to their fellow citizens.

No-responsibility conditionality is profoundly unjust in such cases: not only is Donor wrongfully responsible, at least in part, for the predicament of the very poor; in addition, it proposes to deny the latter assistance on the basis of a self-servingly erroneous diagnostic of the causes of their predicament. Note that, as I defined it, it consists in conditioning the provision of assistance to Beneficiary's lack of responsibility for the fact that it needs it. But the point that Donor may not withhold or withdraw aid from

Beneficiary on the grounds that the latter's political actors are responsible
for their predicament also applies, mutatis mutandis, to cases in which
Donor's regime shares responsibility for the fact that (for example) Beneficiary's regime has carried out a policy of systematic violations of civil
and political rights against one of Beneficiary's ethnic groups. That regime may not then say to Beneficiary, "You are responsible for this policy
and we will therefore withhold / withdraw aid unless you change course."

To be sure, one may disagree with my empirical assessment of contemporary international politics. But even if I (and others) are wrong so to
criticize affluent countries, the normative point survives, to the effect that
a donor that is partly and wrongfully responsible for the situation in which
Beneficiary's population finds itself is not morally justified in withholding
or withdrawing aid *on the grounds* that Beneficiary's regime and population are fully responsible for their country's parlous human rights record.[21]

A Loose End: Aid Conditionality in a Reparative Context

To recapitulate, I have defended very limited forms of aid conditionality.
I have also argued that Donor may not appeal to the claim that Beneficiary is responsible for the fact that it needs more assistance as a reason
for withholding or withdrawing the aid, indeed for making its provision
conditional on human rights reforms—when it is itself responsible, largely
or in part, for Beneficiary's predicament. Although I developed that point
in the context of internal conditionality, it also applies, mutatis mutandis,
to the imposition of external conditions.

As we also saw above, however, it does not follow that Donor may not
attach human rights conditions to the provision of aid. Put differently, the
worry with appeals to responsibility is a worry about a particular kind of
rationale for withholding or withdrawing aid. It is not a worry about the
decision itself so to act. On the contrary, if Donor has wrongfully contributed in the past, or is wrongfully contributing now, to Beneficiary's
predicament, it is under an obligation to provide help at the bar of reparative justice. Accordingly, the question is whether the fact that Donor is
under reparative rather than assistive obligations to provide aid makes a
difference to the kind of the conditions it may attach to the aid. The issue
is not merely of philosophical interest. Belgium, France, and the United

Kingdom, formerly the main three colonial powers, provide conditional aid to sub-Saharan African countries, as do Norway and Sweden. Unlike Norway and Sweden, Belgium, France, and Britain did have colonies in this part of the world. It matters whether or not the presence or absence of a former colonial relationship makes a difference to the kind of conditions that those donors may justifiably impose on those countries.[22]

I do not think that it makes a difference to the requirement that Beneficiary not use the aid to commit human rights violations. By analogy, suppose that Ann stole cash from Bob, as a result of which he is destitute. Sketchily, Ann is under a reparative obligation to restitute the cash and to compensate Bob for the wrongful costs he thereby incurred. Yet she may condition her fulfillment of those obligations to Bob not using the cash to buy weapons with which he will then wrongfully kill his neighbor. More strongly still, she is under a duty of assistance to Bob's neighbor to do so.

Consider now Donor's stipulation that Beneficiary should carry out human rights reforms. Again, it is not clear why Donor's responsibility for the predicament in which Beneficiary's destitute individuals find themselves should make a difference. By analogy, suppose that as a result of Ann's act of theft, Bob finds himself unable to feed his daughter. Ann is under a reparative obligation to Bob to restitute the cash, and to both of them to compensate them for the wrongful costs they thereby incurred. But it would not be wrong of Ann to condition those reparation payments on Bob using what she reparatively owes to Cara to ensure that Cara is fed. In fact, and once again, she is under a duty to Cara to do so.

If I am right, the fact that Ann is responsible for Bob's and Cara's predicament does not make it less justifiable for her to impose such conditions than if someone else had caused it. Similarly, the fact (if and when it is a fact) that Donor's regime is responsible for the predicament of Beneficiary's destitute members does not make it less justifiable for that regime to impose human rights conditions than if a third party had been responsible. What Donor cannot do is appeal to Beneficiary's responsibility for its predicament, thereby occluding its own, as a justification for imposing human rights–based conditionality on the delivery of aid.

It is worth highlighting the practical importance of the point for extant practices. Assume for the sake of argument that former colonial powers such as Belgium, France, and the United Kingdom have by dint of their colonial policies significantly contributed to or have benefited from the predicament, human rights–wise, of their former colonies. Even under those assumptions, those donor countries are not less justified than noncolonial powers in resorting to human rights conditionality. More strongly still, they are under a stronger obligation to do so than if they had not so contributed or benefited, precisely on reparative grounds. There is a risk of course that Donor, by highlighting Beneficiary's human rights failures while hiding its own, is behaving hypocritically. I will return to this issue in Chapter 6.

Conditionality, Paternalism, and Distrust

To summarize, I have argued that Donor may justifiably condition the delivery of aid to Beneficiary's not committing human rights violations and to Beneficiary's implementing specific human rights reforms, so long as the conditions are delineated narrowly and as the aid is targeted to specific policies. On a broadly Walzerian view of political self-determination, however, aid conditionality so circumscribed is morally objectionable, because the more specific Donor's conditions are, the more Donor interferes with Beneficiary's choices. Yet, political communities owe respect to one another as producers of social and political values—so much so that no sovereign political community may justifiably interfere with the internal affairs of another sovereign political community unless the latter commits crimes that "shock the conscience of mankind." When used with respect to rights violations that are less grievously wrong than widespread and extreme abuses, conditionality exhibits a condemnable lack of respect for Beneficiary's members.[23] It does so in two ways. On the one hand, to the extent that Donor's conditions are grounded in judgments about what is best for Beneficiary, and not in what Beneficiary believes is best for its members, such interference constitutes an unacceptably paternalistic interference in Beneficiary's sovereignty—all the more condemnable when Donor gets it wrong. On the other hand, to the extent that Donor's conditions are grounded in a belief that Beneficiary will not or cannot meet the needs of its people unless induced to do so in specific ways, such interference evinces unacceptable distrust. The latter point seems particularly salient in the case of ex ante conditionality, since Donor will not disburse the aid unless Beneficiary has shown itself willing and able to do its bidding. Either way, the objection goes, conditionality attests to a profound and objectionable lack of respect for its supposed beneficiaries.

It is easy to see the force of the objection. But however powerful it might seem, and, indeed, however powerful it often *is* when deployed against the aforementioned measures, it should not lead us to reject conditionality out of hand. For it supposes that a political community is at one with itself save in grievously wrong cases of abuse. However, that supposition clearly is not warranted, even in cases that fall short of grievous abuses. Two points are worth bearing in mind here. First, the leadership might be willing to embark on human rights–promoting reforms, yet be opposed by powerful interest groups and / or a hostile section of the citizenry. Under those circumstances, conditionality passes the buck on to donors, thereby enabling the leadership to neuter those groups.[24]

Second, all too often, the leadership and the social groups that support it *do* engage in seriously oppressive policies toward their vulnerable compatriots. As we saw in Chapters 2 and 3, political organizations are sometimes morally entitled to impose economic sanctions on wrongdoers. To the extent that those sanctions constitute an interference in wrongdoers' economic relationships, they are a form of costs imposition. By virtue of the doctrine of acts and omissions (which I accepted in Chapter 1), they are harder to justify, other things being equal, than withholding aid (positive conditionality) and thereby allowing a cost to befall wrongdoers and innocent bystanders. They are also harder to justify, again other things being equal, than withdrawing aid that one has started providing (negative conditionality). If economic sanctions are morally justified under those circumstances, then a fortiori conditional aid is morally justified under similar circumstances, again other things being equal.

Note that my defense of conditionality against the lack-of-respect objection applies not just to nondemocratic polities but also to regimes whose citizenries democratically opt not to give the aid provided by Donor to its rightful recipients. This is because well-off citizens do not have the right, via their vote and / or regime, to deprive the needy of the resources they need to lead a flourishing life. Conditionality, as I described and defended it earlier in this chapter, is one among several mechanisms thanks to which choices hostile to justice can be blocked. Of course, one may wonder what there is to object to when unjust choices are made by the destitute themselves. To echo Tim Scanlon, what if they wish to build themselves a temple with the aid? Who are we to resist this?

By way of reply: even assuming that we can with reasonable assurance say that such is their genuine preference, insofar as they would thereby deprive their already existing children and future generations of needed resources—indeed, insofar as they would so deprive the dissenting minority, they ought not to be allowed to do so.[25]

That being said, the lack-of-respect objection does have a point. Quite clearly, aid donors and aid beneficiaries often disagree as to the kinds of policies the former can expect the latter to adopt. Some disagreements are likely to strike us as reasonable, while others are likely to seem unreasonable. As I now show, the lack-of-respect objection lacks bite when Beneficiary unreasonably disagrees with Donor; but it comes into its own in cases in which Donor is the unreasonable party and in cases in which Donor and Beneficiary reasonably disagree.[26]

A disagreement is reasonable if both parties are themselves reasonable. All it takes for a disagreement to be unreasonable is for one party to be unreasonable—that is to say, to advance an unreasonable claim. What, then, is an unreasonable claim? I take it for granted that all human beings have rights to the freedoms and resources they need in order to lead a flourishing life. As I noted in Chapter 1, the community of nations claims to endorse those rights—and we can thus take it at its word, all the more so as it is on the right moral track. Suppose, then, that Donor and Beneficiary disagree about a given human right—say, the right to freedom of religion. Beneficiary's leaders hold that only members of the majority religion ought to be allowed to practice their faith, while Donor's leaders insist on freedom of religion for all as a condition for the provision of aid. Insofar as Beneficiary's position is tantamount to denying one of the most fundamental human rights that there is and one, moreover, to which it is ostensibly committed, this particular disagreement is unreasonable. Donor does not wrong those of Beneficiary's members who endorse such discriminatory practices against minority religions or nonbelievers merely by resorting to aid conditionality as a means to induce them to change course.

But now suppose that Donor and Beneficiary agree that the human right to freedom of religion should be enforced for all irrespective of faith. They might nevertheless disagree on the following points: (a) what the content of the right is; (b) whether the right can and ought to be enforced for all here and now; and (c) if so, which policies would best enforce the right.

Disagreements regarding the content of the right are likely to be evaluative. For example, Beneficiary might hold that enforcing the right to freedom of religion is compatible with having an established church or state religion, while Donor might insist that, morally speaking, only a strict separation between church and state will do. Disagreements regarding the aptness of enforcing the right here and now, and if so by which policies, are likely to pertain to matters of empirical facts in general and to considerations of feasibility in particular. For example, Donor and Beneficiary might disagree as to whether enforcing the right here and now is feasible in the light of the religious majority's willingness to tolerate religious minorities. Or they might disagree as to whether Beneficiary does have the resources to enforce the right. Finally, they might agree that both policy p and policy q would work, but disagree as to which of the two would work best.

Who, then, should prevail? Typically, parties in a disagreement as to whether policy p or q is the right policy appeal to two kinds of consideration in support of their views: the available evidence on the one hand, and their epistemic standing on the other hand. The distinction is not hard and fast. Someone might claim that she is in a better position to evaluate the available evidence precisely by dint of her greater expertise in the matter. Conversely, the kind of evidence that a party to the disagreement adduces in favor of her position might tell us something about her epistemic standing. Still, it makes sense to distinguish those two considerations and to ask, first, what evidence there is that a given policy would or not would not be appropriate, and, second, what claim to greater epistemic standing should be regarded as unreasonable in the matter at hand. (Analogously, the fact that I broke my leg does not count as evidence of bone cancer, whereas a scan does. I do not have the epistemic standing to read a scan, whereas an oncologist does.)

Consider first the kind of evidence that might be adduced by advocates and opponents of p. Appealing to the word of God as found in the Bible is not good evidence—it is an article of faith. Appealing to the fact that p has been tried before or elsewhere is good (though not decisive) evidence. Were Beneficiary to insist that God mandates an established church, Donor would be justified in rejecting this position as unreasonable. But it would not be justified in so responding if Beneficiary were to insist that past practices regarding established religions should be taken into account in order to ascertain whether, morally speaking, the right to freedom of religion requires strict separation between church and state.

Of course, simply pointing to some evidence is not enough: what the evidence tells, if anything at all, matters too. It might be inconclusive. Or it might weigh in one direction rather than another. A disagreement between two parties about p is reasonable, thus, only if the evidence as to whether p would work or is the best way to instantiate the human right at issue is inconclusive.

However, the fact that the evidence is inconclusive is not enough to characterize the disagreement as reasonable. Parties might disagree about that very fact. Thus, Beneficiary's leaders might point to the fact that, in some parts of the world, an established religion has not prevented minority religions from flourishing. Donor's leaders might counter that an established religion within Beneficiary would lead to severely discriminatory practices against minorities. At this point, the question of the parties' relative epistemic standing is crucial. Suppose that Donor's and Beneficiary's leaders are what epistemologists call "epistemic peers" and recognize one another as such: they all have similar and relevant knowledge of policy processes, of the political, social, and economic conditions under which p would have to be implemented, and thus of relevant feasibility constraints and likelihood of success. In addition, they all reason competently and in as much awareness as one can expect of their own biases. Suppose further that there are not more experts on Donor's side to argue for p than there are on Beneficiary's side to argue against p and in favor of q. Or suppose that there are more such experts on Donor's side, but that they have been trained in the same kind of universities and in the same theoretical paradigms, and are therefore not likely to have reached their conclusions independently of each other. If so, the fact that there are more of them does not give more credence to their judgment that p. Here, we have a clear case of reasonable disagreement: the evidence for and against p, compared to the evidence for or against q, is inconclusive, and yet the parties, who acknowledge one another as epistemic peers, disagree as to whether p or q.

By implication, then, cases of *un*reasonable disagreement include cases in which the evidence is inconclusive and one side is not as epistemically competent as the other yet maintains its position that the evidence is conclusive; cases in which the evidence is conclusive yet both sides in the disagreement are epistemic peers (this is not as mysterious as it might seem: competent people can and often do make mistakes); and cases in which one side unwarrantedly refuses to recognize that the other side is its epistemic peer or, indeed, has greater expertise than it does, on the basis of which refusal it dismisses the other side's interpretation of the evidence.

The lack-of-respect objection tends to be raised in cases of the latter kind: as critics of extant aid practices point out, aid donors often get it wrong, from a combination of ideological arrogance, entrenched institutional biases, vested interests in maintaining the status quo, and blind faith in their own technological expertise with little regard for local know-how.[27]

Now, suppose that the disagreement between Donor and Beneficiary is unreasonable in the following sense: the best available evidence suggests that the reforms package that Donor seeks to impose is the best way to promote the human rights of Beneficiary's population, and Beneficiary's leaders unwarrantedly refuse to accept this though they agree that this particular human right ought to be protected. It does not seem wrong of Donor to insist, in this case, that it will deliver aid only if Beneficiary implements those reforms.

Suppose next that the disagreement between Donor and Beneficiary is unreasonable, this time in the following sense: the evidence conclusively points against Donor's case for p, Beneficiary's leaders correctly assess on the basis of expert advice that p will, for example, cause considerable hardship for an already struggling population, and Donor's leaders unwarrantedly refuse to give credence to Beneficiary's judgment. In such cases, aid conditionality does smack of colonial interference in the affairs of a sovereign community whose members (let us not forget) are entitled to the aid they are asking for. Moreover, when it rests on an unwarrantedly biased refusal to recognize the other party as an epistemic peer or superior, it instantiates a particularly egregious form of epistemic injustice.

Suppose, finally, that the disagreement between Donor and Beneficiary is a reasonable disagreement. That is to say, there is no conclusive evidence that Donor's preferred policy p would be more effective than Beneficiary's preferred policy q at enforcing a given human right, and Donor and Beneficiary are, and regard one another as, epistemic peers. For example, Donor believes that freedom of religion in Beneficiary requires a strict separation between state and religion, while Beneficiary maintains otherwise. The arguments on both sides are finely balanced. Or suppose that Donor's technical experts believe that proper irrigation in Beneficiary (lack of which is disastrous on human rights grounds) requires taking certain kind of steps, while Beneficiary's own experts disagree. Again, there is no conclusive evidence either way, and no reason for one side to dismiss the other side's experts as incompetent. May Donor resort to conditionality in such cases? Some might think so: they might think that it is up to Donor's experts to exercise their best judgment, and to Donor's leaders to decide, on the basis of expert advice, how to use the funds they are prepared to transfer. I disagree. Remember: ex hypothesi, Beneficiary has a right to the aid, which correlates into Donor's duty to give it. Donor does not own the funds. Rather, the funds are owned by Beneficiary. For Donor under those circumstances to insist that Beneficiary do its bidding evinces condemnable lack of respect. (By implication, were Donor transferring the aid not as a matter of duty but in a supererogatory manner, it might be entitled to impose its own understanding of what the enforcement of human rights requires.)

Crucially, I am not suggesting that, in cases of reasonable disagreement between Donor and Beneficiary as to the aptness of p, either party should weaken its respective judgment that p is or is not the best way to enforce a particular human rights. Epistemologists differ on this point, but for my purposes here, I can remain agnostic. Instead, I am suggesting that irrespective of what Donor ought to believe as to the truth of the statement "*p* is the right policy to adopt under the circumstances," it ought to accept that Beneficiary's view (to the effect that *q* is the right policy) should be implemented.

At this juncture, some readers might wonder whether it still is appropriate to talk of conditionality when donors and beneficiaries negotiate over and agree on conditions. For by stipulation, Donor and Beneficiary agree that the latter needs help to realize certain objectives, agree on those objectives, and reasonably disagree on how to reach them. Under those circumstances, it is appropriate that they should engage in extensive dialogue / negotiations to resolve their differences. It is appropriate, too, to take into account past records of being right or wrong as to which kind of reforms would or would not work, when deciding which set of conditions to propose and accept. To the extent that aid conditionality generally unfolds—or is taken to unfold—against a background of antagonism between donors and beneficiaries, and that, in such cases, the parties in fact cooperate with each other, it seems that the term "aid conditionality" is a misnomer.

I still think that talk of conditionality is apt in such cases. An agreement is not any less conditional for the fact that both parties concur on what constitutes reasonable human rights–based conditions: it remains the case, after all, that aid donors would be justified in withholding or withdrawing the aid, at least at first sight, were beneficiaries not willing to meet the stipulated (and agreed-on) conditions.[28]

In conclusion, nonnegotiable conditionality is morally justified only when the rationale for providing the aid is tied to the realization of specific human rights–based projects, and when Donor correctly assumes, in the light of the available evidence and its epistemic standing relative to Beneficiary's, that the conditions it seeks to impose on Beneficiary are the most likely in general to enforce human rights within Beneficiary. As a matter of fact, I do not know whether disagreements between aid donors and beneficiaries tend to be reasonable or not and, when they are unreasonable, which of donors or beneficiaries advances unreasonable claims. Perhaps most such disagreements are reasonable. Clearly, a full assessment of extant practices in the light of the foregoing considerations is far beyond the scope of this book. It is worth noting however that, in line with the World Food Programme's description of its activities, major aid donors routinely stress the fact that they collaborate with recipients of aid, whom they tend to call partners, rather than treat them as supplicants with a begging bowl.[29]

Aid Conditionality and Effectiveness

At various points throughout this chapter, I have alluded to the possibility that conditionality might not be effective. In this section, I revisit the issue of effectiveness, which dominates the academic literature. The consensus in that literature, as far as one can tell, is that the kind of conditionality practiced by major donors such as the IMF and the World Bank, particularly when focused on structural adjustments along the lines discussed earlier, does not work and should be abandoned on the grounds, precisely, that it proved ineffective (and in fact made things worse). On some views, moreover, aid conditionality in general can be dismissed on those grounds, whereas other accounts suggest that it does work under some, context-dependent circumstances.[30]

It is important to distinguish the question of whether aid works, from the question of whether conditionality works when attached to aid. Of course, if global resource transfers, whether conditional or not, simply do not work let alone make things worse, donors should stop operating them (other than, perhaps, in situations of extreme emergency.) It is not clear, however, that aid always does and necessarily must fail. The normative question at hand, then, is this: assuming for the sake of argument that conditionality is not effective, are donors morally justified, indeed obliged, to exclude it from their arsenal of foreign policy tools?

Insofar as conditionality seeks to change recipients' behavior, and insofar as withholding or withdrawing aid from recalcitrant beneficiary regimes carries significant costs to those regime's destitute populations, one might think that effectiveness is a requirement of justified aid conditionality. On closer scrutiny, however, the issue of effectiveness is somewhat more complex than appears at first sight. When it resorts to aid conditionality, Donor conditions the provision of aid to the realization of certain goals or the adoption of certain policies. Aid conditionality is deemed effective, qua aid conditionality, only if Beneficiary adopts those policies because Donor subjected the delivery of aid to those conditions. Furthermore—and this is crucial—internal conditionality is deemed effective not only if Beneficiary so acts but also if it does achieve those goals thanks to the aid thus provided.

By implication, there are several ways in which aid conditionality might be deemed ineffective—as follows:

(1) Beneficiary receives aid, conditional on fulfilling ex post human rights conditions. Its leadership does not fulfill those conditions.

(2) Beneficiary receives aid, conditional on fulfilling ex ante conditions. Its leadership does not fulfill those conditions.

(3) Beneficiary's leadership does fulfill Donor's conditions (whether ex ante or ex post)—for example, it reforms its parliamentary system and raises social expenditures. However, for reasons beyond its control, the aid provided by Donor does not succeed at improving its members' prospects for a flourishing life. For example, as a result of a civil war in a neighboring country, it is facing an unexpected influx of thousands of refugees, which in turn drains its fledging services.

(4) Same as (3) except that the reason why the aid provided by Donor does not help is that Donor's regime, at the same time as it assists Beneficiary, fans the flame of that civil war.

(5) Beneficiary's leadership does not fulfill Donor's conditions (whether ex ante or ex post), yet for extraneous reasons its citizens are better off in the respects identified by those conditions. For example, Beneficiary does not increase social expenditures, contra Donor's demand that it do so as a means to reduce hunger, but the harvest is better than expected, which leads to less hunger.

(6) Beneficiary's leadership does not fulfill Donor's conditions (whether ex ante or ex post), yet adapts different policies of its own which, together with the help provided by Donor (in ex post cases or in ex ante / in tranches) in fact improve its members' prospects for a flourishing life.

Case (1) is a straightforward failure. The question, then, is whether Donor may justifiably impose ex ante conditions next time Beneficiary asks for help, indeed whether it would be justified in denying its population help altogether. This, in effect, leads us to case (2). As I argued earlier in this chapter, whether conditionality is justified partly depends on whether Beneficiary's population would have received the aid had their leadership been given it unconditionally. If it would not, Donor may justifiably deny the aid from Beneficiary's leadership on pain of being wasteful—even though its having issued conditions has not led Beneficiary's leadership to rescind its unjust policy; it is in that sense that effectiveness is not a necessary condition of a costly omission. It does not follow, however, that Donor may do whatever it wishes to do with the aid. Remember, as we saw in Chapter 1, the affluent hold the resources to which the needy have a right in trust for the latter. If they ought not to disburse those resources—for example for the aforementioned reasons—they ought instead to hold the resources (if possible) in a locked account until such time as circumstances in Beneficiary become propitious; or they ought, if possible and effective, to divert the aid to civil society organizations.

Cases (3) and (4), by contrast, are failures of a rather different kind, in that Beneficiary does in fact comply with Donor's demands. The reason aid conditionality is not effective in case (4) is Donor's doing. As we saw above when discussing the issue of responsibility, it would be profoundly unjust of Donor to invoke ineffectiveness as grounds for withdrawing help from Beneficiary. It would also be unjust, though less grievously so, for Donor to withhold aid from Beneficiary in case (3), given that the latter is not responsible for the failure of the policy.

Cases (5) and (6) are failures in that Beneficiary does not comply, yet its population does see an improvement along dimensions identified by Donor as conditions for the delivery of aid. Is Donor morally justified in tightening up its conditions in the next round of negotiations, indeed in withdrawing or withholding aid as a result of Beneficiary's noncompliance? Suppose that its decision to impose these conditions in the first instance was unjustified (for example, there was unreasonable disagreement to Beneficiary's advantage as to how best to use the aid, or there was reasonable disagreement). In such cases, it seems that Donor cannot charge Beneficiary for using the aid ineffectively and thus cannot decide to discontinue it on that basis. Ineffectiveness seems irrelevant, morally speaking, to Donor's decision to discontinue the aid.

Suppose, now, on the contrary, that Donor was justified in imposing those conditions in the first instance. Granted, Beneficiary's leadership did not do its part. But to deny aid on those grounds, even though ex hypothesi its citizens did witness an improvement in precisely the respects set by Donor, seems wrong. For after all and once again, the resources are not owned by Donor; rather, Donor holds them in trust for Beneficiary's regime, which in turns holds them in trust for its fellow citizens. So long as Beneficiary's regime has done and will continue to do what it ought to do by those individuals, Donor must respect its fiduciary right to the resources its needs in order to fulfill those obligations. The fact that Donor's policy of aid conditionality has failed, qua such policy, is neither here nor there, even though it was justified in adopting it in the first instance.

Conclusion

Let me conclude. In this chapter, I argued that aid conditionality is justified on the grounds and to the extent that providing the aid is tied to the realization of specific human rights–based policies. Attributions of responsibility to Beneficiary for the fact that its population needs assistance, I also argued, do not always warrant withholding or withdrawing aid. This is so either because Beneficiary is not in fact responsible for its predicament, or because even if it is, Donor must at least try to find alternatives to not providing aid, or because Donor is at least in part responsible as well. When Donor is responsible, it is under a reparative obligation to provide assistance—albeit with human rights conditions attached to it.

Furthermore, and as a concession to the lack-of-respect objection, I argued that Donor may not impose nonnegotiable conditions on Beneficiary unless it is warranted in assuming that the conditions it seeks to impose on Beneficiary are the most likely to enforce human rights within Beneficiary. In any other case—in which, that is, Beneficiary is warranted in judging which policy would work, and what is or is not needed, or where there is reasonable disagreement between the parties—nonnegotiable conditionality is not morally justified; negotiated assistance (which does remain conditional) ought to take its place. Finally, I showed that the fact that aid conditionality is not effective does not suffice to show that it is morally unjustified.

My normative account of aid conditionality yields some lessons for actual cases. For example, and as we already saw, policy-specific conditions, such as improving school enrolments or rescinding homophobic legislation may under the circumstances specified here justifiably form part of a conditionality package. By contrast, until fairly recently, aid donors such as the World Bank and the IMF would insist that recipients of loans privatize their utilities sectors, including water—that most basic necessity of all. However, as I noted in Chapter 1, although the protection of private property rights is a requirement of justice, the exclusion of joint ownership over resources is not. In fact, under some circumstances, justice may well require that some resources be jointly and publicly owned. As it happens, the multinational corporations that benefited from the privatization of water sectors imposed huge increases in water bills, including on the very poor, and disconnected water supplies from those unable to pay. Examples include the privatization of the water system in Bolivia and Tanzania, in both cases at the behest of the World Bank. When privatization leads to egregiously unjust outcomes (which it does not always do), of which aid beneficiaries are fully aware and notwithstanding aid donors' convictions to the contrary, it may not justifiably be made a condition for the delivery of aid.[31]

In the case of conditionality as in the case of sanctions, thus, my account aligns with some practices and is profoundly at odds with others.

CHAPTER FIVE

Sovereign Lending, Debt Forgiveness, and Conditionality

IN CHAPTER 1, I averred that socioeconomic justice does not merely require that individuals be given the assistance they need in order to lead a flourishing life—it also requires that they be able to borrow what they need. In Chapter 4, we saw that aid donors are justified in imposing conditions on the fulfillment of their obligation to offer aid as a means to enforce human rights. If so, one might think that lending conditionality is justified a fortiori, for insofar as lenders are under a duty to loan, they may justifiably condition the fulfillment of that duty in the same way as they may justifiably condition the fulfillment of their duty to provide aid.

My aim in this chapter is to explore the ethics of both conditional lending and conditional debt relief as a means to enforce human rights. In line with the book, I focus on sovereign lending—that is to say, on lending by sovereign states or international financial institutions (IFIs) such as the IMF, the World Bank, or the African Development Bank Group, to sovereign states. The sums involved are not trivial (although they look less considerable when compared to global flows of capital). By the end of August 2016, the IMF had committed loans to the tune of $159 billion. By September 2016, the IMF and the World Bank together had granted debt relief worth $76 billion to thirty-six of the poorest countries in the world. The so-called Paris Club, whose members comprise the most powerful economies in the world and thus the sovereign states most exposed to sovereign debt, has made 433 loan-restructuring, debt-relief, and cancellation agreements since its foundation in 1956—to the tune of $583 billion.[1]

I proceed as follows. First, I highlight some important differences between aiding and lending in general, and between the rights and obligations that accrue to parties in aid and lending agreements in particular. Next, I defend the resort to human rights conditionality in cases in which the loan is just and the debt accrued is thereby just. I then turn to the ethics of attaching human rights conditions to the provision of otherwise unjust loans and/or to the granting of relief on—or the cancellation of—unjust debts. I argue that the fact that Lender is willing to grant an unjust loan does not in itself bar its officials from conditioning it on Borrower's compliance with human rights–promoting policies. The same claim holds, I show, with unjust debt conditionality. I also show that the fact that Borrower is responsible for needing a loan or debt relief—when it is responsible—sometimes makes a difference to the moral status of Lender's decision to resort to conditionality. Finally, I examine difficulties inherent in trying to enforce compliance on the part of Borrower.

One final caveat. As with aid, my aim is not to provide an account of the ethics of lending and borrowing in general. Rather, it is to assess whether the well-off, via their states and/or IFIs, are morally justified in imposing human rights–based conditions on the provision of loans and the granting of debt relief, in those cases in which they are under a duty to offer a loan or to grant relief in the first instance. Accordingly, I shall not provide an account of, for example, just or unjust interest rates. Nor shall I consider in any depth the questions of intergenerational justice raised by both lending and borrowing decisions. Nor shall I address the distinct issues raised by private lending and debt forgiveness—as when sovereign actors are indebted to multitudes of individual bondholders and/or so-called vulture funds. Nor do I discuss proposals for dealing with sovereign bankruptcy in general. Nor shall I provide a defense of the view that borrowers are under a pro tanto duty to pay a debt accruing from a just loan: on the contrary, I shall take that view for granted. Finally, cases in which sovereign states are merely permitted to extend loans to other sovereign states, and are not under an obligation of justice to do so, raise separate issues, which I will briefly sketch out in the book's conclusion.[2]

Preliminaries

Aiding versus Lending

As I noted in Chapter 1, duties of distributive justice are duties to give or lend the relevant assistance. Depending on the circumstances, if I have a right to food, then by implication you are under a duty to give it me, to give me the money I need to buy it from someone else, or to give me the help I need to put myself in a position where I will be able to procure the food. You might also be under a duty to lend me the money to buy it, should I be faced with a temporary liquidity shortfall.

Unlike a gift, which one can offer without asking for anything in return, a loan is by definition conditional. When one offers to loan a certain amount of money to another party, one does so on condition, at a minimum, that the borrower pay the money back. However, it is not by definition true of a loan that the repayment should take place according to a certain schedule; nor is it by definition true of a loan that it should be repaid with interest. Indeed, the International Development Association, which is one of the World Bank's two arms (as it were), provides interest-free loans to the governments of the poorest countries in the world. Accordingly, even if one has provided a sound justification for the claim that A may loan money to B, one has not thereby provided a sound justification for the claim that A may justifiably insist that B should repay the loan to a given schedule s within a given timeframe t, or that it may justifiably insist on conditioning the loan offer to the payment of interests to the rate of r percent.

Conditions such as having to repay the principal, pay interest, and pay the loan to schedule s and by time t are what one may call "repayment conditions." My concern in this chapter is with cases in which Lender is willing to loan money to Borrower on condition that Borrower respect human rights as well as comply with repayment conditions.

In Chapter 4, I distinguished between different kinds of conditionality, some of which are relevant to lending. For example, Lender might decide to impose conditions on the granting of a loan that are internal to how the loan is to be used; or it might decide to impose conditions that are external to it. The same considerations apply to debt relief: Lender might accede to Borrower's request for relief on condition that Borrower should use the resource thus freed up toward bringing about human rights, or on condition that Borrower should implement a set of human rights–based policies, though not necessarily thanks to those resources.

I will return to those forms of conditionality at various junctures in the chapter. Meanwhile, I need to make two points about the various ways— some similar, some different—in which aid relationships on the one hand and loan relationships on the other hand create rights, duties, liabilities, immunities, and powers between the parties. (From now on, when I speak of aid, I always mean "gifted aid"—as distinct from a loan that is mandatory at the bar of justice.)

First, to the extent that Borrower's officials have rights, duties, and liabilities with respect to those loans, they do so in a fiduciary capacity. Moreover, Borrower's rights, duties, and liabilities with respect to the loans it obtains from Lender are jointly held by Borrower's individual citizens. With respect to the first point, there is no difference between aid and loans. With respect to the second point, however, there is an important difference. Unlike aid, a loan will have to be repaid over time (unless relief is granted), such that the cohort of citizens who, via their officials, took out the loan will not necessarily overlap with the cohorts of citizens who will have to repay it in full. This raises acute issues of intergenerational justice within Borrower. Given that my focus in this book is on the conditionality of enforcing human rights across political borders (as it were), my concern in this chapter is with just relations between Borrower and Lender. More precisely put, my concern is with just economic relations between Lender's citizens and those citizens of Borrower who were not of age when the loan was taken out and who yet may have to repay it.[3]

Second, to say that Beneficiary has a right to aid against Donor is to say that Beneficiary's interest in having the aid is important enough to place Donor under an obligation to provide it. Even though Donor might be justified in imposing conditions on fulfilling its obligation, the facts remain that Beneficiary has a right to it and that Donor is under a duty to give it (albeit subject to independently justified conditions)—period. Moreover, the conditions that Donor may or must attach to the provision of aid are justified precisely because and only insofar as they are tied to the adoption and implementation of human rights policies. By entering into an agreement with Donor to the effect that it will receive aid so long as it meets those conditions, Beneficiary is not imposing on itself duties that it did not have before.

Some forms of lending are very similar to aid in those respects. As we saw, one can be under a duty to give a loan to someone in need— when that person is temporarily unable to meet her needs by herself. Correlatively, she has a right to the loan. A mandatory-loan agreement between two parties thus does not create rights and duties de novo, not even the borrower's duty to repay the lender: given that she has a pre-agreement right to be offered a loan, she has a pre-agreement duty to repay it if she is offered it. To see this, contrast with loans to which borrowers do not have an independent right. Suppose that Borrower is seeking funds to replace its old railway system. Its citizens enjoy a flourishing life and thus are not owed the funds as a matter of rights, whether in the form of aid or in the form of loans. Lender agrees to extend a loan on condition that Borrower should repeal its homophobic legislation. The loan agreement between Borrower and Lender creates Borrower's right to the money and Lender's duty to provide it as well as rights and duties with respect to repayment modalities (though not with respect to the fulfillment of its obligations to homosexuals). Insofar as I am concerned with the duty to loan, I set those cases aside.

Suppose now that, as a matter of distributive justice, Borrower is entitled to receive money from Lender as a gift, yet Lender offers to loan it instead. In that sense, its offer is unjust. However, given that Lender will not give, they are under a second-best obligation to loan. In this case, too, the loan agreement itself does not confer on Borrower a right to the money and on Lender a duty to provide it, which they did not have before. Were Lender to offer a loan, Borrower's officials would be justified—indeed, might even be under a duty vis-à-vis their compatriots—to accept it. However, Borrower's citizens would not thereby incur repayment obligations to Lender—on the contrary, since the loan would be unjust. Rather, they would owe that obligation to one another (to the extent that, were they to default on the loan, other creditors would be unwilling to grant them credit, and their compatriots' prospects for a flourishing life in the future might be further jeopardized).

It might seem as if the distinction I have just drawn between second-best justified and just loans is somewhat pedantic. It is not. Normatively, it matters deeply whether Lender is fulfilling a first-best or only a second-best obligation to Borrower. In particular, as we shall see below, it makes a difference to Borrower's putative duties to Lender. Empirically, those unjustified loans—assistance that in fact ought to be given as nonrepayable aid as a matter of justice—are the bread and butter of international development. Given that all individuals have rights to the resources they need for a flourishing life, and given that the well-off singularly fail in their correlative obligations of justice to the destitute, the loans extended to the latter by the former via their governments and / or IFIs are unjustified loans. When evaluating extant practices of conditionality, we had better keep that in mind.

We have seen that some of the rights and duties with respect to justified aid conditionality differ from some of the rights and duties accruing to parties in loan agreements. What about agreements pertaining to debt relief? Suppose that the loan was justified in the first instance. If Lender is merely justified in offering relief on the debt, the resulting agreement would confer on it and on Borrower rights and duties that they did not have before. But if Lender is under a duty to provide relief or to cancel the debt altogether, Lender's and Borrower's relevant rights and duties with respect to the relief or cancellation schedule are not created de novo by the resulting agreement; the latter merely states what its parties are in any event required to do.

In cases in which Lender ought not to have offered a loan, on the grounds that Borrower was entitled to get resources as gifted aid, the loan is unjustified and Borrower has a claim that it be cancelled. By entering into a debt cancellation agreement with Lender, Borrower is not acquiring a right to the debt relief (and thus to the monetary resources thereby freed up), and Lender is not placing itself under a duty to cancel the loan, which they respectively did not have before. Rather, they are creating only second-best rights and duties with respect to the debt-relief conditions that they did not have before.

Typology of Loan and Debt Relief Conditionality

As with aid, we must distinguish between different kinds of conditionality. Fortunately, we are not starting from scratch. The distinctions I introduced in Chapter 4 in the context of gifted aid, such as the distinction
between negative and positive, ex ante versus ex post, policy versus outcome, human rights and no-responsibility, and so on, also apply here.
However, there is a particular kind of conditionality that is specific to both
loans and debt relief, and which I shall call "repayment-reforms conditionality." In repayment-reform conditionality, Lender conditions the offer
of a loan to Borrower carrying out reforms aimed at improving chances
that Borrower will be able to repay. (In other words, repayment conditions include interest rates, repayment schedule, etc. Repayment-reforms
conditions are conditions such that, if Borrower meets them, it will be in
a better position to meet its repayment conditions.) Under so-called structural adjustment programs, for example, Lender agrees to loan x so long
as Borrower opens its markets to foreign investments and privatizes its
utilities, which will lead to an increase in GDP and, thereby, in public
revenues. Current examples include the many macroeconomic conditions
that (inter alia) the IMF imposes on borrowers. As the IMF puts it in one
of its factsheets, "The overarching goal is always to restore or maintain
balance of payments viability and macroeconomic stability while setting
the stage for sustained, high-quality growth and, in low-income countries,
for reducing poverty."[4] Those conditions are not restricted to loan offers: they also apply to offers of debt relief and stipulate that Borrower
must conduct policies aimed at enhancing prospects that the remainder
of the loan will be paid.

   With those points in mind, here is a typology of lending and debt relief conditionality:

- Human rights conditionality versus no-responsibility conditionality versus repayment-reforms conditionality
- Internal conditionality (the resources must be used as intended
  and required by human rights) versus external conditionality
  (Lender must, as the price for getting a loan or debt relief, respect
  human rights, though need not use the resources thereby freed up
  to this end specifically)

- Negative conditionality (withdrawing a loan / a promise of debt relief unless conditions are met) versus positive conditionality (granting a loan / offering debt relief so long as conditions are met)
- Ex post conditionality (granting a loan / debt relief at t_1 and asking that conditions be met thereafter) versus ex ante conditionality (granting a loan / debt relief at t_5, or in tranches between t_1 and t_5, so long as conditions are met from t_1 onward)
- Outcome conditionality (granting a loan / debt relief so long as Beneficiary achieves outcome o) versus policy conditionality (granting a loan / debt-relief so long as Beneficiary conducts policy p)
- Comprehensive (with respect to both conditions and the resources accruing from the loan / debt relief) versus targeted (with respect to both the conditions and the resources accruing from the loan / debt relief)

Just Loans, Just Debts

When accounting for the ethics of the conditionality of both loans and debt relief, we must distinguish between cases in which Lender is under a first-best obligation to offer a loan and cases in which it is not morally entitled to do so on the grounds that it ought instead to give the resources for free. In the latter case, Lender acts wrongfully; the loan itself is unjust, even if its repayment conditions are not in themselves unjust. I address just loans (and just debts) in this section, and unjust loans (and unjust debts) in the next section.

Just Loans

Suppose that Lender is under a first-best duty to offer Borrower a loan. The IMF's typical loan instruments fit this particular bill. Rapid credit facility and standby credit facility loans, for example, are issued to low-income countries that urgently need help with a short-term balance of payment problem. Extended credit facility loans, by contrast, are meant to help low-income countries address deeper and longer-terms structural problems. These and other loans as provided by sovereign states and multilateral institutions are solutions to the kind of liquidity crisis I described in Chapter 1 when delineating the content of rights to assistance.[5]

Further, let us suppose that the repayment conditions (interest rate, payment schedule, etc.) are not unjust. As I noted above, Lender might decide, in addition, to impose conditions on the granting of a loan that are internal to how the loan is to be used, or it might decide to impose conditions that are external to it.

HUMAN RIGHTS–BASED CONDITIONALITY

May—indeed must—Lender condition the offer of a loan to Borrower (a) using the loan itself toward respecting the human rights of its citizens, thereby meeting its obligations of justice, or (b) doing what it wants with the loan so long at it meets those obligations?

To the extent that Lender is under a duty to offer a loan to Borrower, its offer should be treated in the same way as the imposition of internal and external conditions on the delivery of aid. Lender may justifiably subject the offer to Borrower's using the loan to meet its obligations to its citizens, so long as (similarly to the case of aid) the conditions it imposes are narrowly specified and the loan is targeted at very specific policies rather than broadly defined outcomes. Lender is also justified in monitoring Borrower's performance if there is no reasonable disagreement as to how best to meet those obligations or if Lender is warranted in making such judgments; the case here is similar to aid. As I noted when discussing aid conditionality, some of those disagreements are broadly technical; others are more political. The point is particularly important in the context of lending, as loans provided by sovereign states and IFIs are often accompanied by the provision of technical expertise that borrowers believe they lack and seek to access.[6] But even if borrowers agree to stipulated technical conditions, lenders are not any less aptly characterized as subjecting the loan to those conditions in the service of human rights, and the loan is not any less conditional for it.

More strongly still, Lender is under a duty to condition the loan offer to the fulfillment by Borrower of its obligation to respect the civil and political rights of both its members and third parties. To see this, suppose that Lender does not do this. Borrower's leadership undertakes to use the loan to, for example, help feed its population, but uses the resources thereby freed up by the loan to stockpile weapons, thanks to which it carries out a policy of unwarranted military aggression toward its neighbor. Or suppose that Borrower uses those resources to fund an oppressive police and security apparatus, thanks to which it violates dissenters' rights to freedom of expression and association. Lender's loan is what is sometimes called an odious loan. Those loans uncover a serious difficulty, which we already encountered in Chapter 4, namely the fungibility of financial resources. Even if Lender ostensibly makes a loan to Borrower on the understanding that the latter will use it toward just ends, there is little that prevents Borrower from pursuing unjust ends thanks to having received the loan, albeit indirectly so.

The point has far-reaching practical and normative implications. Practically speaking, it seems to imply that many of the loans granted by the IMF and the World Bank are unjust loans; among the countries that are eligible for lending assistance under the World Bank's rules, many are ranked the lowest on (inter alia) the Cato Institute's Freedom index and the Democracy Index published by the *Economist*'s Intelligence Unit.[7]

Normatively speaking, IFIs or sovereign states ought not to turn neutrality into a cornerstone of their lending policies, for while (as we shall see below) it is sometimes morally permissible to loan money to unjust regimes, often it is not. Adopting a stance of permanent neutrality is morally wrong insofar as it exposes lenders to the serious risk of making unjustified loans. For all its failings, the Reagan administration made the right decision when it threatened via its IMF officials to suspend loans to Chile in the 1980s, out of (belated) concern for President Pinochet's policy of systematic human rights violations against his opponents. Conversely, Chinese authorities have come under fire for their lending policies in, for example, Sudan. While appearing to conduct a policy of noninterference, China de facto provided support to Sudan's Islamist regime and its genocidal policy in Darfur—with (as far as one can tell and at the time of writing) no discernible improvement in that regime's abysmal human rights record.[8]

Granted, Borrower would see its sovereignty somewhat constrained were it to accept human rights conditions. However, for Lender to offer a loan subject to those conditions is nothing more and nothing less than an attempt to get Borrower to meet its obligations of justice.

REPAYMENT-REFORMS CONDITIONALITY

Mandatory loans nevertheless differ from mandatory aid in one important respect, namely that Lender expects to be repaid. In such cases, Lender conditions the offer of a loan to Borrower carrying out reforms aimed at improving chances that it will be able to meet its repayment obligations. Ex hypothesi, Lender is under a duty to loan x; by implication, it does not have full property rights over x. It does, however, have a right to be compensated for having to defer its use of x. The fact remains that it is at risk of not being repaid that which it is owed. In that light, Lender may justifiably seek to maximize chances that it will be repaid by imposing conditions to that end, at least so long as there is no conclusive evidence to suggest that, in so doing, it would in fact undermine human rights in Borrower.

Suppose, however, that in a given case there is no conclusive evidence, either way, that the repayment reforms would or would not undermine human rights within Borrower. Suppose further that the latter's leaders nevertheless disagree with their counterparts in Lender on this point. Suppose finally that those actors are one another's epistemic peers and acknowledge one another as such; they are locked in a reasonable disagreement. Ought Lender to give way to Borrower, in the same way as Donor, I argued in Chapter 4, ought to give way to Beneficiary? No, precisely because ex hypothesi, Lender is owed the repayments and it may thus exercise greater control over the repayment conditions under which it will make the loan. If the disagreement is reasonable, it is hard to see on what grounds Beneficiary could legitimately object to the imposition of those reforms.

By implication, and a fortiori, Lender may justifiably impose such conditions if the disagreement in which it is locked with Borrower is unreasonable in its favor. But it is not morally justified in so doing if the disagreement is unreasonable in Borrower's favor; in such cases, the lack of respect of objection which, as we saw, has force against aid conditionality, has similar force against loan conditionality.

Conditional Relief and Just Debts

Suppose, then, that at $t1$ Lender grants a loan to Borrower in fulfillment of its obligation to do so, and that the loan is a just loan. At $t5$, Borrower can no longer repay—at least, not without impairing its citizens' prospects for a flourishing life. May Lender resort to either of the forms of conditionality that we have identified so far, as the price to pay for a partial or total debt relief?

CONDITIONALITY AND LENDER'S DUTY TO GRANT RELIEF / CANCEL THE DEBT

Let us assume for the sake of argument that Lender is under a duty to grant Borrower some relief on its debt, or indeed to cancel the debt altogether. By implication, Borrower needs the relief and may not use it to pursue nonjustice-related ends. What conditions, if any, may Lender attach to relief?

As I noted at the outset, since the mid-1990s, IFIs such as the World Bank, the IMF, and the African Development Fund have granted full or partial debt relief to heavily indebted countries under the auspices of the so-called Heavily Indebted Poor Countries (HIPC) Initiative. In so doing, they have followed in the footsteps of the Paris Club. To be considered for debt relief, a country must (inter alia) "have established a track record of reform and sound policies through IMF- and World Bank–supported programs; and have developed a Poverty Reduction Strategy Paper (PRSP) through a broad-based participatory process in the country." The IMF and its partners make it clear that "for debt reduction to have a tangible impact on poverty, the additional money needs to be spent on programs that benefit the poor." As of February 2017, thirty-six countries had obtained full debt relief; another three (Eritrea, Somalia, and Sudan) were in the process of applying for it.[9]

Consider repayment-reform conditions first, whereby Lender seeks to enhance the chances that it will be repaid. If it must provide partial relief, yet may justifiably refuse to cancel the debt in full, it is not unjust on its part to impose such conditions and for the same reason as it may do so when providing a mandatory loan at time $t1$—so long as it does not thereby worsen the predicament of Borrower's citizens. The proviso might seem too obvious to need stating. In practical terms, however, it is far from trivial, insofar as the stated proviso severely constrains Lender's ability to extract resources from Borrower.

Suppose now that Lender is under a duty to cancel the debt altogether. Since Borrower will not have to repay anything, there is no reason for Lender to resort to conditionality of that kind. Here again, the point might seem obvious, but, here again, it does have far-reaching implications. If it turns out that, in any of the aforementioned cases, lenders were under such a duty but instead offered only partial relief, the repayment-reforms conditions that they imposed were unjustified—at least qua repayment reforms. (They may have been justified on the separate grounds that they were coincidentally conducive to improving borrowers' human rights record.)

Consider now human rights–based conditionality. As we saw above, in extant practices, it pertains to poverty reduction—in other words, to the policies aimed at respecting and enforcing the social and economic rights of destitute people. There is no reason not to extend it to the enforcement of civil and political rights. Either way, ex hypothesi, Lender is under a duty to help, on the same grounds as articulated for aid conditionality. This implies that Borrower needs the resources freed up by the relief offer to respect and promote its citizens' human rights, since Lender would not be under such a duty otherwise. We should therefore treat the imposition of such conditions in this case as we did in the case of conditional aid, and can thus endorse those elements of Lender's debt-relief offer that seek to induce Borrower to respect the human rights of its members. Moreover, and by implication, Lender is under a duty to turn down requests for relief when Borrower's regime seeks to use the resources thereby freed up to pursue nonjustice-related ends at the expense of its citizens' human rights.

CONDITIONALITY AND LENDER'S PERMISSION NOT
TO GRANT RELIEF / CANCEL THE DEBT

Suppose now that Lender is not under a duty to grant debt relief, let alone to cancel the debt altogether. There are at least two reasons why that might be so. First, suppose that Borrower's repayment difficulties are not so severe that it could qualify for aid as a matter of justice. In offering debt relief, Lender would in effect gift funds to Borrower. We might think that we should treat Lender's imposition of conditions in this case exactly as we ought to treat the imposition of conditions on nonmandatory gifts. We would be mistaken, for the fact remains that Borrower has not managed to meet its repayment obligations to Lender, which does make a difference to the ethics of some of Lender's conditionality decisions. In particular, in the light of Borrower's behavior, Lender has good reasons to have diminished confidence in Borrower's ability to repay what is left of the loan. It may justifiably subject its debt relief offer to a greater range of, and stricter, reform-repayment conditions than it may do when offering a loan ab initio.

Now suppose that Borrower's difficulties are severe enough that it does qualify for debt relief, but that for Lender to offer it would be harmful to its own population, or a section thereof, or indeed to its future generations—in breach of the no-undue sacrifice proviso. We might think that, in this case, Lender ought not to help Borrower in this way at all. Again, we would be mistaken, for Lender might be able to mitigate those harms by conditioning its offer of help to Borrower favoring Lender's economic agents. Thus, sovereign lenders used to tie their loan offers to borrowers' buying their goods and services. Although the practice has been criticized—notably by the Organisation for Economic Co-operation and Development (OECD)—for depriving borrowers of meaningful policy choices and wrongfully exploiting their vulnerable position, there might be some (admittedly limited cases) where it might be a justified solution to Lender's predicament.[10]

To recapitulate: repayment-reforms conditionality and human rights–based conditionality are morally justified in principle. Furthermore, we cannot read debt conditionality off loan conditionality. The fact that Borrower is failing to pay what it should have paid can make a difference to the conditions that Lender may justifiably impose on it.

Unjust Loans, Unjust Debts

So much for just loans and just debts. Let us now turn to unjust lending practices. A loan is unjust if:

(1) the repayment conditions are unjust—as when, typically, the interests charged by Lender are so high that Borrower simply cannot repay; or,

(2) the loan is taken out for unjust ends—typically by dictators who use the funds thus released to prop up their oppressive regime; or,

(3) Lender ought to have given the money for free; or,

(4) the nonrepayment conditions attached to the loan are in themselves unjust.[11]

To give a contemporary example, in the Greek lending crisis, the IMF and members of the Eurozone are accused in some quarters, notably by the Jubilee Debt Campaign, of imposing both unjust payment terms and unjust political conditions—although it is worth noting that IFIs generally loan on very favorable terms, particularly to the poorest countries. Going further back, Michael Kremer and Seema Jayachandran identify a number of Cold War–era odious loans from the IMF and other sovereign lenders to dictatorships such as President Mobutu's regime in Zaire and President Marcos in the Philippines.[12]

The criticisms leveled at sovereign lenders and IFIs pertain to loans that are unjust on either, some, or all four counts. That said, it is important to distinguish those forms of injustice, not merely for the sake of analytical bookkeeping but also and more importantly because they bear on the justifiability of conditionality in different ways. The questions at hand here, then, are the following: Does the fact that the loan is unjust make it impermissible for Lender to impose human rights–based conditions on its offer? Does the fact that the debt is unjust (that is to say, accrues from an unjust loan) make it impermissible for Lender to cancel it or to offer relief on it subject to such conditions?

Unjust Loans

In asking whether the fact that a loan is unjust makes the imposition of human rights–based conditions impermissible, we are necessarily ruling out from our inquiry unjust loans of type (4), where Borrower sets unjust conditions (unjust, in the sense that those conditions lead to human rights violations). Accordingly, we only need to consider loans that are unjust for reasons highlighted in cases (1) through (3).

ODIOUS LOANS

Let us begin with case (2), describing so-called odious loans. A loan is odious when its beneficiary directly uses it to violate the fundamental human rights of some other party—typically, its citizens—or takes advantage of its fungibility so to act. Typically, odious loans are taken out by dictators, although in principle they can also be taken out by democratically elected leaders who pursue unjust policies. However, it does not follow that loans to dictatorships are never justified, for three reasons. First, Lender may justifiably offer a loan to a dictatorship as a direct inducement toward transitioning into a human rights–respecting democratic regime, or as an indirect means toward such a transition (as when loans contribute to the emergence of a middle class and, thereby, to improved prospects for democratization).

Second, though there might be no prospect in the short and medium term of helping or forcing Borrower into a democratic transition, loans might help alleviate severe poverty. Consider the case of China. It has received millions of dollars in loans from the World Bank since 1947. Yet it is not, by any measure, a democratic regime. At the same time, it has been extraordinarily successful at reducing severe poverty. The figures are astounding. According to the 2016 UN Human Development Report, "China's extreme poverty rate plummeted from 66.5 percent in 1990 to 1.9 percent in 2013." Rapid economic growth fueled by integration in the international economy and its economic and financial institutions have fueled such progress. Granted, rural poverty remains endemic. There is little doubt, however, that at the bar of distributive justice, China has performed outstandingly well, in part (though by no means solely) helped by the World Bank. The costs, at the bar of human rights themselves, of not lending to China at all on the grounds that it is for all intents and purposes a dictatorial regime would be absolutely enormous.[13]

Third, and more controversially still, Lender may sometimes justifiably offer to Borrower a loan that it has very strong reasons to believe would be odious. In Chapter 2, I argued that a regime is morally justified in *not* imposing defensive economic sanctions against arms trades with

Target's oppressive regime if the latter would as a result procure more dangerous weapons from other sources. By parity of reasoning, suppose that if Lender does not offer Borrower this particular loan, Borrower will turn to another lender (Unscrupulous Lender) who not only will not query its ends but will also impose unjust repayment conditions on the loan and thereby further impair Borrower residents' prospects for a flourishing life. On a strict, consequence-insensitive deontological view, whereby agents ought never to be complicitous in wrongdoings, Lender would not be justified in offering the loan as a means to thwart Unscrupulous Lender. But this is too strict. Consequences do matter, and it is conceivable therefore that Lender may so act as the lesser of two evils.

Interestingly, loans to dictators as the lesser of two evils may well offer some scope for human rights–based and repayment-reforms conditionality. On the first count, Borrower's regime might accept some very limited human rights–based conditions in exchange for better repayment terms than it would get from Unscrupulous Lender. On the second count, the question is whether Lender has a claim to being repaid. Given that the loan is odious, it is sometimes held that no repayment is due—at least, not by ordinary members of Borrower who are themselves the most vulnerable to their regime's repressive policies (which policies, moreover, are partly funded by the loan). In that vein, I shall explore presently the implications for repayment-reforms conditionality of the view that under certain conditions lenders are morally obliged to offer relief on debts accruing from odious loans. Meanwhile, however, suppose for the sake of argument that Borrower is under a duty to repay an odious loan. If so, Lender may justifiably impose repayment-reforms conditions on the loan itself, so long as those reforms do not compound the predicament of Borrower's victims. In addition, Lender is under a moral obligation to use the repayments toward the enforcement of human rights, primarily by helping Borrower's victims if it can (for example, by taking on and resettling its refugees) or by assisting other victims of human rights abuses if it cannot.

UNJUST REPAYMENT CONDITIONS

Let us now turn to cases of type (1), where the loan is tied to unjust repayment conditions. Insofar as the loan is unjust on these particular grounds, Lender may not impose conditions on its offer with a view to improving chances that it will be repaid, precisely because it has no claim to being repaid. In other words, it may not resort to repayment-reforms conditionality.

By contrast, it may resort to human rights conditionality. Some might tempted to think, on the contrary, that the fact that it commits an injustice toward Borrower (by offering unjust repayment conditions) deprives it of the standing to enforce the latter's obligations. As I suggested in Chapter 1, however, we would be making a mistake. Remember the case of the Villainous Kidnapper who has wrongfully imprisoned Andrew and Ann. Although Villainous Kidnapper is guilty of the grievous wrongdoing of kidnapping toward Andrew, she may forcibly prevent him from raping Ann without thereby wronging him. By parity of reasoning, the fact that Lender has behaved unjustly toward Borrower does not preclude its justifiably using Borrower's wish for a loan as a means to get it to comply with its obligations of justice.

To be sure, the fact that Lender has behaved unjustly in the past by granting unjust loans may well suggest that it lacks both a good understanding of what would promote human rights within Borrower and the ability and willingness appropriately to monitor Borrower's compliance. Under those circumstances, it is morally appropriate for Lender to offer a loan to Borrower and yet to leave it to a neutral third party to decide which human rights–based conditions Borrower must meet if it is to get the relevant resources. I will return to this issue later on when I address the problems inherent in enforcing conditionality. In any event, even if Lender ought not to design those conditions itself, it may justifiably insist that Borrower should comply with those conditions as designed by third parties.

LOANS INSTEAD OF MANDATED AID

Finally, in cases of type (3), Lender ought to have given the money for free, and the offer to loan is therefore unjust in itself. Accordingly, Lender may not impose conditions on Borrower that would enhance the latter's ability to repay the loan. However, it may impose human rights conditions. As we saw in Chapter 4, Donor may impose human rights conditions on the delivery of aid—conditions, that is, aimed at improving the likelihood that

Beneficiary's members will actually exercise their human rights. By parity of reasoning, it may impose similar conditions to the same end were it to lend the resources instead of giving them. More strongly still, it ought to do so. Granted, it is derelict in its first-best obligation to provide aid. But this does not negate its obligation to help ensure that the human rights of Beneficiary's members will be respected.

Does the fact that Donor ought to have given aid for free make a difference to the stringency of the conditions it may impose on Beneficiary, when acting as a Lender? One might be tempted to think that it does: insofar as Beneficiary-turned-Borrower has to repay the loan, thereby incurring expenses that it would have been spared had Donor-turned-Lender fulfilled its obligation of justice, it behooves the latter to be less strict in its monitoring of the former's performance. I remain unconvinced. What matters is whether or not the conditions thus imposed make it more likely that Borrower's citizens have access to the resources to which they are entitled as a matter of human rights, not whether those conditions attach to something that should have been given for free.

Conditional Relief and Unjust Debts

To recapitulate: it does not follow from the fact that a loan is unjust that Lender is not entitled to insist that Borrower comply with human rights conditions. Still, the loan remains unjust, and Borrower's debt is therefore unjust. How then should we approach the imposition of conditions on the relief of such debts? In some views, a loan between sovereign actors is subject to two fundamentally important tenets, that borrowers generally ought to pay their debt and that, as international law prescribes, treaties must be honored (*pacta sunt servanda*). As I stipulated at the outset of this chapter, I accept the presumption in favor of a pro tanto duty to pay debts accruing from just loans. I also accept the presumption in favor of the duty to honor treaty obligations. However, a number of philosophers and legal scholars have argued that the law has the resources to free a sovereign from its loan obligations when the loan, and consequently the debt, are illegitimate. More controversially still (at least from lawyers' point of view), some scholars, a number of policy makers, and activist movements such as the Jubilee Debt Campaign have also argued that there can be no such thing as a moral duty to repay a unjust debt, and they have called for partial, indeed in some cases complete, debt forgiveness.[14]

In those views, and by implication, Lender is not morally permitted to refuse to cancel unjust debts. If Borrower refuses to pay an unjust debt, Lender simply may not use military force (such as gunboat diplomacy) to force it to do so; nor may it threaten to lock Borrower out of its financial system and to reject loan applications in the future.

I am sympathetic to this point. But even if it is true, it is compatible with the further claim that Lender may justifiably condition the fulfillment of its obligation not to engage in those retaliatory measures on Borrower's compliance with human rights. Standardly, sovereign lenders and IFIs condition the granting of debt relief on Borrower using the repayment amounts toward poverty-alleviation programs. I defended this particular form of conditionality when I examined just debts. The point holds (perhaps surprisingly) even when the debt is unjust. Suppose that Lender ought not to have loaned x to Borrower in the first instance but instead ought to have given it for free. Or suppose that Lender ought not to have loaned x under repayment conditions that made it difficult for Borrower to respect its citizens' human rights. Either way, Lender's duty to cancel the debt is appropriately construed as a duty to provide aid— either a reparative duty, if Lender itself was responsible for or benefited from the unjust debt, or an assistive duty if neither. As we saw in Chapter 4, Donor is morally entitled—indeed required—to condition the provision of aid to Beneficiary's compliance with human rights conditions as a means to help Beneficiary's citizens have better prospects for a flourishing life. By parity of reasoning, it may—indeed must—do so when forgiving debts that Borrower ought not to have accrued in the first instance.[15]

The Problem of Responsibility

We have just seen that Lender may sometimes justifiably impose human rights conditions on the provision of a loan or the relief of debt, as well as repayment-reforms conditions (which it would not have cause to impose were it fulfilling an obligation to provide aid). In this section, I return to the problem of responsibility.

Suppose that Borrower has received loans from Lender in the past, conditional on carrying out human rights reforms. However, Borrower has not succeeded in its endeavors and asks Lender for additional loans. In a worst-case scenario, it is also struggling to pay its debt and asks for relief. It is often claimed, in public discourse about debt crises, that Borrower is responsible for the fact that it needs access to Lender's funds, or that Lender is responsible for Borrower's predicament. Those facts, it is often thought, render it permissible for Lender to refuse to make further loans or to grant relief on the debt.

In Chapter 4, I argued that aid donors should be cautious when attributing to Beneficiary responsibility for its predicament, in the light of the following three considerations:

(1) Even if the predicament of ordinary agents in Beneficiary can be traced solely to recent instances of domestic mismanagement, more often than not those agents are not themselves responsible for those failures.

(2) The regime of a beneficiary political community is often not itself responsible for their country's current predicament; rather, its predecessors are.

(3) Donor countries are often partly and wrongfully responsible for the fact that beneficiary regimes are unable or unwilling to discharge their obligations of justice to their compatriots.

Do the same arguments apply to sovereign lending and debt-relief, bearing in mind that Borrower, in addition to carrying out human rights reforms, must also repay the loan? Suppose that Borrower's regime is itself responsible for past mismanagement. The predicament in which their citizens find themselves (the absence of stipulated human rights reforms and the failure to pay off previous loans) is often not one for which they, as distinct from Borrower's officials, are responsible. In such cases, it would be wrong of Lender to justify not providing a loan on the basis of ascribing responsibility for those failures to those citizens, particularly if it could instead get Borrower to subject itself to more stringent performance reviews on both dimensions (human rights reforms and repayment progress).

The same considerations apply if Borrower's regime, when it asks for a loan, is shouldering the costs of its predecessors' mismanagement. Finally, in some cases Lender might be responsible, and wrongfully so, for the fact that Borrower has not in the past been able to repay its loan and/or carry out human rights reforms. For example, suppose that Lender's decision not to intervene in a neighboring country's civil war—though it could have done so at relatively low cost—causes a mass influx of refugees into Borrower's territory. This is likely to strain Borrower's ability to repay its loan as well as its ability to carry out human rights reforms. However, insofar as Lender wronged Borrower, it is under reparative obligations to the latter's members to compensate them for the harms so incurred. Depending on the nature of its wrongdoing, it might well be under a reparative obligation to cancel the injurious loan, to compensate Borrower for the wrong it committed by offering this particular kind of loan, or to give rather than loan Borrower the resources the latter needs to meet its increased expenditures. In such cases, it is wrong to penalize Borrower by withholding or withdrawing loans on grounds of the latter's responsibility.

That said, there are cases in which Lender may justifiably advert to Borrower's past conduct as a basis for deciding whether to offer a loan or to grant a partial debt relief. First, when discussing gifted aid, I argued that the key question is whether tying the provision to such aid to governmental responsibility is more likely to benefit the poor. Likewise, in the case of mandatory lending, the key question is whether the very poor are more likely to see improvements in their prospects for a flourishing life than if their governments can borrow at will without being subject to fulfilling either repayment-reforms or human rights conditions. It is hard to answer this question in abstraction from the details of specific cases. However, there might well be cases in which no-responsibility conditionality does provide Borrower's regime with a strong incentive to comply with the stipulated conditions.

Second, the decisions that Lender makes, and as a result of which Borrower's regime is struggling to protect the human rights of its residents and / or to repay the loan, might be rightful decisions. In their daily financial life, individuals have to factor into their borrowing decisions the fact that they might find it difficult to repay the loan as a result of lenders' decisions, such as raising interest rates. So long as a lender's decisions are not wrongful and it is not behaving fraudulently, and so long as borrowers have been informed of that possibility, it is not wrong of lenders to regard borrowers' past repayment behavior as an indication of their future ability to repay. By parity of reasoning, if Lender has not acted in such a way as to make it unwarrantedly difficult for Borrower's regime to repay the loans, it may justifiably demand compliance with such conditions as would increase chances that it will be repaid. Were Borrower's regime to act irresponsibly (for example by avoidably failing to plan for such contingencies), and were Lender to suspend loan disbursements, it would still behoove its leaders to consider ways in which they could channel the needed assistance to its rightful recipients.

Third, there might be cases in which neither Borrower nor Lender can be deemed responsible for the former's repayment predicament: instead, the latter can be traced to systemic fragilities in financial markets, which Lender could do very little to alleviate, let alone remedy. Borrower, in other words, is the victim of bad brute luck. Ex hypothesi, however, Lender has a claim to being repaid; subject to the ethical constraints articulated in the previous paragraph, it is not wrong of its leaders that they should seek to improve chances that they will be repaid on future occasions.[16]

The Problem of Enforcement

Suppose that everything I have said so far is true. On the stated grounds and under the stated conditions, lending and debt relief / cancellation conditionality (of the kind at play in this book) is morally justified. Still, some difficulties remain. For a start, in the context of sovereign lending, there are no enforcement mechanisms by which Lender can extract payments from Borrower. Moreover, Lender's interest in getting repaid might and in fact often does stand in tension with the imperative of ensuring that Borrower meet the human rights–based conditions attached to the loan or debt relief. Lender's only way of enforcing human rights conditions is by offering to disburse the loan, grant the relief, or cancel the debt in tranches, and by threatening Borrower to withhold the funds if Borrower fails to comply with the political terms of the agreement. Faced with a recalcitrant Borrower, Lender can either make good on its threat and suspend disbursements or halt its relief/cancellation program, in which case it faces the risk of not being repaid anything it has hitherto loaned and which it is still owed; or it can simply continue to loan, in which case it will have given up on conditionality altogether. This is particularly problematic when conditionality is meant to enforce human rights, since giving up on human rights is not a morally acceptable option.[17]

One way to avoid the tension is to set up an impartial body that would decide when Borrower has met the conditions attached to the loan or debt agreement and whether to restructure the loan by, for example, having Lender change its payment schedule. This would deprive Lender of the incentives to forego conditionality.[18] However, whichever enforcement and monitoring mechanism is chosen might be open to the charge of undue, indeed paternalistic interference in Borrower's affairs. In domestic, private contexts, there are good reasons to resist granting private lenders such as banks or building societies the right to intervene in individual borrowers' day-to-day financial management as a condition for releasing a loan in tranches or for restructuring it. We might think, in particular, that for banks so to treat borrowers would smack of paternalistic interference. And we might be tempted similarly to resist conditionality in the context of sovereign lending.

However, we should not fall prey too easily to the temptation. As we saw earlier, the decisions Borrower's officials have made when taking out previous loans—and which might turn out to have been bad decisions—often cannot be traced to its individual citizens' decisions yet still adversely affect them. Were sovereign lenders to impose and enforce conditions on future loans and to release the funds only subject to satisfactory compliance by appeal to the interests of those members, they would not act paternalistically. This case is in some respects analogous to the situation facing a parent who, now that his bank has raised interest rates, is unable to meet mortgage payments and at the same time to keep himself and his child in the relatively good lifestyle to which they have both been accustomed. It would be objectionably paternalistic for the bank to impose on him conditions relative to his household management and to monitor his compliance before extending the mortgage, by appealing to *his* best interests. But it would not be paternalistic for the bank so to act were it to appeal to *the child's* interest.

To be sure, we may have further, nonpaternalistic reasons to object to the bank's close monitoring of the parent's ability to repay. For example, those reasons might be grounded in the value for the parent-child relationship of parents taking decisions concerning their family without fear of interference from third parties. But those reasons do not apply to relationships between citizens of the same political community, and to relationships between citizens and officials. In fact, those citizens might welcome sovereign lenders' interference in the internal affairs of their political community, particularly if the imposition of conditionality together with close monitoring of their regime's compliance with those conditions would help bring about reforms that powerful minority interests would otherwise resist.

Conclusion

I began by highlighting some important differences between aiding and lending. Aid can in principle be given unconditionally whereas loans cannot. Moreover, in those cases in which aid ought to be given as a matter of justice whereas loans need not be so given, one cannot read the conditionality of lending off the conditionality of aid. Granted, as we saw, some of those conditions are apt in both cases of aid and loans or debt relief, notably the condition that the loan not be used to violate human rights. To illustrate, on those grounds, China's lending policy vis-à-vis Sudan is plausibly regarded as morally objectionable, whereas the U.S. policy vis-à-vis Chile in the 1980s was not.

Furthermore, the fact that a loan is unjust by dint of its repayment conditions or by dint of the fact that it has been granted to a dictatorial regime does not suffice to invalidate as unjust the decision to tie it to human rights–based conditions. The case of China, as a recipient of such loans rather than a provider of them, proved particularly interesting in that regard. In addition, under some circumstances, human rights–based conditionality can also be justified if Lender is responsible for Borrower's inability to repay previous loans or to bring about human rights reforms.

Finally, as we saw throughout the chapter, to the extent that Lender has property rights over the resources it is willing to loan, it may justifiably prioritize its interests in getting repaid—up to a point. In this respect, lending conditionality does differ from aid conditionality. The clause "to the extent" is of course crucial; when the loan is unjust, such that Lender either ought to have given the resources for free, or ought not to have made the loan offer in the first instance, it may not add to this particular injury the insult of seeking to bend Borrower to its will. The same applies, by parity of reasoning, when the debt accruing to Borrower is unjust.

CHAPTER SIX

Tu Quoque

I HAVE ARGUED THROUGHOUT THIS BOOK that under certain conditions, sovereign states and associations thereof (that is to say, their individual citizens, officials, and leaders) may justifiably impose economic sanctions and condition the provision of aid, loans, and/or debt relief on beneficiaries' respect for human rights. More strongly still, they are sometimes under a duty to do so.

Those decisions are often based on moral condemnation of the policies they are meant to stop. Those who conduct those policies (or their supporters) often retort that their accusers are guilty of exactly the same sin or are overly lenient on their equally sinful allies. To illustrate, it does not do for the U.S. to express outrage at the Castro regime's unjust policies and to impose sanctions on Cuba on those grounds, given their own appalling human rights record in Latin America. It does not do for them to impose sanctions on Hamas yet fail properly to condemn Israel's grievously unjust policy vis-à-vis the Palestinians. It does not do for the French governments of the early 1990s to condition the provision of aid to the implementation of democratic reforms while at the same time selling arms to dictators. And it does not do for IFIs to insist on conditionality as a response to recipients' failures to respect their citizens' human rights when those institutions' backers are themselves guilty of human rights violations, indeed are complicitous in beneficiaries' failures. Those actors, it is sometimes objected, are guilty of double standards, behave hypocritically, or both.[1]

This particular objection is aptly labeled "tu quoque." In rhetoric, the phrase refers to the technique that consists in rebutting the arguments of your opponent by pointing out that he is guilty of the same mistake of which he accuses others. In politics and interpersonal morality, where it is ubiquitous, it is used to refer to the complaint, "You too are committing/have committed wrongdoings that are similar to what I have done, and you thus cannot condemn me for it, let alone penalize me for it." Tu quoque, thus, has retaliatory and condemnatory elements.[2]

As we saw throughout the book, the claim that some agents have committed serious human rights violations does not entail that they are not justified in thwarting similar wrongdoings as carried out by other parties. On the contrary, in fact—at the bar of reparative justice, they are sometimes obliged to do so. In other words, I have rejected the retaliatory tu quoque. My concern in this closing chapter is with condemnatory tu quoque. I seek to articulate some of the conditions under which the charge applies, and to set out the kind of considerations that one would need to take into account when evaluating it in the specific context of economic statecraft. To do so, I illustrate my arguments by revisiting some of the cases that we have encountered in the previous chapters. Throughout, I assume that Targets, Beneficiaries, and Borrowers have committed, or are in the process of committing, human rights violations, which in turn warrants the imposition of economic sanctions and/or the imposition of conditions on the provision of aid, loans, or debt relief. The question is whether Senders, Donors, and Lenders are disqualified from morally condemning them by dint of their own wrongful conduct.

I proceed as follows. First, I provide a general account of the forms of conduct which typically elicit tu quoque in simple, individual cases; I also explain what is wrong with those forms of conduct, when they are wrong. Next, I outline some of the difficulties inherent in leveling the charge at agents who act jointly, or at individuals who claim to act on behalf of jointly acting agents, rather than at individuals who act on their own. I then describe instances of economic statecraft where the tu quoque charge is misplaced. These are cases in which Senders and Donors are licensed to condemn the targets of economic sanctions and the putative beneficiaries of assistance conditionality for committing serious right-violations, even though they themselves are similarly guilty. I end by describing cases in which the tu quoque charge is apt.

Two final points. First, as a matter of terminology, when I use the word "Target" in this chapter, I mean the political officials who are the target of sanctioning parties', donors', and lenders' condemnation. Second, most of my examples involve the leadership of a Western state or actor condemning the leadership of a non-Western state for human rights abuses. Accordingly, most of the cases in which I show that the tu quoque charge is apt are cases in which that Western leadership is unjustifiably hypocritical, unjustifiably applies double standards, and so on. I certainly do not mean to suggest that non-Western leaders are never unjustifiably hypocritical or that they never unjustifiably apply double standards, be it when they themselves resort to economic statecraft or are on its receiving end. It so happens, however, that, in the context of this book, economic threats and economic offers are more often applied by Western powers against non-Western powers than vice versa, and that the former routinely ground their decision in moral condemnation of the latter's policies.

Tu Quoque: Understanding the Charge

A First Pass

"You are doing it too!" the wrongdoer says to his critic. The wrongdoer may well agree that the critic is right about the substance of her claim. He may also concede that he may justifiably be subject to retaliatory measures as a result of what he did. What he denies is that she has the standing so to condemn him. To put it conversely, what he affirms is that there is something about her—her character, conduct, and so on—that disqualifies her from issuing an independently and substantively justified moral condemnation.

The charge of tu quoque seems particularly biting when the critic, against whom it is leveled, is not merely stating that his target committed a wrongdoing or, for that matter, is responsible for its predicament. After all, it is open to everyone to say, of anyone else, "you did x, and x is morally wrong," when x *is* morally wrong—open in the sense that for the wrongdoer himself to say it does not make it less true. And, indeed, a wrongdoing critic does something right when he acknowledges that a wrongdoing was committed. Yet—and hence tu quoque—in addition to asserting that his target is acting wrongly, the critic typically evinces the reactive attitudes that, Peter Strawson tells us, are central to attributions of blame and responsibility (such as resentment, anger, a sense of grievance for the injury suffered, or compassion for the wrongdoers' victims). Moreover, the critic implicitly or explicitly compares himself favorably to his target. His criticism rankles, in other words, precisely because he takes the moral high ground.[3]

As we shall see below, there are cases in which the critic is entitled to take the moral high ground even though he is applying double standards or is behaving hypocritically. Often, however, he is not entitled to do that. We—that is to say, all of us, wherever and whoever we are—are one another's moral equals, and ought to regard one another as such. This implies that we ought to judge our moral equals only on the basis of morally relevant factors—whether we judge them noncomparatively (that is to say, for what they each did), or comparatively (that is to say, for what they did in comparison with what we did).

This explains why the critic who invokes double standards or who is a hypocrite is particularly vulnerable to the charge. The critic who applies double standards errs in her comparative moral evaluation of her target in a way that, by unwarrantedly aggrandizing her, thereby unwarrantedly diminishes her target. The hypocrite, for her part, also arrogates moral superiority over the target of her condemnation. But unlike the agent who "merely" applies double standards, the hypocrite, by misleading or attempting to mislead others as to the true nature of her beliefs and / or as to the congruence between her beliefs and her conduct, seeks to protect herself from the moral opprobrium which she heaps on her target. To be sure, the latter ex hypothesi has acted wrongly, or would act wrongly if unchecked, and therefore lacks a claim not to be condemned. But he does have a claim not to be condemned by those who make it seem, or who try to make it seem, as if they themselves ought not to incur the costs of moral opprobrium. It is in that respect that the hypocrite fails to treat her target with the respect she owes him.[4]

Refining the Charge

So far, so good. To get a firmer grip on tu quoque, however, we need a more fine-grained account of what invoking double standards and behaving hypocritically mean.

STANDARD CASES

Suppose that Dominic believes that it is morally wrong of women, but not of men, to have sex outside marriage. This is a clear case of a double standard: Dominic advances a specious reason—namely, the mere fact of gender—in support of his differential treatment of women and thus unwarrantedly exposes the latter to moral sanctions while unwarrantedly exonerating men. Note that one can be guilty of unwarrantedly applying double standards diachronically. Suppose that Debra shares Dominic's view on gender and extramarital sex. She herself used to have extramarital affairs but is now faithful to her husband. When openly criticizing women who have extramarital sex, she finds spurious reasons as to why she somehow is excused for acting as she did. This is a common example of a double standard—not merely in ordinary life, but, as we shall see, in international politics too.

Meanwhile, here is a standard example of hypocritical behavior: Henry, a married man, genuinely believes that extramarital sex is morally wrong; he openly professes this belief and condemns anyone who does not share that belief and/or who has sex outside marriage. But he often has secret sexual encounters with prostitutes. Henry fails to live up to the standards he sets himself and others; indeed, it is an interesting feature of this case that he is not guilty of the kind of double standard that operates in Dominic's or Debra's reasoning. Henry, though, is a hypocrite, for he is deceitful. In this particular case, he lies, but the charge of hypocrisy would also hold if he merely pretended to believe in "no sex outside marriage," for example as a means to ingratiate himself with the traditionalist wing of the political party that he hopes to lead. Furthermore, Henry also invites the charge of hypocrisy if he used to have sex with prostitutes while already married, yet fails to disclose it when condemning married people who currently do. Finally, the charge would also hold if he attempted to deceive and failed. Suppose that, unbeknownst to him, Henry's "audience" is fully aware that he is having sex with prostitutes, and/or is motivated by political ambition rather than a commitment to obeying God's command. Henry is an unsuccessful hypocrite, but a hypocrite nonetheless. By implication, as soon as Henry realizes that his behavior is not a secret, he can no longer be aptly called a hypocrite even if he persists in his own behavior.[5]

REFINING THE ACCOUNT

There is another layer of complexity to consider. Suppose that Bob unjustifiably assaults Ann. Andrew condemns Bob for so doing. Bob retorts that Andrew is not in a position to condemn, for he too is guilty of grievously assaulting an innocent person without justification. We would naturally think that Bob has a point. However, as G. A. Cohen notes in his wonderful discussion of the issue, we must distinguish between cases in which Andrew is not involved in the very same wrongdoing for which he condemns Bob, and cases in which he is involved.[6] Furthermore, with respect to the second kind of cases (and to add to Cohen's argument), we need to draw an additional distinction, between cases in which Andrew is merely complicitous in Bob's wrongdoing and cases in which Andrew acted in such a way as to make it particularly difficult or costly for Bob not to commit the wrongdoing. Consider the following scenarios, where Andrew condemns Bob for killing Ann:

(1) Andrew culpably kills Victor. Bob culpably kills Ann.
(2) Andrew knowingly and culpably provides Bob with the weapon that the latter will use culpably to kill Ann.
(3) Andrew culpably puts Bob under pressure to kill Ann, failing which he will subject Bob to harsh retaliatory measures.
(4) Andrew culpably threatens Bob's life. Bob can survive only if he kills Ann.

In all four cases, Bob acts wrongly and Andrew lacks the standing morally to condemn him for killing Ann. However, other things equal, it is worse for Andrew to apply double standards or to be hypocritical when he is involved in Bob's wrongdoing than when he is not. Furthermore, as we move down through the cases, Andrew is increasingly involved in Ann's wrongful death. Thus, it is pro tanto worse of him to condemn Bob in (4) than in (3), in (3) than in (2), and in (2) than in (1).

Suppose now that Andrew is remorseful and has begun fulfilling the reparative obligations he has incurred as a result of (contributing to) killing Ann. Does he thereby regain some of his standing to condemn Bob for what the latter did to Ann? I do not think so. Of course, he can say, in acknowledgement of their wrongdoing, "what *we* did (whether separately or together) was wrong." He can also condemn Bob for not being remorseful and for not fulfilling his reparative obligations toward Ann and her family. But what he cannot do is condemn Bob for the initial assault without, at the same time, condemning himself. However profound his remorse and however well he does by Ann's memory and her family, he can never erase the fact that he committed that wrongdoing (in (1)), indeed, that he did so with Bob (in (2)), that he would have punished Bob had Bob desisted (in (3)), and that he forced Bob to choose between his life and Ann's (in (4)). Given how oblivious officials of developed countries are of their own regimes' present and past involvement in human rights abuses abroad, the point is worth stressing here and will be worth remembering later on.

From Interpersonal Morality to Foreign Policy: Some Difficulties

Insofar as tu quoque is a response to unwarranted moral condemnation, it can only be leveled at critics whose wrongdoing is such that they ought not to condemn. In this book, I deal with political actors who, in that capacity, condemn their counterparts for human rights violations. Accordingly, my main concern in this chapter is not with the hypocrisy or the tendency to apply double standards of (for example) a married politician who claims to support traditional family values and is caught propositioning underage prostitutes. Nor is my concern with a presidential candidate who, while on the campaign trail, claims to abide by certain moral political principles (such as an absolute prohibition on the use of torture) and yet once elected routinely authorizes the use of torture on suspected terrorists. Rather, my concern is with cases in which, acting (or claiming to act) on behalf of their fellow citizens, political officials condemn another regime/citizenry, even although their own regime/citizenry have in the past committed, and/or are now committing human rights violations.

Here are some of the difficulties raised by the deployment of tu quoque against those actors. Let us suppose that the leadership of country A openly and publicly condemns country B for its highly repressive policies toward its LGBT citizens. In response, B's leaders note that A's leadership and well-off citizens are derelict in their own obligations toward their religious minorities, and claim that A's leadership is therefore not in a position to condemn them. By raising tu quoque, and thus counter-criticizing A's leadership, B's leaders make the following three assumptions. First, they assume that committing a human rights violation is sufficient to lose the standing to condemn. Second, they assume that there is such a thing as a collective agent, A's leadership, which has a collective intention to conduct such policies and (in hypocrisy cases) a collective intention to (attempt to) deceive, if not necessarily the world at large, at least the target of its moral condemnation—namely B. Third, they assume that this collective agent is appropriately held morally responsible both for repressing its religious minorities and for dishonestly and / or hypocritically criticizing B.

All three assumptions are problematic. Let me start with the second and third assumptions. They are both in tension with the view, which is at the heart of moral individualism (and, thereby, human rights–based morality), that there is no such thing as a collective agent of which it makes sense to say, not just that it acts but that it can be held morally responsible for those actions above and beyond its members' individual responsibility. To be sure, and as I noted in Chapter 1, a plausible way to reconcile that view with the fact of individuals acting jointly is to construe those acts as directed to particular goals, each contributing to a joint enterprise, and to conceive of those agents as being aware of what other, similarly situated agents are doing toward that enterprise. On this account, attributions of responsibility for the outcomes of the joint enterprise track each individual members' acts. But the difficulty remains of establishing who, within a group, exactly is responsible for what, and thus who exactly is vulnerable to tu quoque and who is not.[7]

The following example nicely illustrates the point. In the spring and early summer of 2017, a coalition of Arab Gulf states, led by Saudi Arabia, cut off diplomatic ties with Qatar and subjected it to trade sanctions, on the grounds that it had long provided funding for Islamist terrorists operating in the region. Suppose, arguendo, that the allegation is correct (I am not claiming that it is). Yet, although the Saudi kingdom is indeed vulnerable to radical Islamist terrorism, and although its regime is at the forefront of the struggle against those movements, it has also long been accused of indirectly supporting the latter by funding radical Islamist schools and mosques in various parts of the world, and by knowingly failing to thwart donations to such groups from wealthy private actors. Again, suppose arguendo that this allegation is correct too. (And, again, I am not claiming that it is.) If so, the pot, it seems, is calling the kettle black. But who, exactly, is the pot? *If* the allegation against the Saudi regime is correct, relevantly situated members of the Saudi regime can be described as acting jointly with their colleagues toward the goals of supporting fundamentalist Islam and to share responsibility for consequent acts of terrorism. Insofar as they do not admit to that latter fact (and again, so long as the allegation is correct—which it may not be), those agents are making themselves vulnerable to tu quoque for criticizing the Qatari leadership as they did. But for all we know, there may be other members of the Saudi regime who do not so criticize the Qataris and who therefore are not vulnerable to tu quoque. Consequently, even if (to repeat) both allegations are correct, it does not make sense to say that Saudi Arabia is hypocritical in its condemnation (and concomitant sanctions policy) of Qatar.[8]

The problems this case illustrates are not unique to foreign policy. In this particular context, however, the difficulties inherent in ascribing responsibility for wrongdoing and for dishonest condemnation of other wrongdoers are rendered particularly acute by lack of knowledge about the other parties' individual acts, commitments, and intentions, and by the multilayered processes by which political decisions are made.[9]

Finally, consider the first assumption, to the effect that committing human rights violations causes one to lose one's standing to condemn agents who also commit human rights violations. This does not seem quite right. We may perhaps readily agree that a critic who commits more of the same kind of human rights violations, or who commits a qualitatively worse human rights violation than his target, lacks the standing to condemn. But it does not follow that a critic who commits fewer of the same kind of human rights violation, or a less bad human rights violation, also lacks the standing to condemn. Sometimes, of course, he does. Suppose that one-time culpable murderer W_2 condemns five-time culpable murderer W_1 for having killed more often than he did. Ceteris paribus, it seems wrong of W_2 to do this: some wrongdoings are qualitatively such that their authors simply may not condemn other wrongdoers for committing more of the same. If W_2 may not condemn W_1 in this case, and if the reason why he may not do so is that he too committed murder, W_1 can level the tu quoque charge even though he is a multiple offender.[10]

Yet there comes a point where the number of a given kind of human rights violations that one commits does make a difference to one's standing to condemn other wrongdoers. Suppose that W_1 commits vastly more murders than one-time murderer W_2. We can handle this case in two ways. Either we hold that past a certain numerical threshold, one may be justifiably condemned by those who commit fewer violations of the same serious kind. Or we say that, past that threshold, a qualitatively different wrongdoing has been committed. In this case, we might have to describe W_1 as having committed the qualitatively different wrongdoing of a massacre, and thus as not being immune from W_2's condemnation.

If this is correct, before leveling tu quoque, Critic's target (or, for that matter, bystanders) must have some sense of how much weight to assign to quantity versus quality. This is hard enough to do in individual cases. It is harder still in collective-cum-political cases, for in those cases, the scale of seriousness along which to rank those violations is likely to be much greater (from one policeman beating up one citizen, to large-scale genocidal campaigns, and everything else in between), as are the numbers of violations (from one victim to hundreds of thousands). Furthermore, as soon as one brings qualitative differences between human rights violations into play, one faces the challenge of identifying precisely what kind of violation is being committed and why having committed this particular kind of violation undermines (or not) one's standing to condemn. Again, the difficulty is not unique to collective-cum-political cases but it is particularly acute in such contexts.

Those various complexities should not lead us to infer that the tu quoque charge cannot have purchase in the context of political agency in general, and complex foreign policy decisions in particular. True, B's leaders and citizens, neutral third parties, and A's dissenters can only proceed on the basis of what A's leaders, officials, and citizens profess to believe in, what policies they actually implement, and (if we are lucky) some information about public opinion with respect to the policies in question within A. And so all that they can say—but, indeed, what they can sometimes say—is that, on the balance of the best available evidence, it seems that at least some of B's leaders, officials, and citizens apply double standards, and / or are hypocritical, and / or occlude their wrongful involvement, in their condemnation of A's policies. From now on, I shall use the phrases "A (or Critic) condemns B (or Target)," and "B levels tu quoque against A," to refer to those various claims. Although my points in the remainder of the chapter apply to citizens as well as officials of the political community whom I label "Critic," foreign policy decisions and the pronouncements on which they are seemingly based (be they condemnatory or laudatory) is made by officials. Accordingly, and for the sake of expository simplicity, I shall focus on leaders and officials.

Rejecting Tu Quoque

In this section, I consider cases in which those who are subject to economic sanctions or denied assistance on the grounds that they are guilty of human rights violations may not object to being condemned by foreign policy actors who impose those measures on them yet themselves commit similar wrongdoings.

For tu quoque to hold, it must be the case that relevantly situated Critic's officials are hypocritical or that they apply double standards, whether or not they are involved in Target's wrongdoings. It must also be the case that they act unjustifiably in being / doing so and thus by condemning Target. In this section, I argue that Critic's officials do not always in fact so behave, and that when they do, they are sometimes justified in so doing.

The Conduct Requirement

Let us consider the first condition—which we may call the conduct requirement—by using the United States as an illustrative example. The United States has routinely condemned foreign regimes for committing grievous human rights violations and has imposed sanctions or conditioned the delivery of aid on the basis of that condemnation. In response, the targets of those critics as well as third parties have no less routinely countered that the U.S. human rights record, both at home and abroad, is far from blemish-free. In the light of the difficulties raised by the collective-cum-institutional context of this reciprocal mudslinging, the tu quoque charge holds only if relevantly situated American officials (American presidents, leaders of Congress, top members of the cabinet, the upper echelons of the military, etc.) have individually and jointly committed the human rights violations that, their target claims, undermine their standing to condemn. As a matter of fact, it does hold for the American public officials who have contributed over time to the appalling abuses committed by many regimes in Latin America. Crucially, however, contemporaneity is relevant to the conduct requirement. To see this, consider a different example: the public officials of aspiring nuclear powers whose efforts at acquiring nuclear weapons are thwarted nowadays via sanctions by the current American administration may not charge the American administration with tu quoque just on the grounds that the United States is the only country so far that has resorted to nuclear warfare. That decision was taken over seventy years ago by a completely different set of officials, and insofar as current officials do not meet the conduct requirement, they should not be (counter) condemned for it and it alone. (I say that the public officials of aspiring nuclear powers cannot invoke that past event *alone* as a basis for their condemnation. But if they can show, in addition, that the current administration has failed properly to express regret at its predecessors' decision to drop the bomb, they may well have a case, so long as their targets unjustifiably apply double standards and / or are unjustifiably hypocritical. Remember Debra, who condemns sexually promiscuous women but finds spurious reasons to justify her own past promiscuous behavior.)

Justified Conduct

Suppose now that Critic's target correctly claims that Critic's officials and citizens conduct themselves in ways that might warrant tu quoque. Still, it does not follow that those members of Critic are vulnerable to the charge, for as we shall now see, they are sometimes justified in so acting, and thus do not lose their standing to condemn Target's wrongdoing.

JUSTIFIED DOUBLE STANDARDS

Consider the charge of applying double standards as leveled against Critic whose alleged wrongdoing is independent of Target's wrongdoing. Take, as an example, the sanctions that the United Nations Security Council (UNSC) has imposed against North Korea's regime in response to the latter's decisions to conduct nuclear tests. Assume for the sake of argument that nuclear proliferation in that region is a threat to collective security and, thereby, a threat to the human rights of the hundreds of thousands of individuals who would be caught in a regional war. All five permanent members of the UNSC, themselves nuclear powers, are signatories to the 1968 Nuclear Proliferation Treaty (NPT). North Korea declared in 2003 that it was withdrawing from the NPT—though its failure to withdraw within the mandated notification period has led some to argue that it is still bound by the treaty. Now, of the many rationales for the sanctions regime, one in particular exposes some of the permanent members of the UNSC to the charge of wrongfully applying double standards, while the other does not. On the one hand, the UNSC and its member states might hold that North Korea is a party to the treaty and that by conducting those tests, it fails in its treaty obligations not to acquire nuclear weapons. If so, the officials of the UNSC permanent member states are guilty of illicitly applying double standards if they themselves are derelict in their own treaty obligations—notably their obligation not to increase and develop their own arsenal. They act illicitly, for there is no principled reason to hold North Korea to its treaty obligations while exempting, for example, Russia and the United States from them.

On the other hand, member states' officials might hold that, irrespective of the NPT, North Korea cannot be trusted with nuclear weapons whereas they, nuclear member states of the Council, can. In so claiming, they would be applying double standards to their own conduct and to North Korea. Yet, they may perhaps have a principled reason for doing so, namely that North Korea is far more likely to use those weapons, notably against its southern neighbor, than they are. Granted, it may be that

Kim Jong-un's threats to launch nuclear attacks are nothing but vacuous bellicose posturing, that in fact he and his regime pose no greater nuclear threat to collective security than the United States or Russia, and that the UNCS are perfectly aware of that. If so, the member states' officials would be illicitly applying double standards. But if they are right that Kim Jong-un does pose a greater threat, then they do not lose their standing to condemn him on that count, and the fact that they are applying double standards to him is no grounds for subjecting them to tu quoque.

JUSTIFIED HYPOCRISY

What about hypocrisy? The hypocrite, you recall, does not merely fail to act as he preaches—he seeks to disguise his true beliefs and / or the fact that his actions are not congruent with the beliefs that he expresses (whether those beliefs are his true beliefs or not). There clearly are cases in which he is justified in so acting, indeed is obliged to do so. The often-discussed deceitful Nazi, who professes ideological commitment to the regime yet abhors its ideals and covertly opposes it is a paradigmatic example of a justified hypocrite. (By contrast, the person who does believe in the ideology, yet does not have the willpower to implement it and somehow succeeds in hiding that fact is not a justified hypocrite qua hypocrite. For what makes his conduct right is the fact that he is not killing Jews, not the fact that he pretends to do so.)[11]

Similarly, one can imagine cases in which the relevant officials of a political community are justifiably deceiving (or attempting to deceive) the target or beneficiaries of their policy of conditionality as to the nature of their beliefs, the lack of congruence of their professed beliefs and their actions, or both. They do so by lying outright, or by omitting to tell the truth. This is not as mysterious as it seems: hypocrisy can sometimes help political actors reach compromises thanks to which they put a stop to human rights violations.[12] Some of the instances of sanctions and conditionality that we encountered in this book, and the condemnatory stand on the basis of which they were defended, illustrate the point well—at least, on a generous construal of what the leadership of sanctioning states and donors were trying to do. Consider, for example, sanctions against apartheid South Africa. The latter's regime was routinely condemned for its abhorrently racist laws and policies. Yet, some of the sanctioning states were themselves either failing to abolish apartheid-like discriminations of their own or had actively championed racist policies in the past—and failed openly to acknowledge it. Thus, India's successive regimes, which were some of the most openly vocal opponents of apartheid and proponents of economic sanctions against the South African regime, were at the same time failing to end the severely discriminatory and yet illegal and unconstitutional practice of untouchability. Likewise, successive regimes of former colonial power France, at the same time as endorsing sanctions against South Africa, were failing to acknowledge, publicly and openly, the racist underpinnings of France's colonial empire.[13] In both cases, however, it is not entirely implausible to aver that, whatever their actual motives may have been, Indian and French leaders may have been justified in occluding the most unpalatable dimensions of their respective domestic and colonial policies. Indian society in the late 1950s, shortly after Independence, might not have been able to cope with an outright denunciation by its leaders of untouchability. In France, political elites would not have countenanced a similar denunciation of colonial practices (both before and during decolonization) in which some of them had been directly involved, and might instead have turned against the sanctions against South Africa.

Perhaps I am wrong. Perhaps it would have been possible for Indian and French governments openly to acknowledge their respective countries' moral failures without incurring the aforementioned costs. If so, in those two cases, the charge of unjustified hypocrisy, and thus tu quoque, would hold. The point remains, though, that in principle, it is quite possible that tu quoque is not aptly deployed against the kind of moral condemnation on which the resort to economic statecraft often relies, even when its targets do in fact behave hypocritically.

JUSTIFIED SHARED INVOLVEMENT

Consider, finally, cases in which Critic is involved in the very wrongdoings for which it condemns its targets—more precisely, involved in ways that license us to say they were acting jointly with the latter and can be said to share responsibility for those wrongdoings. We might be tempted to think that agents who are jointly involved in an unjust collective venture cannot do so justifiably. Were they to condemn fellow contributors, they would be vulnerable to tu quoque simply by dint of their involvement. We would be mistaken, however. For it does not follow from the fact that a joint venture is unjust that its contributors unjustifiably contribute to it; in fact, they might be contributing to a specific, and itself just, aspect of the overall joint venture.[14] This is not incompatible with condemning that venture. In a sense, this is what partial sanctions combined with inducements in the form of aid and loans amount to. By providing such inducements, donors may end up enabling the commission of serious human rights violations by beneficiaries—not least because aid is fungible. They might be justified in so doing, however, if the alternative would be worse—if, for example, the beneficiary dictatorial regime which they support would be toppled and replaced by a genocidal regime. However, the fact that propping up the dictatorial regime is the lesser of two evils does not deprive donors of the standing to condemn it for its worst excesses. Donors-cum-senders, thus, could block the shared involvement variant of condemnatory tu quoque by pointing out that they are justified in getting involved (in this case, as a means to forestall further and worse human rights violations in the region).

Endorsing Condemnatory Tu Quoque

To recapitulate, the fact that a political actor commits the very same (kind of) acts for which she condemns other political actors does not cause her to lose the standing to issue such condemnation, for, after all, she may well be justified in being hypocritical, and/or in applying double standards, and/or in being jointly involved in those acts.

That said, quite often, and as we saw throughout this book, political actors who resort to sanctions or to conditional assistance do behave unjustifiably qua critics of their policies' targets. Their officials often commit qualitatively similar or worse human rights violations, and/or they often jointly commit vastly more of the same kind of violations. In addition, they often share responsibility for Target's failures to respect human rights—

to varying degrees perhaps, but without justification. Those actors do lack the standing to condemn the targets of their sanctions and the beneficiaries of their development programs. In this section, I illustrate the point by highlighting cases that justifiably elicit tu quoque.

Unjustified Double Standards

Let us begin with the case of illicit double standards—again, starting with independently committed wrongdoings. Return to the case of successive American administrations, which have recurrently condemned Cuban authorities for their bad domestic human rights record and have justified sanctions on those grounds. As we saw, some of those officials were themselves guilty of contributing to human rights abuses in other Latin American countries. It is hard to think of a plausible justification for their support for General Pinochet's regime in Chile, for Manuel Noriega's regime in Panama, or for Argentina's junta. The charge of tu quoque does have force in such cases.

To be sure, those American officials might retort that they "merely" contributed to human rights violations carried out against non-Americans, whereas Castro's regime committed human rights violations against fellow Cubans. This, they might say, points to a salient difference between the two cases. This putative defense calls for two responses. First, at the bar of human rights–based justice this will not work, for there is no greater obligation not to violate the human rights of one's fellow residents than there is not to violate the human rights of foreigners.

Second, successive U.S. administrations and their relevantly situated officials have committed grievous human rights violations against a large section of their own citizenry—to wit, African Americans—while refusing to acknowledge it. I have in mind the ways in which the penal system, both state and federal, continues to discriminate, in more or less subtle ways, against those individuals, particularly men, from stop-and-search operations to the classification of criminal offences, decisions to prosecute, and sentencing decisions. Granted, what those U.S. officials have done, indeed are still doing, to so many African Americans, is not as wrong as what the Castro's officials have done to Cubans. But it has reached a threshold of wrongness, as it were, such that U.S. administrations lack the standing to condemn. If I am right, in so condemning Cuba they unwarrantedly hold its administration to a double standard and arrogate moral superiority over the latter. Therein lies their wrongdoing. Even if U.S. officials have been correct in their assessment of the Cuban regime's human rights record (and there are good reasons to believe that they have), they have erred in their comparative judgment and have thus failed to treat their Cuban counterparts and the citizens on whose behalf the latter have acted with the respect they owed them.[15]

Unjustified Hypocrisy

Let us turn now to unjustified hypocrisy. Imagine a political community whose regime, via its officials, claims to be against torture and yet provides military aid to other regimes on the condition that they do not (inter alia) engage in "torture or cruel, inhuman, or degrading treatment." Those words are lifted straight out of the 1961 U.S. Foreign Assistance Act (section 116). Suppose that those officials do in fact sanction, or at the very least turn a blind eye to, acts of torture by their own forces (as the U.S. civilian and military leadership did during and in the aftermath of the 2003 war in Iraq). Suppose that the regime also provides direct assistance to torture-practicing regimes (as the U.S. civilian and military leadership also did, indeed have done, indeed are still alleged to be doing, for example, with respect to Israel and Egypt).[16] Moreover, it attempts to hide what its forces are doing and refuses to acknowledge that the beneficiaries of its assistance are practicing torture (again, something that successive administrations have routinely done and failed to do, respectively). Suppose, finally, that there is no overriding justification for that regime so to act. By condemning regimes that practice torture and by misleading (or attempting to mislead) the world at large about its true beliefs and / or the lack of congruence between its beliefs and its actions, this particular Critic arrogates moral superiority over the target of its condemnation while attempting to protect itself from moral opprobrium. Therein lies its wrongdoing—one that is worse, other things equal, than the imposition of double standards, precisely because it involves deception.

Unjustified Shared Involvement

In cases of shared involvement, and whether Critic merely imposes double standards or is hypocritical about its own conduct (for example by attempting to cover up its wrongdoing), Critic loses its standing to condemn precisely by dint of its responsibility for the human rights violations for which it condemns Target. Consider, first, cases in which Critic actually contributes to those violations. The Iran-Contra scandal, which nearly derailed Reagan's administration in the late 1980s, illustrates the point well. In 1984, Congress banned the use of federal funds to support right-wing militias—the so-called contras—that were seeking to overthrow the socialist Sandinista government in Nicaragua. However, at the behest of President Reagan and other top-level officials in his administration, Lieutenant-Colonel Oliver North, one of the deputy directors of the National Security Council, set up a complex system designed to fund the contras covertly. A central plank of that system consisted of selling arms to Iran—in direct and covert violation of the different legislative instruments that, since 1979, had explicitly banned such sales.

There is so much for which to criticize Reagan's administration that it is hard to know where to begin. It clearly was unjustifiably hypocritical: it claimed to block arms exports to Iran while covertly facilitating them, and professed a commitment to human rights while covertly participating in the contras' campaigns of atrocities against civilians. Furthermore, it also illicitly applied double standards by harshly condemning communist regimes for their repressive policies while openly praising right-wing militias for theirs. But the most striking feature of the Iran-Contra affair is that, while openly and vociferously condemning Iranian leaders for violating the rights of Iranian citizens and for supporting international terrorism, the Reagan administration was in fact providing the Iranian leaders with the means to do so—in breach of its own legislation to boot. The Regan administration, more than anyone one can think of, lacked the standing to condemn Iranian officials.[17]

Consider now cases in which Critic culpably violates Target's rights and where Target can defend those rights only by violating the human rights of some of Critic's citizens. This is the kind of case that Cohen had in mind when discussing tu quoque in the context of foreign policy.

The specific, real-life example that led him to write the article in question is worth discussing. It involves the then Israeli ambassador in London, who acknowledged in a BBC4 interview that those whom he charged with wrongdoing—the Palestinians—had a legitimate end (to wit, building an independent state) but condemned them for resorting to terrorism as a means to achieve that end. Cohen's objection is that Israel itself made it impossible for the Palestinians to resort to legitimate means such as a regular army, full diplomatic standing, and so on, while at the same time conceding that the Palestinians had a grievance. According to Cohen, whether or not the Palestinians did in fact have such a grievance, the Israeli ambassador simply could not, as a spokesperson for the state of Israel, condemn the Palestinians for using illegitimate means, when the state of Israel did little itself to address what it accepted was a grievance.[18]

I agree with Cohen, but for my purposes in this chapter, a more relevant case is one in which the person who is being condemned does have a legitimate grievance, whether or not her critic concedes the point. Let us assume for the sake of argument that the Palestinians have a jointly held right to independent statehood, conditional on their willingness to recognize the sovereignty of the state of Israel. Let us also assume that even if the Palestinians were willing to recognize the state of Israel, a majority of Israelis, both citizens and officials in power, would nevertheless be determined to prevent them from having an independent and well-functioning state. Let us further suppose that, under those circumstances, the Palestinians would be permanently deprived of the legitimate means by which they could achieve that end and would have no choice but to resort to terrorism. Even though (I submit) Hamas would act grievously wrongly by resorting to terrorism as an instrument of foreign policy, Israel's regime would lack the standing to condemn them for doing so. In fact, so would the U.S. administration, at least to the extent that its continuing support for Israel's regime was a contributing factor to the Palestinians' predicament. If I am right, under the stipulated circumstances, neither Israeli nor U.S. officials had the standing to condemn those terrorist tactics. This of course does not in any way undermine the two-pronged view that Hamas does warrant condemning in general and that other political actors might well have the standing to do so.

Conclusion

In this chapter, I have scrutinized the claim that political actors who justify resorting to economic statecraft (through sanctions or when offering
assistance) by pointing to and condemning their target's parlous human
rights record often illicitly apply double standards, are guilty of hypocrisy, or are themselves implicated in the wrongdoings they condemn. As
we saw, the charges of double standards and hypocrisy do not always
apply. I have not provided a view, in these particular respects, on every
single one of the cases of sanctions or conditional offers we have encountered in this book. Rather, my aim has been to articulate the kind and
range of considerations that we ought to bear in mind when leveling and
evaluating tu quoque. Although my focus has been on its deployment in
the context of economic statecraft, the foregoing discussion has purchase
in other contexts.

Conclusion

IT IS TIME TO CONCLUDE. I noted at the outset that economic state-craft has long been a key instrument for the realization of geopolitical goals. In the last few decades or so, it has regularly been and continues to be used as a means to enforce human rights. Hence the normative puzzle with which we started. To the extent that economic statecraft consists in imposing trade and financial sanctions and thereby in interfering with free trade, it seemingly stands in tension with the human right to private property. To the extent that it consists in withholding or withdrawing material assistance, including from the very poor, it seemingly stands in tension with the human right to receive such assistance. And yet I argued that under certain conditions political actors such as states, coalitions of states, and international organizations are morally justified in resorting to economic sanctions, conditional aid, and conditional lending as a means to enforce human rights.

At first, this seemed a relatively uncontroversial view. Yet, the devil has been in the detail. As we saw throughout, decisions to resort to economic statecraft are constrained by the imperatives of necessity, proportionality, and effectiveness suitably construed. Moreover, they admit of different justifications, depending on the kinds of goods and agents to which they apply. In addition, they must be evaluated, morally speaking, in the light of the following two considerations. First, insofar as economic sanctions and conditional offers of assistance are meant to stop, deter, and induce unjust regimes and their officials, they rely on attributions of both individual and collective responsibility for those wrongdoings. Second, they rely on judgments to the effect that they are, or on the contrary are not, effective, proportionate, and necessary. Yet, those judgments are often the locus of fierce disagreement between political actors, not least because they are made under conditions of epistemic uncertainty. Under those conditions, and as I averred in the introduction (verbatim), when deciding whether or not to resort to economic statecraft, we must pay attention to the wrongful damage those measures might cause—more specifically whether we would wrongfully deprive agents of the freedoms and resources to which they have rights. Other things being equal, we ought to err on the side of helping, or not interfering with, those whom we in fact are not under a duty to help or may interfere with, for the sake of ensuring that we do not wrongfully fail to help, or wrongfully interfere with, those whom we must help or let free. When things are not equal, what we must do depends on the degree of uncertainty under which we operate, the probability that the damage will eventuate and the magnitude of both the damage that we risk causing and the damage that we risk not preventing if we do not act. The less certain we are, the more cautious we should be.

Subject to and bearing in mind those considerations, I have defended the following views, which are worth setting out here in somewhat discursive form.

Economic Sanctions

(1) Primary and secondary comprehensive sanctions (against all agents and / or all goods): No.

(2) Primary and secondary targeted sanctions (against some agents and / or some categories of goods):

    a) Yes, in fact mandatory (and in some cases subject to victims' presumptive consent), with respect to:

        • narrow strategic goods (e.g., weapons);

        • single purpose goods (e.g., weapons);

- indirectly contributing goods (e.g., goods at discounted prices, favorable (private) loans);
- wide strategic goods (e.g., luxury products).

b) Presumptively no, in most cases, with respect to dual-purpose goods (e.g., oil)

Thus, to rehearse some of my recurrent examples, and subject to the facts being as stated here to the best of my knowledge, highly targeted sanctions on President Kim Jong-un, President Putin, President Assad, and former president Mugabe, and their top advisers, policy makers, and law enforcement and military officials are justified on my account. More comprehensive sanctions against a wide range of Cuban, Russian, and North Korean agents are not.

Aid Conditionality

(3) No-responsibility-based: Yes if it solves the problem of moral hazard. No in many cases, and particularly if Donor is itself partly and wrongfully responsible for Beneficiary's predicament.

(4) Human rights conditionality: Yes, in fact mandatory, and in the following instances:

- internal conditions (whereby the aid is conditional on its not being used to violate human rights, or on its being used toward specific human rights reforms);
- external conditions (whereby the aid is conditional on the adoption of human rights reforms, albeit not with the aid thus provided);
- negative conditionality (whereby the aid will be withdrawn failing compliance);
- positive conditionality (whereby the aid will be withheld failing compliance);
- policy conditionality (whereby the aid is attached to policies, not outcomes);
- targeted conditionality (whereby the aid is for specific, rather than wide-scale, projects).

On those grounds, I have expressed considerable skepticism, in line with many commentators, about the large-scale reforms, notably in the direction of privatization, that international financial institutions have used to impose on recipients of assistance. By contrast, the imposition of more modest conditions, pertaining to very specific projects such as increasing school enrollment (Cambodia) or putting pressure on homophobic regimes (Uganda) is morally justified. This is subject to there being no reasonable disagreement between donors and beneficiaries or no unreasonable disagreement in favor of beneficiaries; it is also subject to donors seeking to find alternative and effective ways of channeling the aid to their intended beneficiaries when faced with a recalcitrant regime.

Lending and Debt Forgiveness Conditionality

(5) Responsibility conditionality: Yes, so long as it solves the problem of moral hazard, and / or Borrower's difficulties in repaying a just loan can be traced to systemic fragilities in the international financial system.

(6) Human rights conditionality: Yes. Insofar as Lender is under a duty to offer a loan or grant relief to Borrower, its offer should be treated in the same way as the imposition of conditions on the delivery of aid. Mutatis mutandis, the conclusions set out at (4) above hold in those cases too. The Reagan administration's lending policy toward Chile was justified at the bar of human rights conditionality; the Chinese authorities' lending policy toward Sudan was not. Human rights conditionality can in some circumstances be justified even if the loan is an odious loan, or if it is unjust by dint of its repayment conditions, or if Lender ought in fact to have given the resources for free. The loans that successive Chinese regimes secured from sovereign lenders and thanks to which millions of individuals were lifted out of destitution illustrate the point.

(7) Repayment-reforms conditionality (whereby Lender conditions the offer of a loan to Borrower carrying out reforms aimed at improving chances that Borrower will be able to repay the loan, whether in full or, if relief is granted, in part): Yes, subject to the

following conditions: the loan is just; lenders and borrowers reasonably disagree as to the degree to which those conditions would impair human rights, or the disagreement between them is unreasonable in favor of lenders.

The headline news, in other words, is this: economic sanctions and conditional offers of assistance are morally justified, but only in very few cases, because they are highly constrained by the requirements of necessity, proportionality, and effectiveness, and because the problem of uncertainty is so deep.

As I noted at the outset of this book, economic statecraft is by no means the only way in which sovereign actors and associations thereof seek to enforce universal human rights. Nor is it used only as such a way. In fact, both economic sanctions and conditional offers of economic assistance are routinely deployed in the pursuit of ends which have little to do with human rights: territorial expansion, strengthening military alliances and spheres of geopolitical influence, domestic economic prosperity, and so on. This was so in 400 BC, and it continues to be so now. The complex ethical issues that economic statecraft raises when deployed to those ends warrant further and separate inquiry. Still, my arguments about human rights–based economic statecraft yield some preliminary, if speculative, thoughts.

Consider economic sanctions first. Suppose that state Blue acts within its rights by pursuing a given policy. Is Red justified in imposing economic sanctions on Blue as a means to force a policy change in alignment with Red's own interests? Clearly, Red may not so act as a means to get Blue to help Red pursue unjust ends. For example, it may not make g exports to Blue conditional on the Blue letting Red's air force use Blue's airbases— when it intends to use those airbases as a launch pad for an unjust military aggression on another country. The presumption in favor of international free trade may not be overridden by the pursuit of grievously unjust ends, of which a military aggression without a just cause is one.

Suppose now that Red's condition is not that Blue should commit a wrongdoing. Its condition, rather, is that Blue should surrender its rights over, for example, part of its territory, or with respect to trading with other countries toward which Red is unwarrantedly hostile. In such cases too, Red may not so act—any more than it may invade Blue militarily as a means to get Blue to cede that to which it has a right. In so far as Blue acts within its rights by conducting its foreign and domestic policy, its agents have not forfeited their property rights over those holdings, and Red does not have an overriding justification to infringe on those rights as a means to get Blue to change course.

Let us now turn to aid. Suppose that Red conditions the delivery of assistance to the latter being used, not to further the life prospects of Blue's members but, rather, to further some end of Red's. Most obviously, Red may not so act if Blue's members do not already lead a flourishing life or if Red has not fulfilled its reparative obligations to Blue, since it would thereby breach its obligations of justice to the latter by withdrawing or withholding the assistance. However, if Blue's members already have the resources they need or have obtained reparations from Red, and if their regime asks Red for material assistance (for example, toward major structural projects), Red may so act. Of course, as a matter of fact, it is extraordinarily unlikely that Red would be willing to give the funds and not expect repayment. Be that as it may, should it decide to act in a supererogatory manner, it may justifiably subject its offer to the fulfillment by Blue of (nonwrongful) conditions. For example, it may justifiably insist that Blue should use Red's firms to carry the job, or that Blue should agree to enter into a defensive alliance as the price to pay for getting the funds.

Finally, what about loans and debt relief? Suppose that Red conditions its offer to Blue (a) using the funds, in part or in whole, to promote some geopolitical interest(s) of Red's, or (b) doing what it wants with the funds but separately promoting those interests. As with aid, Red may not so act if it is under a duty to offer assistance of this kind. But if it is not under a duty to provide the loan or to offer relief on the debt, the case is similar to supererogatory help. Accordingly, it is hard to see how one could object to Red's conditions, so long as Red does not direct Blue to embark on wrongful policies. Red's and Blue's situation is relevantly similar to that of a car dealer who offers a loan to his client on condition that the latter buy one of his cars, or to that of a bank that offers a complex loan to its client on condition that the latter lease it commercial premises below market rates.

In both cases, it is true that Red is constraining Blue's ability rightfully to shape its collective future. At the same time, Blue will be able to conduct policies that, were it not for x, it would not be able to conduct. It is

also true that Red displays a form of patriotic partiality when it asks for
political conditions that favor its own citizens. Yet, ex hypothesi, it has
met its assistive and reparative obligations and is acting within the scope
of its legitimate political prerogative. Subject (once more) to the aforementioned proviso, there is little to object to in such cases.

Were the Athenians, thus, objectively justified in imposing trade sanctions on Megara? Probably not, at least on the assumption that Corinth
did have a claim to expand its navy in response to Athens' own domination
of the Mediterranean. There are also reasons to doubt that the Hanseatic League and the papacy were objectively justified in using embargoes
and boycotts as a means to bolster their geostrategic ambitions. Louis
XIV's offer to Charles II, for its part, was not morally untainted either.
Finally, there is much to find objectionable in the kind of economic arm-
twisting in which the North Atlantic and the Soviet blocs engaged during
the Cold War, or in which, as Russia's foreign policy toward Ukraine
seems to attest, powerful nations still engage for the sake of morally ques-
tionable goals.

To some, those claims will undoubtedly come across as hopelessly
naïve. They might say that Athens had no choice but to put pressure on
Corinth at Megara's expense—what else could she do, when her prestige
and prosperity depended on it? They might insist that Louis XIV had to
bribe Charles II—what else could he do, when faced with a bellicose William of Orange? They might claim that American administrations had
to impose sanctions against Cuba as a way to restrict the Soviet Union's
sphere of influence in Latin America—what else could they do, when faced
with encroachments by a totalitarian regime on what they had long regarded as their exclusive domain? They might argue that President Putin
has to put economic pressure on Ukraine—what else can he do, faced with
his country's geostrategic decline on its western border?

By *their* lights, and on the basis of the evidence available to them,
leaders of the present may not so act, whereas leaders of the past, by contrast, may well have been justified in so acting, at least in some cases. By
our lights, none of them were, at least not objectively so. This does not
mean that we may blame them. But it does mean that, when evaluating
economic statecraft, we should resist the allure of realpolitik and heed the
demands of justice.

Notes

Acknowledgments

Index

Notes

Introduction

1. The term "economic statecraft" was introduced into mainstream political science literature by David Baldwin, whose study remains a classic. See D. A. Baldwin, *Economic Statecraft* (Princeton, NJ: Princeton University Press, 1985). For an excellent historical overview, see R. D. Blackwill and J. M. Harris, *War by Other Means: Geoeconomics and Statecraft* (Cambridge, MA: Belknap Press of Harvard University Press, 2016). For specific examples see, e.g., R. J. Bonner, "The Megarian Decrees," *Classical Philology* 16, no. 3 (1921): 238–245; B. R. MacDonald, "The Megarian Decree," *Historia: Zeitschrift für Alte Geschichte* 32, no. 4 (1983): 385–410; P. A. Brunt, "The Megarian Decree," *American Journal of Philology* 72, no. 3 (1951): 269–282; S. Stantchev, "The Medieval Origins of Embargo as a Policy Tool," *History of Political Thought* 33, no. 3 (2012): 373–399.

2. The academic study of coercive diplomacy has its source in, inter alia, Thomas Schelling's seminal work on conflict strategies and Alexander George's early work on coercive alternatives to war (see T. C. Schelling, *The Strategy of Conflict* [Cambridge, MA: Harvard University Press, 1960]; A. L. George, *Forceful Persuasion: Coercive Diplomacy as an Alternative to War* [Washington, DC: United States Institute of Peace, 1991]). It has generated a growing literature from international relations and foreign policy scholars. See, e.g., R. J. Art and P. M. Cronin, eds., *The United States and Coercive Diplomacy* (Washington, DC: United States Institute of Peace, 2003); L. Freedman ed., *Strategic Coercion: Concepts and Cases* (Oxford: Oxford University Press, 1998); P. V. Jakobsen, "Coercive Diplomacy: Countering War-Threatening Crises and Armed Conflicts," in *Contemporary Security Studies,* ed. A. Collins (Oxford: Oxford Universisty Press, 2007), 279–293; F. McGillivray

and A. C. Stam, "Political Institutions, Coercive Diplomacy, and the Duration of Economic Sanctions," *Journal of Conflict Resolution* 48, no. 2 (2004): 154–172; J. A. Nathan, *Soldiers, Statecraft, and History: Coercive Diplomacy and International Order* (Westport, CT: Praeger, 2002); K. A. Schultz, *Democracy and Coercive Diplomacy* (Cambridge: Cambridge University Press, 2001); P. G. Lauren, G. A. Craig, and A. L. George, *Force and Statecraft: Diplomatic Challenges of Our Time,* 5th ed. (Oxford: Oxford University Press, 2014). The ethics of negotiations is sometimes addressed in journals of business studies. See, e.g., A. Strudler, "On the Ethics of Deception in Negotiation," *Business Ethics Quarterly* 5, no. 4 (1995): 805–822.

3. Here are some notable exceptions to philosophers' neglect of foreign policy: M. Blake, *Justice and Foreign Policy* (Oxford: Oxford University Press, 2013); M. Risse, *On Global Justice* (Princeton, NJ: Princeton University Press, 2012); J. Pattison, *The Alternatives to War: From Sanctions to Nonviolence* (Oxford: Oxford University Press, 2018). Book-length works on the morality of war include C. Fabre, *Cosmopolitan War* (Oxford: Oxford University Press, 2012); H. Frowe, *Defensive Killing* (Oxford: Oxford University Press, 2014); J. McMahan, *Killing in War* (Oxford: Clarendon, 2009); R. J. Norman, *Ethics, Killing, and War* (Cambridge: Cambridge University Press, 1995); D. Rodin, *War and Self-Defense* (Oxford: Clarendon, 2002); and, last but not least, M. Walzer, *Just and Unjust Wars: A Moral Argument with Historical Illustrations,* 5th ed. (New York: Basic Books, 2015).

4. For a fascinating account of the combined use of sanctions and conditional assistance involving North Korea, see S. Haggard and M. Noland, *Hard Target: Sanctions, Inducements, and the Case of North Korea* (Stanford, CA: Stanford University Press, 2017).

5. On economic diplomacy writ large, see G. A. Pigman, *Contemporary Diplomacy: Representation and Communication in a Globalized World* (Cambridge: Polity, 2010), ch. 9; G. R. Berridge, *Diplomacy: Theory and Practice,* 4th ed. (Basingstoke: Palgrave Macmillan, 2010), ch. 14; R. P. Barston, *Modern Diplomacy,* 4th ed. (Abingdon, Oxon: Routledge, 2014), ch. 9; S. Woolcock and N. Bayne, "Economic Diplomacy," in *Oxford Handbook of Modern Diplomacy,* ed. A. F. Cooper, J. Heine, and R. Thakur (Oxford: Oxford University Press, 2013), 385–401. On individual boycotts, see W. Hussain, "Is Ethical Consumerism an Impermissible Form of Vigilantism?," *Philosophy & Public Affairs* 40, no. 2 (2012): 111–143. On the use of economic instruments against transnational terrorist networks, see, e.g., J. Lepgold, "Hypotheses on Vulnerability: Are Terrorists and Drug Traffickers Coercible?," in *Strategic Coercion: Concepts and Cases,* ed. L. Freedman (Oxford: Oxford University Press, 1998), 131–150. On cyberattacks of the kind described here, see, e.g., Blackwill and Harris, *War by Other Means.*

6. On the methodology of hypothetical examples, see K. Brownlee and Z. Stemplowska, "Thought Experiments," in *Methods in Analytical Political Theory,* ed. A. Blau (Cambridge: Cambridge University Press, 2017), 21–45.

7. J. Wolff, *Ethics and Public Policy: A Philosophical Inquiry* (London: Routledge, 2011), 194–195. For a particularly good example of a normatively informed engagement with institutional design in the context of justice in trade, see Risse, *On Global Justice,* ch. 18.

1. Human Rights

1. The philosophical literature on human rights is staggeringly vast. For a very useful and recent state-of-the art discussion, see R. Cruft, M. S. Liao, and M. Renzo, eds., *Philosophical Foundations of Human Rights* (Oxford: Oxford University Press, 2015). For the view that human rights are pre-institutional rights, see, e.g., A. Gewirth, *Human Rights* (Chicago: University of Chicago Press, 1982); J. Griffin, *On Human Rights* (Oxford: Oxford University Press, 2008); M. C. Nussbaum, "Capabilities and Human Rights," *Fordham Law Review* 66 (1997): 273-300; T. Pogge, *World Poverty and Human Rights* (Cambridge: Polity Press, 2002); A. K. Sen, "Elements of a Theory of Human Rights," *Philosophy & Public Affairs* 32, no. 4 (2004): 315-356; J. Tasioulas, "The Moral Reality of Human Rights," in *Freedom From Poverty as a Human Right: Who Owes What to the Very Poor?*, ed. T. Pogge (Oxford: Oxford University Press, 2007), 75-102; J. Tasioulas, "Human Rights, Legitimacy, and International Law," *American Journal of Jurisprudence* 58, no. 1 (2013): 1-25.

   By contrast, on the so-called political conception of human rights, the latter refer to norms which play a particular role in international political practices. For prominent defenses of the political conception, see C. R. Beitz, *The Idea of Human Rights* (Oxford: Oxford University Press, 2009); A. E. Buchanan, *The Heart of Human Rights* (Oxford: Oxford University Press, 2014); J. Rawls, *The Law of Peoples: With the Idea of Public Reason Revisited* (Cambridge, MA: Harvard University Press, 1999); J. Raz, "Human Rights in the Emerging World Order," *Transnational Legal Theory* 1 (2010): 31-47. In a 2017 article, Julio Montero develops an account which, he claims, bridges the gap between those conceptions—by emphasizing the duties of the international community as a whole. I am sympathetic to view that there are such duties, but not to his rejection of cosmopolitan humanism. See J. Montero, "International Human Rights Obligations within the States System: The Avoidance Account," *Journal of Political Philosophy* 25, no. 4 (2017): 19e-39e.

2. For defenses of the interest theory of rights, see, e.g., J. Raz, *The Morality of Freedom* (Oxford: Clarendon, 1986), ch. 7; M. H. Kramer, "Getting Rights Right," in *Rights, Wrongs, and Responsibilities*, ed. M. H. Kramer (Basingstoke: Palgrave, 2001), 28-95. I defend this conception of a flourishing life (which I also call a decent life) in C. Fabre, *Social Rights under the Constitution: Government and the Decent Life* (Oxford: Clarendon, 2000), ch. 1.

3. Those remarks hide a number of difficulties, which I need not tackle here. In particular, I am aware that the word "presumptive" as I use it here would not satisfy lawyers, who (I believe) use it in the epistemic sense, but I cannot think of another suitable term. I am grateful to Hassan Dindjer, John Gardner, and Frederick Wilmot-Smith for helping me clarifying my thoughts in this passage.

4. For a sophisticated defense of egalitarian cosmopolitanism, see S. Caney, *Justice Beyond Borders: A Global Political Theory* (Oxford: Oxford University Press, 2005). A full-blown egalitarian conception of justice might draw different implications for conditionality: it might, for example, endorse sanctions in a greater range of cases.

5. The point is overlooked in the relevant literature, though there is growing recognition of its importance See, in particular, M. Meyer, "The Right to Credit," *Journal*

of Political Philosophy (forthcoming); M. Hudon, "Should Access to Credit Be a Right?," *Journal of Business Ethics* 84, no. 1 (2009): 17–28; N. Dobos, "The Democratization of Credit," *Journal of Social Philosophy* 43, no. 1 (2012): 50–63.

6. There is a vast literature on second-best (or conditional) obligations of that kind. The locus classicus is F. Jackson and R. Pargetter, "Oughts, Options, and Actualism," *Philosophical Review* 95, no. 2 (1986): 233–255.

7. For a classic defense of a currency exchange levy, see J. Tobin, "A Proposal for Monetary Reform," *Eastern Economic Journal* 29, no. 4 (2003): 519–526. For normative defenses of levies on international financial transactions, see A. James, *Fairness in Practice: A Social Contract for a Global Economy* (Oxford: Oxford University Press, 2013), ch. 8; G. Wollner, "Justice in Finance: The Normative Case for an International Financial Transaction Tax," *Journal of Political Philosophy* 22, no. 4 (2014): 458–485. For an illuminating account of the ways in which various forms of international taxation can serve global justice, see G. Brock, "Taxation and Global Justice: Closing the Gap between Theory and Practice," *Journal of Social Philosophy* 39, no. 2 (2008): 161–184.

8. I defend the view that justice under certain conditions requires that resource be jointly owned in C. Fabre, "Justice, Fairness, and World Ownership," *Law and Philosophy* 21, no. 3 (2002): 249–273. For an illuminating defense of the view that the Earth belongs to humankind in common, which is compatible with limited private property rights over its constituent resources, see M. Risse, *On Global Justice* (Princeton, NJ: Princeton University Press, 2012), esp. ch. 6.

9. See W. N. Hohfeld, *Fundamental Conceptions as Applied in Judicial Reasoning* (New Haven, CT: Yale University Press, 1919). For a classic analysis of the incidents of ownership, see A. M. Honoré, "Ownership," in *Oxford Essays in Jurisprudence*, ed. A. G. Guest (Oxford: Oxford University Press, 1961), 104–147.

10. For recent defenses of constrained free trade, see C. Brandi, "On the Fairness of the Multilateral Trading System," *Moral Philosophy and Politics* 1, no. 2 (2014): 227–247; A. James, "A Theory of Fairness in Trade," *Moral Philosophy and Politics* 1, no. 2 (2014): 177–200; James, *Fairness in Practice;* M. Risse and G. Wollner, "Three Images of Trade: On the Place of Trade in a Theory of Global Justice," *Moral Philosophy and Politics* 1, no. 2 (2014): 201–225; Risse, *On Global Justice,* ch. 14; A. Walton, "Do Moral Duties Arise from Global Trade?," *Moral Philosophy and Politics* 1, no. 2 (2014): 249–268.

11. In drawing that distinction I follow Christian Barry and Gerhard Øverland—though they couch it in terms of harm, not cost. See Barry and Øverland, *Responding to Global Poverty: Harm, Responsibility and Agency* (Cambridge: Cambridge University Press, 2016), ch. 5. As they show, there are different ways of enabling harm. As they also show, to the extent that the affluent wrongfully harm the poor, they do so largely by enabling rather than by doing harm. This of course does not render their consequent obligations trivial.

12. For a recent and rich defense of the view that the duty of assistance imposes "moderate costs" on the affluent, see Barry and Øverland, *Responding to Global Poverty,* esp. ch. 2. For a recent critique of this kind of view, see J. Montero, "Human Rights, Personal Responsibility, and Human Dignity: What Are Our Moral Duties

to Promote the Universal Realization of Human Rights?," *Human Rights Review* 18, no. 1 (2017): 67–85.

13. For an account of reparations in international law, see, e.g., D. Shelton, *Remedies in International Human Rights Law*, 3rd ed. (Oxford: Oxford University Press, 2015); R. Falk, "Reparations, International Law, and Global Justice: A New Frontier," in *The Handbook of Reparations*, ed. P. De Greiff (Oxford: Oxford University Press, 2008), 478–503. In 2006, the UN General Assembly adopted *Basic Principles and Guidelines on the Right to a Remedy and Reparation*. For philosophical defenses of the "Beneficiaries Pay Principle," see, e.g., J. J. Thomson, "Preferential Hiring," *Philosophy & Public Affairs* 2, no. 4 (1973): 364–384; D. Butt, *Rectifying International Injustice: Principles of Compensation and Restitution between Nations* (Oxford: Oxford University Press, 2009), 117–30; A. Pasternak, "Voluntary Benefits from Wrongdoing," *Journal of Applied Philosophy* 31, no. 4 (2014): 377–391. For philosophical objections to the principle, see, e.g., R. Huseby, "Should the Beneficiaries Pay?," *Politics, Philosophy & Economics* 14, no. 2 (2015): 209–225; C. Knight, "Benefiting from Injustice and Brute Luck," *Social Theory and Practice* 39, no. 4 (2013): 581–598; K. Lippert-Rasmussen, "Affirmative Action, Historical Injustice, and the Concept of Beneficiaries," *Journal of Political Philosophy* 25, no. 1 (2017): 72–90.

14. M. Capriati, "The Universal Scope of Positive Duties Correlative to Human Rights," *Utilitas*, 2018, 1e–24e. See also E. Ashford, "The Duties Imposed by the Human Right to Basic Necessities," in *Freedom from Poverty as a Human Right: Who Owes What to the Very Poor?*, ed. T. Pogge (Oxford: Oxford University Press, 2007), 183–218; Tasioulas, "The Moral Reality of Human Rights"; L. Wenar, "Responsibility and Severe Poverty," in Pogge, *Freedom from Poverty*, 255–274.

15. See L. Wenar, *Blood Oil: Tyrants, Violence, and the Rules That Run the World* (Oxford: Oxford University Press, 2016). The account of individual responsibility for collective outcomes on which I rely is adapted from Christopher Kutz's well-known view. See Kutz, *Complicity: Ethics and Law for a Collective Age* (Cambridge: Cambridge University Press, 2000).

16. Here too, I follow Capriati's argument. See Capriati, "The Universal Scope of Positive Duties." See also R. E. Goodin, "What Is So Special about Our Fellow Countrymen?," *Ethics* 98, no. 4 (1988): 663–686. See also Wenar, "Responsibility and Severe Poverty"; S. Caney, "Global Poverty and Human Rights: The Case for Positive Duties," in Pogge, *Freedom from Poverty*, 275–302. For a recent and illuminating discussion of the role of political institutions in delivering global justice, see Risse, *On Global Justice*, pt. 4.

17. J. C. Rubenstein, *Between Samaritans and States: The Political Ethics of Humanitarian INGOs* (Oxford: Oxford University Press, 2015). I am grateful to Jacob Levy for drawing my attention to this book.

18. Those few paragraphs hide a number of nuances and complications which readers versed in defense ethics in general and the ethics of war in particular will undoubtedly have spotted. Let me mention a few useful sources (out of an ever-growing literature): J. McMahan, *Killing in War* (Oxford: Clarendon, 2009); H. Frowe, *Defensive Killing* (Oxford: Oxford University Press, 2014); J. Quong, "Killing in

Self-Defence," *Ethics* 119 (2009): 507–537; J. Quong, "Liability to Defensive Harm," *Philosophy & Public Affairs* 40, no. 1 (2012): 45–77; J. Quong, "Proportionality, Liability, and Defensive Harm," *Philosohpy & Public Affairs* 43, no. 2 (2015): 144–173; S. Lazar, "Necessity in Self-Defense and War," *Philosophy & Public Affairs* 40, no. 1 (2012): 3–44; D. Rodin, *War and Self-Defense* (Oxford: Clarendon, 2002); J. M. Firth and J. Quong, "Necessity, Moral Liability, and Defensive Harm," *Law and Philosophy* 31, no. 6 (2012): 673–701.

I need to make another terminological point. When I use one-to-one cases involving a wrongdoer and a victim, I usually assume that the wrongdoer is a male and the victim a female. This enables me to use different gendered pronouns and possessive adjectives and, thereby, to achieve a greater degree of expository clarity. Allocating the male pronoun to wrongdoers and the female pronouns to victims should in no way be taken to imply that I subscribe to the grotesquely incorrect view that women, and only women, are victims and that men, and only men, are wrong-doers. However, in the context of state-based human rights abuses, it remains the case that far many more men than women are in positions of institutional power worldwide (and the more so the more high-powered the officials are), and thus in a position to abuse the human rights of both men and women. In that sense, my linguistic choice better reflects reality than the alternative would do.

19. For a fascinating discussion of the judgments which agents should reach with respect to their own wrongful contributions and which the state should reach with respect to citizens' contributions under conditions of epistemic uncertainty, see Barry and Øverland, *Responding to Global Poverty,* ch. 10. For clear articulations of different ways of understanding the precautionary principle, as well as accounts of different forms of uncertainty, see, e.g., N. A. Manson, "Formulating the Precautionary Principle," *Environmental Ethics* 24 (2002): 263–274; S. O. Hansson, "Decision Making under Great Uncertainty," *Philosophy of the Social Sciences* 26, no. 3 (1996): 369–386; S. M. Gardiner, "A Core Precautionary Principle," *Journal of Political Philosophy* 14, no. 1 (2006): 33–60.

2. Economic Sanctions

1. Details for the sanctions regimes as applied by the United Nations can be found on the UN's website at http://www.un.org. Details for the sanctions regimes as applied by the United States can be found on the U.S. Treasury's website at https://www .treasury.gov. For details of sanctions as applied by the European Union, see "Consolidated List of Sanctions," European Union External Action Service, August 18, 2015, https://eeas.europa.eu/headquarters/headquarters-homepage_en /8442/Consolidated%20list%20of%20sanctions. An overview of all extant sanctions regimes would take up too much space. For a classic empirical review of dozens of cases, see G. C. Hufbauer, J. J. Schott, and K. A. Elliott, *Economic Sanctions Reconsidered: Supplemental Case Histories,* 2nd ed. (Washington, DC: Institute for International Economics, 1990); G. C. Hufbauer, J. J. Schott, and K. A. Elliott, *Economic Sanctions Reconsidered: History and Current Policy,* 2nd ed. (Washington,

DC: Institute for International Economics, 1990). For recent overviews of UN
sanctions for the period from 1991 through 2013, one of the best resources is the
Targeted Sanctions Consortium (TSC), a network of over fifty scholars and
practitioners working in that field. Its findings, both quantitative and qualitative, can
be found at the Targeted Sanctions Consortium Database, accessed October 27,
2017, http://graduateinstitute.ch/home/research/centresandprogrammes/global
-governance/research-projects/UN_Targeted_Sanctions/targeted-sanctions
-consortium-da.html. Although the TSC's work focuses on UN sanctions, the
databases contain useful information on other sanctioning parties. Another helpful
source is the Threat and Imposition of Sanctions Database at https://www.unc.edu
/~bapat/TIES.htm. Finally, two particularly useful and recent works on targeted
sanctions warrant mentioning here: T. J. Biersteker, S. E. Eckert, and M. Tourinho,
eds., *Targeted Sanctions: The Impacts and Effectiveness of United Nations Action*
(Cambridge: Cambridge University Press, 2016); M. Eriksson, *Targeting Peace:
Understanding UN and EU Sanctions* (London: Routledge, 2016).

2. For details of the EU sanctions against Russia, see "EU Sanctions against Russia
over Ukraine Crisis," European Union Newsroom, updated January 15, 2018,
https://europa.eu/newsroom/highlights/special-coverage/eu-sanctions-against-russia
-over-ukraine-crisis_en. For details of the U.S. sanctions, see "Ukraine and Russian
Sanctions," U.S. Department of State, accessed November 14, 2017, https://www
.state.gov/e/eb/tfs/spi/ukrainerussia/. On the case of Venezuela, see J. M. Brown,
"EU Agrees Sanctions on Venezuelan Government," *Financial Times* (London),
November 13, 2017.

3. For U.S. sanctions against Syria, see https://www.state.gov/e/eb/tfs/spi/syria/. For
a useful UK briefing, see "Embargoes and Sanctions on Syria," Department for
International Trade and Export Control Joint Unit, updated January 28, 2015,
https://www.gov.uk/guidance/sanctions-on-syria. Of the plethora of articles and
news reports dating from June and July 2017 on the issuing of sanctions against Qatar
by Saudi Arabia, Egypt, Bahrain, and the United Arab Emirates, the following is a
useful summary: S. Kerr, "Saudi Arabia, UAE, Bahrain, and Egypt Cut Ties with
Qatar," *Financial Times* (London), June 5, 2017.

4. On U.S. sanctions against Iran and North Korea, see in particular the website for the
U.S. Department of the Treasury, Office of Foreign Assets Control, Sanctions
Programs and Information, last updated January 9, 2018, https://www.treasury.gov
/resource-center/sanctions/Pages/default.aspx. For EU sanctions, see "Sanctions:
How and When the EU Adopts Restrictive Measures," Council of the European
Union, last reviewed November 22, 2017, http://www.consilium.europa.eu/en
/policies/sanctions/.

5. See, e.g., A. Charron and C. Portela, "The UN, Regional Sanctions and Africa,"
International Affairs 91, no. 6 (2015): 1369–1385. The African Union's press release
regarding the 2015 sanctions against Burundi, last updated October 19, 2015, can be
found at http://www.peaceau.org/en/article/communique-of-the-551st-meeting-of
-the-peace-and-security-council. For interesting discussions of the AU and the
ECWAS stand regarding unconstitutional regime change, see T. J. Bassett and
S. Straus, "Defending Democracy in Côte d'Ivoire: Africa Takes a Stand," *Foreign*

Affairs 90, no. 4 (2011): 130–140. See also A. Charron, "Sanctions and Africa: United Nations and Regional Responses," in *Responding to Conflict in Africa: The United Nations and Regional Organizations,* ed. J. Boulden (London: Palgrave Macmillan, 2013), 77–98.

6. See, e.g., D. A. Baldwin, *Economic Statecraft* (Princeton, NJ: Princeton University Press, 1985), 214–224, though the labels "narrow" and "wide" are mine. Joy Gordon's distinction between indirect and direct sanctions maps onto the distinction between sanctions applied to wide strategic goods and sanctions applied to narrow strategic goods. See J. Gordon, "A Peaceful, Silent, Deadly Remedy: The Ethics of Economic Sanctions," *Ethics & International Affairs* 13, no. 1 (1999): 123–142.

7. For interesting studies on the impact of U.S. sanctions on U.S. firms, see, e.g., G. C. Hufbauer and K. A. Elliott, "US Economic Sanctions: Their Impact on Trade, Jobs, and Wages," (working paper, Peterson Institute for International Economics, April, 1999), https://piie.com/publications/working-papers/us-economic-sanctions-their -impact-trade-jobs-and-wages; R. N. Nass, "Economic Sanctions: Too Much of a Bad Thing," Brookings Policy Brief Series, June 1, 1998, https://www.brookings.edu /research/economic-sanctions-too-much-of-a-bad-thing/; R. M. Nelson, "U.S. Sanctions and Russia's Economy," Congressional Research Service, February 17, 2017, https://www.fas.org/sgp/crs/row/R43895.pdf.

8. I thank Christian Barry for this point.

9. For discussions of sanctions in the light of just war theory, see, e.g., Gordon, "A Peaceful, Silent, Deadly Remedy"; G. A. Lopez, "More Ethical than Not: Sanctions as Surgical Tools: Response to 'A Peaceful, Silent, Deadly Remedy,'" *Ethics & International Affairs* 13, no. 1 (1999): 143–148; G. A. Lopez, "In Defense of Smart Sanctions: A Response to Joy Gordon," *Ethics & International Affairs* 26, no. 1 (2012): 135–146; A. C. Pierce, "Just War Principles and Economic Sanctions," *Ethics & International Affairs* 10, no. 1 (1996): 99–113; O. O'Donovan, *The Just War Revisited* (Cambridge: Cambridge University Press, 2003), ch. 4; N. Milaninia, "*Jus ad bellum economicum* and *jus in bello economico:* The Limits of Economic Sanctions Under the Paradigm of International Humanitarian Law," in *Economic Sanctions under International Law,* ed. A. Z. Marossi and M. R. Bassett (The Hague: T. M. C. Asser, 2015), 95–124; A. Winkler, "Just Sanctions," *Human Rights Quarterly* 21, no. 1 (1999): 133–155; J. Babic and A. Jokic, "The Ethics of International Sanctions: The Case of Yugoslavia," *Fletcher Forum of World Affairs* 24, no. 1 (2000): 87–101; J. Pattison, "The Morality of Sanctions," *Social Philosophy and Policy* 32, no. 1 (2015): 192–215; J. Pattison, *The Alternatives to War: From Sanctions to Nonviolence* (Oxford: Oxford University Press, 2018), ch. 3.

10. I defend this view in "Cosmopolitanism and Wars of Self-Defence," in *The Morality of Defensive War,* ed. C. Fabre and S. Lazar (Oxford: Oxford University Press, 2014), 90–114. The issue is discussed at some length in that collection of essays.

11. For a recent discussion of the empirical point, including a good state-of-the-art section, see G. P. R. Wallace, "Regime Type, Issues of Contention, and Economic Sanctions: Re-evaluating the Economic Peace between Democracies," *Journal of Peace Research* 50, no. 4 (2013): 479–493. For a powerful philosophical defense of

economic sanctions against liberal democracies, see A. Pasternak, "Sanctioning Liberal Democracies," *Political Studies* 57, no. 1 (2009): 54–74.

12. This list of goods draws on allegations regarding Teodoro Obiang's extravagant lifestyle. At the time of this writing, Obiang, the president's son, is the vice president of Equatorial Guinea. Equatorial Guinea is the richest African country in terms of GDP per capita, thanks to its oil resources. Yet, according to a number of sources, not least Human Rights Watch, it also has one of the most corrupt, violently abusive regimes in the world, with dismal records in education and health in particular. See "'Manna from Heaven'? How Health and Education Pay the Price for Self-Dealing in Equatorial Guinea," Human Rights Watch, June 15, 2017, https://www.hrw.org/report/2017/06/15/manna-heaven/how-health-and-education-pay-price-self-dealing-equatorial-guinea. See also L. Wenar, *Blood Oil: Tyrants, Violence, and the Rules That Run the World* (Oxford: Oxford University Press, 2016), 70–71 and 250–251.

13. For the view that North Korea's regime would not survive a total ban on oil, see, e.g., T. Munroe and J. Chung, "For North Korea, Cutting Off Oil Supplies Would Be Devastating," Reuters, April 13, 2017, https://in.reuters.com/article/northkorea-nuclear-china-oil/for-north-korea-cutting-off-oil-supplies-would-be-devastating-idINKBN17F179. For a dissenting view, see D. Tweed and S. Stapczynski, "North Korea May Copy Nazi Germany If Total Oil Ban Takes Effect," *Bloomberg: The Quint,* updated September 23, 2017, https://www.bloombergquint.com/politics/2017/09/15/north-korea-may-copy-nazi-germany-if-total-oil-ban-takes-effect.

14. The claim that the costs attendant on thwarting human rights violations must in principle be allocated in proportion to wrongdoers' contribution to those deeds is not without its critics. For a strong defense of an alternative principle, to the effect that the costs of remedying unjust policies in general must be distributed equally between citizens of a democratic state (when the violations are committed by the latter), see A. Pasternak, "Sharing the Costs of Political Injustices," *Politics, Philosophy & Economics* 10, no. 2 (2011): 188–210.

15. Y. Yang, "Chinese Traders Fret about North Korea Sanctions," *Financial Times* (London), September 4, 2017; "Why Sanctions against North Korea Are Causing Pain in China," *Bloomberg Businessweek,* updated September 21, 2017.

16. For details of U.S. sanctions, see "Announcement of Treasury Sanctions on Entities within the Financial Services and Energy Sectors of Russia, against Arms or Related Materiel Entities, and Those Undermining Ukraine's Sovereignty," U.S. Department of the Treasury, press release, July 16, 2014, https://www.treasury.gov/press-center/press-releases/Pages/jl2572.aspx. For details of the EU sanctions, see "Legislation," *Official Journal of the European Union* 57, no. L 271 (September 12, 2014), http://eur-lex.europa.eu/legal-content/EN/TXT/PDF/?uri=OJ:L:2014:271:FULL&from=EN.

17. Or, as Warren Quinn famously put it, the right to threaten is derived from the right to protect. See W. Quinn, "The Right to Threaten and the Right to Punish," *Philosophy & Public Affairs* 14, no. 4 (1985): 327–373.

18. For discussions of the paradox in the context of nuclear deterrence, see, e.g., G. S. Kavka, *Moral Paradoxes of Nuclear Deterrence* (Cambridge: Cambridge University Press, 1987); A. Kenny, *The Logic of Deterrence* (Chicago: University of Chicago

Press, 1985). For good objections to the paradox, see, e.g., J. McMahan, "Deterrence and Deontology," *Ethics* 95, no. 3 (1985): 517-536.

19. See N. L. Miller, "The Secret Success of Nonproliferation Sanctions," *International Organization* 68, no. 4 (2014): 913-944. Of course, concern for human rights is not the only reason why nuclear powers, notably the United States, seek to combat proliferation. But it is one such reason, and one moreover that has normative force and is relevant to the present inquiry.

20. V. Tadros, *The Ends of Harm: The Moral Foundations of Criminal Law* (Oxford: Oxford University Press, 2011), ch. 13; V. Tadros, *Wrongs and Crimes* (Oxford: Oxford University Press, 2016), ch. 4. The Kantian objection to deterrence is usually deployed in the context of justifying punishment, and indeed, Tadros's aim is to defend a deterrence theory of punishment. But the objection can in principle be raised against general deterrence tout court—not merely punitive deterrence. By the same token, Tadros's moves are not local to deterrent punishment and warrant examining here.

21. Tadros, *Wrongs and Crimes,* 65-66. Suppose that there is no such thing as an impersonal obligation. If so, Tadros's second defense of deterrence fails, as does this particular case for economic sanctions. This would give us yet more reason to be skeptical of this particular policy.

22. For an empirical study of the problem of escalation, with regard to nuclear disarmament in North Korea, see S. Haggard and M. Noland, *Hard Target: Sanctions, Inducements, and the Case of North Korea* (Stanford, CA: Stanford University Press, 2017), chs. 6-7. Some of the most sophisticated arguments about risks of escalation in armed conflicts appear in the literature on nuclear deterrence. Many writers in that literature appeal to probabilistic reasoning, as I do here. Yet some, notably Robert Goodin, explicitly reject those appeals. See R. E. Goodin, "Nuclear Disarmament as a Moral Certainty," *Ethics* 95, no. 3 (1985): 641-658. Importantly, Goodin's skepticism unfolds against a set of assumptions which, he himself acknowledges, might not always obtain—notably the fact that a war in which nuclear weapons would be deployed would in all likelihood descend into a full scale, all-out, world-ending nuclear holocaust.

23. For particularly eloquent defenses of the objection, see Gordon, "A Peaceful, Silent, Deadly Remedy"; J. Gordon, "Reply to George A. Lopez's 'More Ethical than Not,'" *Ethics & International Affairs* 13, no. 1 (1999): 149-150; J. Gordon, "Smart Sanctions Revisited," *Ethics & International Affairs* 25 (2011): 315-335; J. Gordon, "Extraterritoriality: Issues of Overbreadth and the Chilling Effect in the Cases of Cuba and Iran," *Harvard International Law Journal* 57 (January 2016), http://www.harvardilj .org/wp-content/uploads/January-2016_Vol-57_Gordon.pdf, esp. 7-8.

24. R. Olearchyk, "Ukraine Imposes Sanctions on Russian-Owned Banks," *Financial Times* (London), March 16, 2017. Russia's policy was deemed illegal by a nonbinding vote of the UN General Assembly on March 27, 2014. See "General Assembly Adopts Resolution Calling upon States Not to Recognize Changes in Status of Crimean Region," United Nations Meeting Coverage, https://www.un.org/press/en/2014 /ga11493.doc.htm.

25. The conclusion I reach here is similar to James Pattison's claim that economic sanctions can be a fair way to distribute the costs attendant on responding to rights violations. See Pattison, "The Morality of Sanctions," 208–210.

26. In the case of the 2003 war on Iraq, and according to reputable sources, private firms together secured about $138 billion worth of contracts relating to military logistics, reconstruction, and private security. See A. Fifield, "Contractors Reap $138 Billion from Iraq War," *Financial Times* (London), March 18, 2013, https://www.ft.com/content /7f435f04-8c05-11e2-b001-00144feabdc0. On the case of Iran, see, e.g., M. McAuliff, "Iran Sanctions Cost the U.S. Billions: Study," *Huffington Post,* July 15, 2014, https://www.huffingtonpost.com/2014/07/14/iran-sanctions-us-cost_n_5585803.html.

27. For recent discussions of feasibility constraints and their role in theories of justice, see, e.g., D. Estlund, "Utopophobia," *Philosophy & Public Affairs* 42, no. 2 (2014): 113–134; H. Lawford-Smith, "Understanding Political Feasibility," *Journal of Political Philosophy* 21, no. 3 (2013): 243–259; A. Baderin, "Two Forms of Realism in Political Theory," *European Journal of Political Theory* 13, no. 2 (2014): 132–153; D. Miller, "Political Philosophy for Earthlings," in *Political Theory: Methods and Approaches,* ed. D. Leopold and M. Stears (Oxford: Oxford University Press, 2008), 29–48; P. Gilbert and H. Lawford-Smith, "Political Feasibility: A Conceptual Exploration," *Political Studies* 60, no. 4 (2012): 809–825; M. Jensen, "The Limits of Practical Possibility," *Journal of Political Philosophy* 17, no. 2 (2009): 168–184; J. Räikkä, "The Feasibility Condition in Political Theory," *Journal of Political Philosophy* 6, no. 1 (1998): 27–40.

28. On the Oil for Food Programme and the steps which led to its adoption, see "Oil for Food," accessed October 24, 2017, http://www.un.org/Depts/oip/background/index .html. On its failings see, e.g., S. Otterman, "Iraq: Oil for Food Scandal," Council on Foreign Relations, last updated October 28, 2005, at http://www.cfr.org/iraq/iraq -oil-food-scandal/. One of the most widely made claims about those sanctions is that they led to a serious increase in child mortality. There are strong reasons for believing that those reports were exaggerated. See T. Dyson and V. Cetorelli, "Changing Views on Child Mortality and Economic Sanctions in Iraq: A History of Lies, Damned lies and Statistics," *BMJ Global Health* 2 (2017), http://gh.bmj.com /content/2/2/e000311.

29. Against the view that intervening agents are solely responsible, see, e.g., M. J. Zimmerman, "Intervening Agents and Moral Responsibility," in "Philosophy and the Law," special issue, *Philosophical Quarterly* 35, no. 141 (1985): 347–358.

30. The points I make in this paragraph draw on the view, notably defended by McMahan, that combatants may under certain conditions shift the harms of their humanitarian intervention onto noncombatants who benefit from it. See J. Mc-Mahan, "The Just Distribution of Harm Between Combatants and Noncombatants," *Philosophy & Public Affairs* 38, no. 4 (2010): 342–379. See also Pattison, "The Morality of Sanctions."

31. For the second reason, see T. C. Schelling, *The Strategy of Conflict,* 2nd ed. (Cambridge, MA: Harvard University Press, 1980), 159. For discussions of consent and economic sanctions, see Pattison, "The Morality of Sanctions."

32. See, e.g., A. Buchanan, "Self-Determination, Revolution, and Intervention," *Ethics* 126, no. 2 (2016): 447–473, 460n10. The difficulty is only one of the reasons why Buchanan resists the consent requirement.

33. J. Parry, "Defensive Harm, Consent, and Intervention," *Philosohpy & Public Affairs* 45, no. 4 (2017): 356–396.

34. I provide a longer defense of consent in general and presumptive consent in particular; see C. Fabre, "Permissible Rescue Killings," *Proceedings of the Aristotelian Society* 109, no. 1, pt. 2 (2009): 149–164; C. Fabre, *Cosmopolitan War* (Oxford: Oxford University Press, 2012), 175–178. On the importance of consent, see also N. A. Davis, R. Keshen, and J. McMahan, eds., *Ethics and Humanity: Themes from the Philosophy of Jonathan Glover* (Oxford: Oxford University Press, 2010). Two points. First, in relation to consent, I use the word "presumptive" in the epistemic sense—that is, "We have reason to presume that X consents unless and until we have stronger reasons to believe otherwise." Second, my claim here is that the victims' presumptive consent to a sanctions policy is a necessary condition for a decision to adopt that policy at *t1* to be justified, not that it is sufficient. A dictator's victims might presumptively consent to a humanitarian intervention at the outset, hoping that a new and just regime might quickly be established. Yet, had they known that the intervention would in fact make things worse, they would not have consented to it at the outset. *Ex post,* then, we would conclude that the intervention was not objectively justified. The case of Iraq in 2003 comes to mind. I am grateful to Mathias Risse for pressing me on this and for supplying the example.

35. I defend that view in the case of war in *Cosmopolitan War,* 82. For skepticism, see J. McMahan, "Self-Defense Against Justified Threateners," in *How We Fight: Ethics in War,* ed. H. Frowe and G. Lang (Oxford: Oxford University Press, 2014), 104–137.

36. W. Godwin, *Enquiry Concerning Political Justice* (London: G. G. J. and J. Robinson, 1793), bk. 2, "Of Justice."

37. This point is about proportionality in relation to the good ends that Sender is pursuing. As such, it is compatible with my earlier claim that comprehensive sanctions which are meant deliberately to target ordinary North Koreans who contribute to their regime's unjust policy are a disproportionate response to their individual contributions.

38. In their influential study, Hufbauer, Schott, and Elliott argue that sanctions have been effective in a third of the 116 cases they examine. Their findings have been criticized by, among others, Robert Pape in a pair of widely cited articles. See Hufbauer, Schott, and Elliott, *Economic Sanctions Reconsidered: Supplemental Case Histories;* Hufbauer, Schott, and Elliott, *Economic Sanctions Reconsidered: History and Current Policy;* R. A. Pape, "Why Economic Sanctions Do Not Work," *International Security* 22, no. 2 (1997): 90–136; R. A. Pape, "Why Economic Sanctions Still Do Not Work," *International Security* 23, no. 1 (1998): 66–77. For an illuminating study of the effectiveness of sanctions in the South African case, see N. C. Crawford and A. Klotz, eds., *How Sanctions Work: Lessons from South Africa* (New York: St. Martin's, 1999). For the view that the effectiveness of sanctions partly depends on the nature of the authoritarian regime against which they are applied (as personalist or military), see A. Escribà-Folch and J. Wright, "Dealing with Tyranny:

International Sanctions and the Survival of Authoritarian Rulers," *International Studies Quarterly* 54, no. 2 (2010): 335–359. For the view that economic sanctions tend to worsen oppressive regimes' human rights records, see D. Peksen, "Economic Sanctions and Human Security: The Public Health Effect of Economic Sanctions," *Foreign Policy Analysis* 7, no. 3 (2011): 237–251. Finally, sanctions might be deemed ineffective insofar as they make it more likely that the targeted state will be subject to military aggression on the part of nonsanctioning states *and* as military aggression would itself be ineffective at enforcing human rights. See, e.g., T. M. Peterson and A. C. Drury, "Sanctioning Violence: The Effect of Third-Party Economic Coercion on Militarized Conflict," *Journal of Conflict Resolution* 55 (2011): 580–605.

39. See E. A. Ellis, "The Ethics of Economic Sanctions," *Internet Encyclopedia of Philosophy,* accessed Febrfuary 8, 2018, http://www.iep.utm.edu/eth-ec-s/. On the Zimbabwe case, see "Embargoes and Sanctions on Zimbabwe," Department for International Trade, Foreign & Commonwealth Office, and Export Control Joint Unit, last updated June 4, 2013, https://www.gov.uk/guidance/arms-embargo-on -zimbabwe, and "Zimbabwe Sanctions," U.S. Department of the Treasury, accessed October 23, 2017, https://www.treasury.gov/resource-center/sanctions/Programs /pages/zimb.aspx.

40. On the issue of collaboration with wrongdoers, see, e.g., R. E. Goodin and C. Lepora, *On Complicity and Compromise* (Oxford: Oxford University Press, 2013). For a similar point, see Pattison, *Alternatives to War,* 46–47.

41. See Baldwin, *Economic Statecraft,* 263.

3. Secondary Sanctions

1. The relevant legislation and explanatory notes can be found at the Department of Treasury Resource Center, last updated January 12, 2018, https://www.treasury.gov /resource-center/sanctions/Programs/Pages/Programs.aspx. For a clear historical account of the U.S. sanctions against Cuba through the early 1990s, see K. S. Wong, "The Cuban Democracy Act of 1992: The Extraterritorial Scope of Section 1706(a)," *University of Pennsylvania Journal of International Law* 14, no. 4 (1994): 651–682. On the fall 2017 discussion of extending sanctions against North Korea, see "Executive Order: Blocking Property of the Government of North Korea and the Workers' Party of Korea, and Prohibiting Certain Transactions with Respect to North Korea," press release, March 16, 2016, https://www.whitehouse.gov/the-press -office/2016/03/16/executive-order-blocking-property-government-north-korea-and -workers. For academic discussions of those cases, see, e.g., J. Gordon, "Extraterri- toriality: Issues of Overbreadth and the Chilling Effect in the Cases of Cuba and Iran," *Harvard International Law Journal,* January 18, 2016, esp. 7–8; J. A. Meyer, "Second Thoughts on Secondary Sanctions," *University of Pennsylania Journal of International Law* 30, no. 3 (2009): 905–968.

2. See, e.g., C. Mills, "Will Europe Rebel against U.S. Sanctions?," *National Interest,* August 3, 2017, http://nationalinterest.org/feature/will-europe-rebel-against-us -sanctions-21782; J. Brunsden, "EU Caught in Crossfire of US's Russia Sanctions

Move," *Financial Times*, July 4, 2017, https://www.ft.com/content/236aa73a-7073
-11e7-93ff-99f383b09ff9.

3. For a summary of those sanctions, see "European Union: Restrictive Measures
(Sanctions) in Force," European Commission, Service for Foreign Policy Instruments, updated July 7, 2016, http://eeas.europa.eu/cfsp/sanctions/docs/measures_en
.pdf. At the time of writing, Britain was still a member of the EU and those sanctions
were therefore binding on its citizens.

4. See "Security Council Fails to Adopt Draft Resolution on Syria That Would Have
Threatened Sanctions, Due to Negative Votes of China, Russian Federation," UN
Security Council, July 19, 2012, http://www.un.org/press/en/2012/sc10714.doc.htm.
Another veto occurred on February 28, 2017. See "Syria War: Russia and China Veto
Sanctions," *BBC News*, http://www.bbc.co.uk/news/world-middle-east-39116854.

5. I can do little more than skim the surface of this hugely complex field. For a classic
introduction to private international law, to which much of what I say here owes, see
A. Briggs, *The Conflict of Laws*, 3rd ed. (Oxford: Oxford University Press, 2013). For
illuminating accounts and defenses of comity and its underlying rationale, see A.
Briggs, "The Principle of Comity in Private International Law," vol. 354 of *Collected
Courses of the Hague Academy of International Law* (Nijhoff, Leiden: Brill, 2011);
T. Endicott, "Comity among Authorities," *Current Legal Problems* 68, no. 1 (2015):
1–26. As Briggs notes, the principle is far from being accepted by all common-law
courts as a norm for judicial decisions (as distinct from a norm for state conduct).

6. L. Wenar, *Blood Oil: Tyrants, Violence, and the Rules That Run the World* (Oxford:
Oxford University Press, 2016), 202. Further information on the British system is
available at BGS: Minerals UK, accessed September 29, 2017, http://www.bgs.ac.uk
/mineralsUK/planning/legislation/mineralOwnership.html.

7. For discussions of the principles of nationality, protection, passive personality, and
universal jurisdiction in the context of international criminal law, see, e.g., B.
Broomhall, *International Justice and the International Criminal Court: Between
Sovereignty and the Rule of Law* (Oxford: Oxford University Press, 2004); L.
Reydams, *Universal Jurisdiction: International and Municipal Legal Perspectives*
(Oxford: Oxford University Press, 2003); J. Crawford and I. Brownlie, *Brownlie's
Principles of Public International Law*, 8th ed. (Oxford: Oxford University Press, 2012),
chs. 21 and 30; A. Cassese, *International Criminal Law*, 2nd ed. (Oxford: Oxford
University Press, 2008), ch. 16; A. Chehtman, *The Philosophical Foundations of
Extraterritorial Punishment* (Oxford: Oxford University Press, 2010).

8. For a defense of secondary sanctions that appeals to the principles of nationality and
territoriality, see Meyer, "Second Thoughts on Secondary Sanctions." Meyer argues
that in law only those two principles, and neither protection nor universal jurisdiction,
can justify sanctions.

9. The United States has also argued that the nationality principle allows it to extend
sanctions to foreign subsidiaries of U.S. companies. This has proved controversial,
particularly in the case of sanctions against Cuba. In response to this policy, some
countries, notably Canada, have imposed countermeasures aimed at mitigating the
adverse consequences of those sanctions—thereby confronting those companies with

the dilemma of having to comply with Canadian legislation at the risk of falling foul of the U.S. sanctions, or complying with the latter at the risk of falling foul of the former. For exploration, see Wong, "The Cuban Democracy Act of 1992"; H. L. Clark, "Dealing with U.S. Extraterritorial Sanctions and Foreign Counter-measures," *University of Pennsylvania Journal of International Economic Law* 25 (2004): 455–489. I shall return to this below. Clark notes that the extension of the notion of nationality to companies owned by Sender's nationals wherever they are contravenes customary international law, whereby companies acquire the nationality of the state under which law it is registered.

10. As Annette Zimmermann pointed out to me, agents who produce goods from within Sender might wish for those goods not to reach Target, precisely on the grounds that Target's regime is guilty of grievous human rights violations. However, due to the complexities of global trade, they are not always in a position to exercise such control—which furnishes Sender's regime with a further reason for applying the principle of goods territoriality. I am grateful to Zimmermann for helping me clarify my thoughts in this paragraph.

11. For a very good discussion of this point, see L. Wenar, "Coercion in Cross-Border Property Rights," *Social Philosophy and Policy* 32, no. 1 (2015): 171–191, esp. 180–181; Wenar, *Blood Oil,* chs. 10 and 11. More generally, international law does restrict municipal property law with respect to rights to use, exclude, and transfer. See J. G. Sprankling, *The International Law of Property* (Oxford: Oxford University Press, 2014), esp. ch. 3.

12. See "Sudan and Darfur Sanctions," U.S. Department of the Treasury, Resource Center, accessed November 20, 2017, https://www.treasury.gov/resource-center /sanctions/Programs/Pages/sudan.aspx. For discussion, see Meyer, "Second Thoughts on Secondary Sanctions," 931–932. Attempts by the UN to apply sanctions against the Sudanese regime and warring factions since the mid-2000s repeatedly failed, not least because China consistently opposed such measures. See M. Nichols, "China Questions U.S. Threat of UN Sanctions on South Sudan," Reuters, February 27, 2015, http://www.reuters.com/article/us-southsudan-un -sanctions-idUSKBN0LV2FR20150227.

13. These points are not straw men: I am grateful to the participants at the LSE's Popper Seminar held on January 12, 2016, and at the Current Legal Problems Lecture held on February 25, 2016, for raising them.

14. See, e.g., R. Mohamad, "Unilateral Sanctions in International Law: A Quest for Legality," in *Economic Sanctions under International Law: Unilateralism, Multilateralism, Legitimacy, and Consequences,* ed. A. Z. Marossi and M. R. Bassett (The Hague: T.M.C. Asser, 2015), 71–81. For a qualified defense of multilateral sanctions, see also Meyer, "Second Thoughts on Secondary Sanctions." For primary sources on the UN extant sanctions regimes, see the Security Council Report, http://www.securitycouncilreport.org/sanctions/.

15. Meyer, "Second Thoughts on Secondary Sanctions," 931–932.

16. UNSC Resolution 2375 (2017) "Strengthening Sanctions on North Korea," https://usun.state.gov/remarks/7969.

4. Conditional Aid

1. For a useful historical overview of different forms of conditionality since World War II, see O. Stokke, "Aid and Political Conditionality: Core Issues and State of the Art," in *Aid and Political Conditionality,* ed. O. Stokke (London: Cass, 1995), 1–87; D. Moyo, *Dead Aid: Why Aid Is Not Working and How There Is a Better Way for Africa* (London: Penguin, 2010), ch. 2. See also G. Cumming, *Aid to Africa: French and British Policies from the Cold War to the New Millenium* (Aldershot: Ashgate, 2001) for a good summary of various ways of defining aid (p. 13) and an illuminating historical overview (chs. 2 and 3).

2. For the view that access to the justice system is a requirement of justice, see F. Wilmot-Smith, "Necessity or Ideology?," *London Review of Books* 36, no. 21 (2014): 15–17.

3. Recent critical works on the degree to which global aid has stymied, rather than helped, poverty alleviation, include W. Easterly, *The White Man's Burden: Why the West's Efforts to Aid the Rest Have Done So Much Ill and So Little Good* (Oxford: Oxford University Press, 2006); Moyo, *Dead Aid;* P. Collier, *The Bottom Billion: Why the Poorest Countries Are Failing and What Can Be Done About It* (Oxford: Oxford University Press, 2008); B. Ramalingam, *Aid on the Edge of Chaos: Rethinking International Cooperation in a Complex World* (Oxford: Oxford University Press, 2013). I return to this issue throughout the chapter.

4. For a classic defense of luck egalitarianism and the no-responsibility condition, see R. Dworkin, "What Is Equality? Part 1: Equality of Welfare," *Philosophy & Public Affairs* 10, no. 3 (1981): 185–246; R. Dworkin, "What Is Equality? Part 2: Equality of Resources," *Philosophy & Public Affairs* 10, no. 4 (1981): 283–345. For trenchant criticisms, see, e.g., E. S. Anderson, "What Is the Point of Equality?," *Ethics* 109, no. 2 (1999): 287–337.

5. For a good overview of those different forms of conditionality as applied to overseas aid, see, e.g., H. Bedoya, S. Koeberle, P. Silarsky, and G. Verheyen, eds., *Conditionality Revisited: Concepts, Experiences, and Lessons* (Washington, DC: World Bank, 2005).

6. It is worth noting that external and internal conditions can also pertain to ends which are not related to human rights. Thus, Donor can be described as imposing an internal condition on Beneficiary's receipt of the aid when it says, "Unless you use the aid to serve our own geopolitical interests, we will not help you." Likewise, Donor can be described as imposing an external condition when it says to Beneficiary, "We will not give you the assistance you need unless you agree to lease us one of your naval bases for our navy." Because my concern in this book is with aid conditionality as a means to enforce human rights, I will not deal with such cases—save for a few remarks in the book's conclusion.

7. See, e.g., J. K. Boyce, *Investing In Peace: Aid and Conditionality after Civil Wars* (Oxford: Oxford: Oxford University Press, 2002). For a discussion of moral hazard and conditionality in general, see, e.g., P. Mosley and J. Hudson, *Aid, Conditionality and Moral Hazard: Discussion Papers in Development Economics* (Reading: University of Reading, 1996). For a discussion of the issue in connection with North

Korea, which received conditional international assistance to cope with famine in the mid-1990s, see S. Haggard and M. Noland, *Hard Target: Sanctions, Inducements, and the Case of North Korea* (Stanford, CA: Stanford University Press, 2017), ch. 4.

8. See Stokke, "Aid and Political Conditionality," 14–15.

9. I am grateful to Simon Caney for raising this possibility.

10. For a skeptical take on moving to policy conditionality, however, see A. G. Dijkstra, "The Effectiveness of Policy Conditionality: Eight Country Experiences," *Development and Change* 33, no. 2 (2002): 307–334. For an endorsement of very specific policy conditionality, see, e.g., Easterly, *White Man's Burden*, esp. 154–157, 179, and ch. 6.

11. UN World Food Programme, "Take-Home Ration Programme: WFP Cambodia," April 2, 2010, video, WFP in Action, http://www.wfp.org/videos/take-home-ration -programme-wfp-cambodia.

12. For an influential critique of international aid donors along those lines, see, e.g., N. Woods, *The Globalizers: The IMF, the World Bank, and Their Borrowers* (Ithaca, NY: Cornell University Press, 2006). Out of the huge literature on the Washington Consensus, the following works are particularly useful: N. Serra and J. E. Stiglitz, eds., *The Washington Consensus Reconsidered: Towards a New Global Governance* (Oxford: Oxford University Press, 2008); J. Stiglitz, *Globalization and Its Discontents* (London: Allen Lane, 2002); M. R. Abouharb and D. Cingranelli, *Human Rights and Structural Adjustment* (Cambridge: Cambridge University Press, 2007); Easterly, *White Man's Burden;* W. Easterly, *The Tyranny of Experts: Economists, Dictators, and the Forgotten Rights of the Poor* (New York: Basic Books, 2013). For a review by Action Aid of such practices dating from the mid-2000s, see *What Progress? A Shadow Review of World Bank Conditionality*, 2006, accessed December 8, 2017, https://www.actionaid.org.uk/sites/default/files/what_progress.pdf.

13. For a statement of the Millennium Challenge Corporation's mission and values, see https://www.mcc.gov/about/values, accessed on 15/11/2017. For the French and UK case, see Cumming, *Aid to Africa*.

14. For details of the legislation, see "Uganda Passes Tough New Anti-Gay Law," *Al Jazeera*, December 20, 2013, http://america.aljazeera.com/articles/2013/12/20/uganda -passes-toughnewlawagainsthomosexuality.html. For reports of funding cuts, see "Uganda Hit with Foreign Aid Cuts over Anti-Gay Law," *Al Jazeera*, February 27, 2014, http://america.aljazeera.com/articles/2014/2/27/uganda-hit-with -foreignaidcutsoverantigaylaw.html.

15. For a powerful articulation of the view that NGOs are not necessarily a panacea, see J. C. Rubenstein, *Between Samaritans and States: The Political Ethics of Humanitarian INGOs* (Oxford: Oxford University Press, 2015). On the influence of evangelical organizations in Uganda, see, e.g., J. K. Arinaitwe, "How US Evangelicals Are Shaping Development in Uganda," *Al Jazeera,* July 25, 2014, http://www .aljazeera.com/indepth/opinion/2014/07/us-evangelicals-uganda -201472413592026813 7.html; A. O'Hehir, "'God Loves Uganda': Africa's Terrifying Christian Revival," *Salon,* October 9, 2013, https://www.salon.com/2013/10/09/god _loves_uganda_africas_terrifying_christian_revival/; M. Blake, "Meet the

American Pastor Behind Uganda's Anti-Gay Crackdown," *Mother Jones,* March 10, 2014, http://www.motherjones.com/politics/2014/03/scott-lively-anti-gay-law-uganda/; F. Nzwili, "Uganda's Anti-Gay Bill Refocuses Attention on US Evangelical Influence," *Christian Science Monitor,* February 25, 2014, https://www.csmonitor .com/World/2014/0225/Uganda-s-anti-gay-bill-refocuses-attention-on-US -evangelical-influence. I am grateful to Alexa Zeitz for helping me better understand this particular example.

16. It might be thought that my claim in this paragraph contradicts the conclusion I reached in connection with internal conditionality in the previous subsection. There, I noted that Donor may justifiably withdraw resources from Beneficiary's regime if the latter uses the aid to violate human rights. The point applies, I argued, to Beneficiary's destitute members who support those violations. Here, I claim that Beneficiary's destitute members who support human rights violations may neverthe-less have a claim to the aid, if withholding the aid from them would constitute a disproportionate cost. The reason why those two claims are not mutually inconsistent is this. In the case of internal conditionality, the aid would be used to commit human rights violations and thus would not help those destitute individuals anyway. In the case of external conditionality, it might be used to help them, and it thus pays to inquire whether withdrawing or withholding it would be a disproportionate response.

17. I am grateful to Christian Barry and Mathias Risse for pressing me on this.

18. J. Rawls, *The Law of Peoples: With the Idea of Public Reason Revisited* (Cambridge, MA: Harvard University Press, 1999), 117–119. The names "Profligate" and "Thrifty" are mine. For a view similar to Rawls, see D. Miller, "Justice and Global Inequality," in *Inequality, Globalization and World Politics,* ed. A. Hurrell and N. Woods (Oxford: Oxford University Press, 1999), 187–210.

19. I owe this point to Christian Barry.

20. I am grateful to Marco Meyer for pressing me on this.

21. For devastating indictments of the extent to which rich countries contribute to global poverty by supporting oppressors, see, e.g., T. Pogge, *World Poverty and Human Rights* (Cambridge: Polity Press, 2002); L. Wenar, *Blood Oil: Tyrants, Violence, and the Rules That Run the World* (Oxford: Oxford University Press, 2016). For criticisms of no-responsibility conditionality along the lines articulated here, see, e.g., Stokke, "Aid and Political Conditionality"; Easterly, *Tyranny of Experts.*

22. As a matter of fact, there are reasons for thinking that French and British foreign aid policies toward their former colonies have been shaped at least in part by that relationship. For a very interesting study, see Cumming, *Aid to Africa,* esp. ch. 4. There is a larger empirical and fascinating issue at stake here, namely the extent to which the European Union's relationship with African, Caribbean, and Pacific countries has been shaped by a shared colonial past. See, e.g., K. Nicolaïdis, B. Sèbe, and G. Maas, eds., *Echoes of Empire: Memory, Identity and Colonial Legacies* (London: Tauris, 2015), pt. 3. For a philosophical account of the duties of global justice as grounded in colonial wrongdoings, see L. Ypi, R. E. Goodin, and C. Barry, "Associative Duties, Global Justice, and the Colonies," *Philosophy & Public Affairs* 37, no. 2 (2009): 103–135.

23. What I call the broadly Walzerian view is drawn from the following works by Michael Walzer: M. Walzer, *Just and Unjust Wars: A Moral Argument with Historical Illustrations,* 5th ed. (New York: Basic Books, 2015), chs. 4 and 6; M. Walzer, *Spheres of Justice: A Defense of Pluralism and Equality* (New York: Basic Books, 1983); M. Walzer, "Philosophy and Democracy," *Political Theory* 9, no. 3 (1981): 379–399. For the Walzerian view as deployed in the context of conditional aid, see V. Collingwood, "Assistance with Fewer Strings Attached," *Ethics & International Affairs* 17, no. 1 (2003): 55–67. See also H. W. Singer, "Aid Conditionality" (IDS discussion paper, Institute of Development Studies, University of Sussex, 1994). I am grateful to Anna Goppel and Pranay Sanklecha for helping me improve my arguments in this section.

    It is worth noting that although the charge as stated here is most often raised against aid conditionality, it can also apply to economic sanctions—in particular to secondary sanctions. The thought would be this: by refusing to recognize a third party's jurisdictional sovereignty with respect to transactions between its own agents and Target, Sender is behaving toward that third party as a colonial power. My response below to the objection as raised against aid conditionality applies, mutatis mutandis, against the objection as raised against sanctions.

24. For a similar point, see R. W. Grant, *Strings Attached: Untangling the Ethics of Incentives* (Princeton, NJ: Princeton University Press, 2011), 76.

25. See T. M. Scanlon, "Preferences and Urgency," *Journal of Philosophy* 72, no. 19 (1975): 655–669. I defend at some length the view that democracy does not override justice in C. Fabre, *Social Rights under the Constitution: Government and the Decent Life* (Oxford: Clarendon, 2000). I am grateful to Simon Caney for pressing me on this.

26. The notion of reasonable disagreement has received a good deal of attention in political philosophy since the publication of John Rawls's *Political Liberalism* in 1993; see J. Rawls, *Political Liberalism* (New York: Columbia University Press, 1993). Some of the most interesting works on this topic, on which I freely draw here, are: A. Gutmann and D. F. Thompson, *Democracy and Disagreement* (Cambridge, MA: Harvard University Press, 1996); G. F. Gaus, *Justificatory Liberalism: An Essay on Epistemology and Political Theory* (Oxford: Oxford University Press, 1996); J. Waldron, *Law and Disagreement* (Oxford: Clarendon, 1999); J. Quong, *Liberalism without Perfection* (Oxford: Oxford University Press, 2011); C. McMahon, *Reasonable Disagreement: A Theory of Political Morality* (Cambridge: Cambridge University Press, 2009). In this section, I also make use of the following works in epistemology and its intersection with ethics: A. I. Goldman, "Experts: Which Ones Should You Trust?," *Philosophy and Phenomenological Research* 63, no. 1 (2001): 85–110; L. Trinkaus Zagzebski, *Epistemic Authority: A Theory of Trust, Authority, and Autonomy in Belief* (Oxford: Oxford University Press, 2012); R. Feldman and T. A. Warfield, eds., *Disagreement* (Oxford: Oxford University Press, 2010); M. Fricker, *Epistemic Injustice: Power and the Ethics of Knowing* (Oxford: Oxford University Press, 2007).

27. For a withering critique of aid and lending conditionality along those lines, see Easterly, *Tyranny of Experts,* and Goldman, "Experts: Which Ones Should You Trust?"

28. I thank Sam Bruce for this point. For interesting discussions of supposed tensions between conditionality and beneficiaries' ownership of aid programs, see, e.g., Bedoya, Koeberle, Silarsky, and Verheyen, *Conditionality Revisited*. A full normative account of diplomatic negotiations writ large is beyond the scope of this book. It would need to address two further and interrelated issues: the imbalance between rich and poor countries' expert resources (which imbalance is itself, more often than not, the product of systemic injustice) and procedural constraints on such negotiations. I briefly tackle the latter issue in C. Fabre, *Cosmopolitan Peace* (Oxford: Oxford University Press, 2016), 102–113.

29. See World Food Programme, "Program Design," accessed October 24, 2017, http://www1.wfp.org/programme-design.

30. In addition to the works I have cited in this chapter, see R. C. Riddell, *Does Foreign Aid Really Work?* (Oxford: Oxford University Press, 2007), esp. ch. 14; P. Collier, P. Guillaumont, S. Guillaumont, and J. W. Gunning, "Redesigning Conditionality," *World Development* 25, no. 9 (1997): 1399–1407; T. Killick, "Principals, Agents and the Failings of Conditionality," *Journal of International Development* 9, no. 4 (1997): 483–495; T. Killick, *Aid and the Political Economy of Policy Change* (London: Routledge, 1998); T. Mkandawire, "Aid, Accountability and Democracy in Africa," *Social Research* 77, no. 4 (2010): 1149–1182. The radical thesis that aid simply does not work, period, has been advanced by, inter alia, Dambisa Moyo and William Easterly. The more nuanced thesis that aid can under certain conditions help its intended beneficiaries has been defended by, inter alia, Paul Collier, Jeffrey Sachs, and Christian Barry and Gerhard Øverland. See Moyo, *Dead Aid*; Easterly, *Tyranny of Experts*; Collier, *Bottom Billion*; J. Sachs, *The End of Poverty: Growing the World's Wealth in an Age of Extremes* (London: Penguin, 2005); C. Barry and G. Øverland, *Responding to Global Poverty: Harm, Responsibility and Agency* (Cambridge: Cambridge University Press, 2016), 63–71.

31. For a fascinating discussion of the politics and harmful effects of water privatization, see K. J. Bakker, *Privatizing Water: Governance Failure and the World's Urban Water Crisis* (Ithaca, NY: Cornell University Press, 2010). On Bolivia's case specifically, see Abouharb and Cingranelli, *Human Rights and Structural Adjustment*, 141. Tanzania renationalized its water networks and supplies in 2005.

5. Sovereign Lending, Debt Forgiveness, and Conditionality

1. Relevant resources can be found on the IMF's and World Bank's respective websites: http://www.imf.org; http://www.worldbank.org.

2. For a defense of that view, together with a broader philosophical account of debt in general, see A. X. Douglas, *The Philosophy of Debt* (London: Routledge, 2015).

3. For helpful discussions of those intergenerational issues, see, e.g., S. G. Reddy, "International Debt: The Constructive Implications of Some Moral Mathematics," *Ethics & International Affairs* 21, no. 1 (2007): 33–48; C. Dimitriu, "Are States Entitled to Default on the Sovereign Debts Incurred by Governments in the Past?," *Ethical Perspectives* 22, no. 3 (2015): 369–393. The claim that taking out a loan might, as a

result of regime change, create intergenerational injustice comports with the individualistic underpinnings of cosmopolitan justice. As Odette Lienau argues, historically the norm that sovereign debts must be repaid notwithstanding regime change relies on statist conceptions of sovereignty. Such conceptions as applied to international finance are out of step (she convincingly argues) with encroachments on state sovereignty as instantiated in, for example, international criminal law. See O. Lienau, *Rethinking Sovereign Debt: Politics, Reputation, and Legitimacy in Modern Finance* (Cambridge, MA: Harvard University Press, 2014), esp. chs. 1 and 8.

4. See "Factsheet," International Monetary Fund, http://www.imf.org/en/About /Factsheets/Sheets/2016/08/02/21/28/IMF-Conditionality.

5. Comprehensive information about the IMF's various lending instruments can be found at the IMF factsheet, http://www.imf.org/en/About/Factsheets/IMF-Lending.

6. I am grateful to Tim Besley for pressing me on this.

7. See "Borrowing Countries," International Development Association, accessed October 4, 2017, http://ida.worldbank.org/about/borrowing-countries; "Human Freedom Index," CATO Institute, accessed October 4, 2017, https://www.cato.org /human-freedom-index; "Democracy Index," *The Economist,* https://infographics .economist.com/2017/DemocracyIndex. The charge that IFIs help authoritarian regimes maintain their rule has been made repeatedly in academic and activist circles. See, e.g., W. Easterly, *The White Man's Burden: Why the West's Efforts to Aid the Rest Have Done So Much Ill and So Little Good* (Oxford: Oxford University Press, 2006), esp. 131–138.

8. Of course, whether those institutions, notably the IMF and World Bank, are in fact politically neutral is a matter for (heated) debate. For a general discussion of the issue, see N. Woods, *The Globalizers: The IMF, the World Bank, and Their Borrowers* (Ithaca, NY: Cornell University Press, 2006). On the supposed neutrality of IFIs in general, and the case of the United States and Chile, see M. R. Abouharb and D. Cingranelli, *Human Rights and Structural Adjustment* (Cambridge: Cambridge University Press, 2007), 34–35 and 105, respectively. On China and Sudan, see, e.g., C. Alden, D. Large, and R. S. de Oliveira, eds., *China Returns to Africa: A Rising Power and a Continent Embrace* (New York: Columbia University Press, 2008).

9. "Debt Relief under the Heavily Indebted Poor Countries (HIPC) Initiative," International Money Fund, November 3, 2017, http://www.imf.org/en/About /Factsheets/Sheets/2016/08/01/16/11/Debt-Relief-Under-the-Heavily-Indebted-Poor -Countries-Initiative.

10. For the OECD's stance on tied v. untied development assistance, see "Untying Aid: The Right to Choose," accessed October 20, 2017, http://www.oecd.org /development/untyingaidtherighttochoose.htm#history.

11. For a similar typology, see J. Hanlon, "Defining 'Illegitimate Debt': When Creditors Should Be Liable for Improper Loans," in *Sovereign Debt at the Crossroads: Challenges and Proposals for Resolving the Third World Debt Crisis,* ed. C. Jochnick and F. A. Preston (Oxford: Oxford University Press, 2006), 125–126. Examples of unjust nonrepayment conditions include the stipulation that Borrower should

embark on an unjust policy; more frequently, they include stipulations that Borrower should give preferential treatment to Lender's firms when opening its markets. This is unjust to the extent that Borrower's business sector lacks opportunities to develop as a result. The loans that China provided to Angola from the 1990s onward come to mind here. True, thanks to those loans, Angola's authoritarian and rights-violating regime managed to start reconstructing the country following a devastating civil war, but the loans were conditioned on Chinese firms, many of which were state-based, carrying out 70 percent of the contracts. Of course, Borrower's business sector might not be in a position to take up the work when the loan is issued. The worry, though, is that it is not afforded a chance to do so, which in turn might foster long-term dependency, contra the demands of justice, on Lender. See M. E. Ferreira, "China in Angola: Just a Passion for Oil?," in Alden, Large, and Oliveira, *China Returns*, 295–317.

12. See S. Jayachandran and M. Kremer, "Odious Debt," in Jochnick and Preston, *Sovereign Debt at the Crossroads*, 215–225. For the charge that the IMF derives unfair benefits from its lending practices, see "'Cancel Greek Debt' Projected on German Embassy in London," Jubilee Debt Campaign, accessed October 20, 2017, http:// jubileedebt.org.uk/campaigns/cancel-greek-debt. On the claim that IFIs offer favorable repayment terms, see, e.g., "What Is IDA?," International Development Association, accessed October 20, 2017, http://ida.worldbank.org/about/what-ida.

13. *Human Development Report 2016*, UN Human Development Programme, http://hdr .undp.org/sites/default/files/2016_human_development_report.pdf, 26. The global poverty rate is defined as having $1.90 or less to live on per day. On the World Bank's involvement in China from the bank's perspective, see "The World Bank in China," accessed October 24, 2017, http://www.worldbank.org/en/country/china. I am grateful to Mathias Risse for drawing my attention to this example and helping clarify my thoughts in this paragraph and the previous one.

14. I provide an account of just treaty obligations in C. Fabre, *Cosmopolitan Peace* (Oxford: Oxford University Press, 2016), 90–101. Note that I am not endorsing the norm *pacta sunt servanda* in the unqualified form in which it is invoked in international politics: whether there is an obligation to abide by treaties and, by implication, to pay the debts created by loan agreements depends on the moral status of the relevant provisions. For powerful arguments against the norm in its unqualified form, see G. Wollner, "Morally Bankrupt: International Financial Governance and the Ethics of Sovereign Default," *Journal of Political Philosophy* December 5, 2017, http://onlinelibrary.wiley.com/doi/10.1111/jopp.12151/full; Dimitriu, "Are States Entitled to Default?" The philosophical and philosophically informed legal literature on odious debts is growing. See, e.g., C. Barry, "Sovereign Debt, Human Rights, and Policy Conditionality," *Journal of Political Philosophy* 19, no. 3 (2011): 282–305; C. Barry and L. Tomitova, "Fairness in Sovereign Debt," *Ethics & International Affairs* 21, no. S1 (2007): 41–79; Hanlon, "Defining 'Illegitimate Debt'"; Jayachandran and Kremer, "Odious Debt"; J. King, *The Doctrine of Odious Debt in International Law* (Cambridge: Cambridge University Press, 2016); J. Shafter, "The Due Diligence Model: A New Approach to the Problem of Odious Debts," *Ethics & International Affairs* 21, no. 1 (2007): 49–67; C. Dimitriu, "Odious

Debts: A Moral Account," *Jurisprudence* 6, no. 3 (2015): 470–491. The website for the Jubilee Debt Campaign contains extensive resources; see http://jubileedebt .org.uk.

15. For the IMF debt relief mechanisms and conditions, see "Debt Relief under the Heavily Indebted," International Money Fund. For an interesting discussion of the connection between the duty to provide aid and the duty to cancel illegitimate debts, see Barry, "Sovereign Debt, Human Rights, and Policy Conditionality"; S. Arslanalp and P. B. Henry, "Helping the Poor to Help Themselves: Debt Relief or Aid?," in Jochnick and Preston, *Sovereign Debt at the Crossroads*, 174–193; J. Boorman, "Dealing Comprehensively, and Justly, with Sovereign Debt," in Jochnick and Preston, *Sovereign Debt at the Crossroads*, 226–245.

16. For an illuminating normative account of the role of different kinds of luck in financial crises, see J. Linarelli, "Debt in Just Societies," Social Science Research Network, last revised August 3, 2017, https://papers.ssrn.com/sol3/papers.cfm ?abstract_id=2837505; J. Linarelli, "Luck, Justice and Systemic Financial Risk," *Journal of Applied Philosophy* 34, no. 3 (2017): 331–352. Linarelli focuses on private lending, but his framework is helpful for sovereign debt cases.

17. My argument here closely follows R. Ramcharan, *Reputation, Debt, and Policy Conditionality* (Washington, DC: International Monetary Fund, 2003). Ramcharan presents his argument in the context of the conditionality of debt.

18. See, e.g., Barry, "Sovereign Debt, Human Rights, and Policy Conditionality."

6. Tu Quoque

1. For examples of the charge as leveled against U.S. foreign policy in general, see, e.g., M. Lynch, "Lie to Me: Sanctions on Iraq, Moral Argument and the International Politics of Hypocrisy," in *Moral Limit and Possibility in World Politics,* ed. R. M. Price (Cambridge: Cambridge University Press, 2008), 165–196; D. Glaser, "Does Hypocrisy Matter? The Case of US Foreign Policy," *Review of International Studies* 32, no. 2 (2006): 251–268. For the French case, see G. Cumming, *Aid to Africa: French and British Policies from the Cold War to the New Millenium* (Aldershot: Ashgate, 2001), 107–108. In international law, the charge is expressed in the doctrine of estoppel, whereby a state that committed a particular deed against or in relation to another state cannot then sue the latter for doing exactly the same. See, e.g., T. M. Franck, *Fairness in International Law and Institutions* (Oxford: Oxford University Press, 1997), 51–53.

2. In his often-cited book *Organized Hypocrisy*, Stephen Krasner argues that the international system of states is nothing but a system of organized hypocrisy, in which states claim to respect the norms of sovereignty but in fact do not. The main problem with his account is that it does not distinguish hypocrisy from political-cum-moral weakness and double standards. See S. D. Krasner, *Sovereignty: Organized Hypocrisy* (Princeton, NJ: Princeton University Press, 1999).

3. See P. F. Strawson, "Freedom and Resentment," *Proceedings of the British Academy* 48 (1962): 1–25. Note that my concern here is with the standing to *blame,* or *condemn*

another agent for doing *x*—not with the standing to offer a justification for the claim that doing *x* is morally wrong. For a recent and illuminating account of the latter kind of standing, see J. Frick, "What We Owe to Hypocrites: Contractualism and the Speaker-Relativity of Justification," *Philosohpy & Public Affairs* 44, no. 4 (2016): 223-265.

4. See R. J. Wallace, "Hypocrisy, Moral Address, and the Equal Standing of Persons," *Philosophy & Public Affairs* 38, no. 4 (2010): 307-341. See also C. McKinnon, "Hypocrisy, with a Note on Integrity," *American Philosophical Quarterly* 28, no. 4 (1991): 321-330; K. Lippert-Rasmussen, "Who Can I Blame?," in *Autonomy and the Self,* ed. M. Kühler and N. Jelinek (Dordrecht: Springer, 2013), 295-316. As Kasper Lippert-Rasmussen rightly pointed out to me in private correspondence, unwarrantedly holding others to lower standards than those that one applies to oneself is to fail to treat them as moral equals. In this chapter, however, I am concerned with cases in which the critic condemns others for acting wrongly although he unwarrantedly exempts himself from the same duty.

5. For the view that the imposition of double standards is neither necessary nor sufficient for the charge of hypocrisy to stick, see, e.g., B. Szabados and E. Soifer, *Hypocrisy: Ethical Investigations* (Peterborough, ON: Broadview, 2004), ch. 11, esp. 232 and 236. For the view (contrary to my point about deception) that hypocrisy need not involve deception, see, e.g., S. Smilansky, "On Practicing What We Preach," *American Philosophical Quarterly* 31, no. 1 (1994): 73-79. For the view that hypocrisy is simply the failure to do as one preaches, see P. A. Furia, "Democratic Citizenship and the Hypocrisy of Leaders," *Polity* 41, no. 1 (2009): 113-133. In addition to those works, my discussion of hypocrisy in this section owes much to the following: R. Crisp and C. Cowton, "Hypocrisy and Moral Seriousness," *American Philosophical Quarterly* 31, no. 4 (1994): 343-349; R. W. Grant, *Hypocrisy and Integrity: Machiavelli, Rousseau, and the Ethics of Politics* (Chicago: University of Chicago Press, 1997); J. C. Isaac, "Hypocrisy and the Limits of Debunking It," *Polity* 34, no. 1 (2001): 31-35; McKinnon, "Hypocrisy, with a Note on Integrity"; J. N. Shklar, *Ordinary Vices* (Cambridge, MA: Belknap Press of Harvard University Press, 1984); D. Statman, "Hypocrisy and Self-deception," *Philosophical Psychology* 10, no. 1 (1997): 57-75; B. Szabados, "Hypocrisy," *Canadian Journal of Philosophy* 9, no. 2 (1979): 195-210; Wallace, "Hypocrisy, Moral Address"; D. Runciman, *Political Hypocrisy: The Mask of Power, from Hobbes to Orwell and Beyond* (Princeton, NJ: Princeton University Press, 2008). O. J. Herstein, "Understanding Standing: Permission to Deflect Reasons," *Philosophical Studies* 174, no. 12 (2017): 3109-3132; A. M. Smith, "On Being Responsible and Holding Responsible," *Journal of Ethics* 11, no. 4 (2007): 465-484; M. Friedman, "How to Blame People Responsibly," *Journal of Value Inquiry* 47, no. 3 (2013): 271-284; T. M. Scanlon, *Moral Dimensions: Permissibility, Meaning, Blame* (Cambridge, MA: Harvard University Press, 2008), ch. 5.

6. G. A. Cohen, "Casting the First Stone: Who Can, and Who Can't, Condemn the Terrorists?," in *Finding Oneself in the Other,* ed. M Otsuka (Princeton, NJ: Princeton University Press, 2013), 115-133. See also Lippert-Rasmussen, "Who Can I Blame?"

7. Prominent defenders of collective agency include, inter alia, L. May, *The Morality of Groups: The Collective Responsibility, Group-Based Harm, and Corporate Rights* (Notre Dame, IN: University of Notre Dame Press, 1989); C. List and P. Pettit, *Group Agency: The Possibility, Design, and Status of Corporate Agents* (Oxford: Oxford University Press, 2011); M. Gilbert, *On Social Facts* (London: Routledge, 1989); M. Gilbert, *Joint Commitment: How We Make the Social World* (Oxford: Oxford University Press, 2013). One of the most pressing questions, for collective agency accounts, is that of whether—and if so how—to allocate to citizens responsibility for what their state, seen as a corporate agent, does. For an illuminating discussion, see in particular A. Pasternak, "From Corporate Moral Agency to Corporate Rights," *Law & Ethics of Human Rights* 11, no. 1 (2017): 135–159; A. Pasternak, "Limiting States' Corporate Responsibility," *Journal of Political Philosophy* 21, no. 4 (2013): 361–381; A. Pasternak, "Sharing the Costs of Political Injustices," *Politics, Philosophy & Economics* 10, no. 2 (2011): 188–210.

8. See S. Kerr, "Saudi Arabia, UAE, Bahrain, and Egypt Cut Ties with Qatar," *Financial Times* (London), June 5, 2017. On the claim that the Saudis both fight and, albeit unwittingly, abet terrorism, see S. Shane, "Saudis and Extremism: 'Both the Arsonists and the Firefighters,'" *New York Times,* August 25, 2016.

9. On the ways in which institutional processes make it difficult to level the charge of hypocrisy, see S. Dovi, "'Making the World Safe for Hypocrisy?,'" *Polity* 34, no. 1 (2001): 3–30; Glaser, "Does Hypocrisy Matter?" In his interesting comparative study of French and British aid policy both during and after the Cold War, Gordon Cumming persuasively argues that the decentralized nature of French bureaucracy makes it harder for the French government to deliver a consistent policy. This provides another illustration of my point. See Cumming, *Aid to Africa,* esp. chs. 7 to 9.

10. My remarks in this paragraph draw on G. A. Cohen's illuminating attempt to "narrow the scope of *Tu Quoque*" (as he puts it). The difficulties also apply in the individual cases that Cohen considers (if I pilfer a small sum of money from the office petty cash reserve, do I lose the standing to condemn my colleague who has stolen far more? Do I lose the standing to condemn the rapist?). See Cohen, "Casting the First Stone."

11. See, e.g., E. F. Kittay, "On Hypocrisy," *Metaphilosophy* 13, nos. 3–4 (1982): 277–289; Crisp and Cowton, "Hypocrisy and Moral Seriousness."

12. For arguments along those lines, see, notably, Shklar, *Ordinary Vices;* Grant, *Hypocrisy and Integrity.* For a more critical take, see Dovi, "'Making the World Safe for Hypocrisy?'"

13. The French did not properly begin to reckon with their colonial past until the 1990s. For interesting discussions of this issue, see, e.g., F. Barclay, ed., *France's Colonial Legacies: Memory, Identity and Narrative* (Cardiff: University of Wales Press, 2013).

14. For exploration of this issue in the context of participation in unjust wars, see S. Bazargan, "The Permissibility of Aiding and Abetting Unjust Wars," *Journal of Moral Philosophy* 8, no. 4 (2011): 513–529; V. Tadros, "Unjust Wars Worth Fighting For," *Journal of Practical Ethics* 4, no. 1 (2016): 52–78.

15. There are scores of reports on this issue, based on official U.S. data. For an overview, see the report Human Rights Watch produced for the United Nations in 2014:

https://www.hrw.org/sites/default/files/related_material/2014%20HRW%20US%20
CERD.pdf. I am grateful to Zofia Stemplowska for pressing me on the points raised
in these paragraphs.

16. For reports to the effect that those two countries routinely practice torture, see the
following damning reports by Amnesty International: "Israel and Occupied
Palestinian Territories 2016 / 2017," accessed November 28, 2017, https://www
.amnesty.org/en/countries/middle-east-and-north-africa/israel-and-occupied
-palestinian-territories/report-israel-and-occupied-palestinian-territories/; "Egypt:
Hundreds Disappeared and Tortured amid Wave of Brutal Repression," July 13,
2016, https://www.amnesty.org/en/latest/news/2016/07/egypt-hundreds-disappeared
-and-tortured-amid-wave-of-brutal-repression.

17. The Iran-Contra scandal is bewilderingly complex. For good contemporaneous
summaries, see, e.g., J. Canham-Clyne, "Business as Usual: Iran-Contra and the
National Security State," *World Policy Journal* 9, no. 4 (1992): 617–637; C. A.
Rubenberg, "US Policy toward Nicaragua and Iran and the Iran-Contra Affair:
Reflections on the Continuity of American Foreign Policy," *Third World Quarterly*
10, no. 4 (1988): 1467–1504; D. J. Scheffer, "U.S. Law and the Iran-Contra Affair,"
American Journal of International Law 81, no. 3 (1987): 696–723. These works are
also a good source for American policy in Latin America in general.

18. Cohen, "Casting the First Stone."

Acknowledgments

Writing acknowledgments is one of my favorite tasks. I must begin by thanking the Warden and Fellows of All Souls College for their ongoing material and intellectual support. This is the first book I have written from start to finish while at All Souls. To belong to this wonderful and somewhat strange institution is an astounding privilege, of which I am conscious every day.

Early draft chapters were presented at the following seminars, workshops, and venues: the Warwick Political Theory Workshop, the Nuffield Political Theory Workshop, the Montreal *Group de Recherche Interuniversitaire en Philosophie Politique,* the University of Toronto's Center for Ethics, the LSE Popper Seminar, the Graz Conference on Global Justice, the Oxford CSSJ Seminar, the Oxford Department for Continuing Education, and the University of Birmingham's Center for Global Justice. An extended version of Chapter 3, on secondary sanctions, was initially delivered in 2016 at University College London as a Current Legal Problems lecture and, at Jeffrey King's invitation, appeared as "Secondary Economic Sanctions" in the associated journal, *Current Legal Problems*, Vol. 69, No. 1 (2016): 259–288, published by Oxford University Press. I thank Jeff and the anonymous reviewers for their constructive and generous feedback on the draft. The article is reprinted here, with some updates and revisions.

At Oxford, I have been blessed with wonderful students and colleagues. In the winter of 2017, Simon Caney and I organized a seminar series on his own book manuscript as well as this one. Simon's gentle encouragements and incisive comments, not to mention the students' active contributions to our discussions, revived my flagging faith in the project. In October 2017, at a crucial juncture in the redrafting, Kalypso Nicolaïdis generously organized a workshop on the almost-final draft—with considerable administrative support from Barnaby King. I am grateful to both organizers and audiences for their helpful suggestions.

Many people went beyond the call of duty and provided excellent written comments on draft chapters: Jessica Begon, Tim Besley, Samuel Bruce, Joseph Carens, Negar Habibi, Thomas Hurka, Yukinori Iwaki, Jeff King, Joseph Lacey, Meira Levinson, Kasper Lippert-Rasmussen, Marco Meyer, David Miller, Kalypso Nicolaïdis, Fergus Peace, Victor Tadros, Patrick Tomlin, and Annette Zimmermann. Chris O'Flaherty, Royal Navy Hudson Visiting Fellow at St Antony's College, Oxford (2017–2018), sent me twelve pages of feedback and saved me from several factual errors, for which I am deeply grateful.

Christian Barry and Mathias Risse read the penultimate draft for Harvard University Press and showed extraordinary engagement with the project. Taken together, their written reports contained some of the most constructive and helpful comments I have ever received on a book-length typescript. Christian and Mathias could be forgiven for not wanting to read a word of it ever again. If they ever did, they would see that I do not agree with all of their objections and that I have not taken up all of their expository and substantive suggestions. But they would also see that every chapter bears their intellectual footprints.

Last but not least, at Harvard University Press, Ian Malcolm shepherded me through the process from the very beginning and provided invaluable intellectual support, while Melody Negron, Carol Noble, Stephanie Vyce, and Olivia Woods heaved the book over the finishing line. To all, I extend heartfelt thanks.

Index